PORTRAYALS
—— OF ——
REVOLUTION

Images, Debates and Patterns of Thought on the French Revolution

Noel Parker

Southern Illinois University Press
Carbondale and Edwardsville

Published in the United States, its dependencies, and Canada by
Southern Illinois University Press, P.O. Box 3697, Carbondale,
IL 62902–3697

First published 1990 by
Harvester Wheatsheaf,
66 Wood Lane End, Hemel Hempstead,
Hertfordshire, HP2 4RG
A division of
Simon & Schuster International Group

Printed and bound in Great Britain by
BPCC Wheatons Ltd, Exeter

Set by Photoprint, Torquay
in Garamond 11/12½

Library of Congress Cataloging-in-Publication Data
Parker, Noel, 1945–
    Portrayals of revolution: images, debates and patterns of
thought on the French Revolution/Noel Parker.
        p.   cm.
    1. France—History—Revolution, 1789–1799—Public opinion.
2. Public opinion—France.   3. Arts and revolutions—France.
4. France—History—Revolution.   1789–1799—Literature and the
revolution.   5. France—History—Revolution, 1789–1799—
Historiography.   I. Title.
DC158.8.P37   1990
944.04—dc20
                                                89–26365
                                                CIP
    ISBN 0–8093–1684–6

Contents

Acknowledgements

Many people have contributed to the strengths of this book, though its shortcomings must remain my responsibility. In particular, a number of colleagues and friends have been generous enough to read and comment upon earlier (usually denser) components and drafts. Martin Barker, John Fauvel, Carolyn Harding, David Held, Russell Keat, Maunagh Kelly, Jonathan Ree, Mike Sonenscher, Mark Whitaker and Gwynn Williams are all owed a debt of gratitude for that assistance. Almost equally as valuable in the task has been the practical support and tolerance of my parents and various colleagues in the Open University, North-West Region, who, in a strictly personal capacity, have been persistently helpful to me during the years of preparation. In this connection, I should like to mention Juliet Swift in particular.

Introduction: The Revolution as an Event in Culture

By any standards, the French Revolution was an extraordinary historical event. It altered the direction not only of French history but also, more widely, of European history. There will always be debate on how it did so, and on whether this was to the good. But this book is not a *direct* historical study of the Revolution. It has considerable historical content, but it does not contribute new evidence to the arguments of historians as to what brought the Revolution about, or what its effects were. Instead, it marshals material already available to show how the Revolution has been portrayed in various forms of culture, including historical writing. To that extent, it is intended to analyse and assess the ideas of the Revolution which historians, and others, may have.

There are two special features of the French Revolution which attracted me to it as a subject. Firstly, those involved, at least during the first years (up until the mid-1790s), were self-consciously trying to reconstitute a social order and form a society from scratch. Secondly, this period threw up quite a quantity of new culture, much of which tried to fit in to this reconstructive purpose. These two features are connected. Culture generated in the Revolution tried to address its audience in a way that would help to integrate the latter into the 'nation' which was supposedly engaged in reconstituting itself. In the portrayals of the Revolution we find a struggle to resolve two related issues thrown up in that effort to reconstruct: the problem of how to think of the new basis of a social unity which, it was believed, would reorganize society; and the peculiar character of the present moment in the movement of history.

The role of culture in the reconstitution of the social order was taken very seriously by those involved in the Revolution. Witness the

1

lengthy debates and the plethora of schemes for national education to disseminate a common culture across the length and breadth of the nation.[1] Indeed, the continuing legacy of the French Revolution included a national system of education greatly in advance of that of France's neighbours, and the *idéologue* movement which, through its attempt to systematize the theoretical basis for national education, first gave currency to our modern notion of ideology and provided the premisses of Comtean sociology.

Many of the great names of the Revolution appear among those putting forward schemes in the debates: Mirabeau, Talleyrand, Condorcet, Danton, Robespierre. The diffusion of an appropriate common culture was thought to be so fundamental that the obligation to provide it was even written into the revolutionary constitutions. As Condorcet explained it, education would improve the human race, teaching the people the meaning of justice, rendering them more able, adapting them to change, reducing inequality and dependence, and thus preventing a return to tyranny.[2] Danton was more graphic in describing the intimate relationship between people and nation which education could engender:

> What is individual reason against that of the nation? Who amongst us is unaware of the dangers that perpetual isolation can produce? It is in the schools of the nation that the child will be suckled on republican milk. The Republic is one and indivisible. Public education must relate to this centre of unity.[3]

A similar importance was attributed to the teaching of the French language. In proposing a scheme to reform and generalize the use of French, Abbé Grégoire argued that 'knowledge and the use of the national language is essential to preserve freedom.'[4]

A striking aspect of these schemes was that they included not just the education of children (such as we would think of today) but also programmes of organized regular public festivals and celebrations. These events, which will be considered more closely in Chapter 2, were described by Robespierre as 'essential to public education'.[5] They were foremost among the means to educate adults in civic values. For the revolutionaries, the purpose of education was to diffuse appropriate culture to all levels and all ages in society. Those involved thought that culture was a vital component in the cohesion of the Revolution.

Overall, this book considers the style, the tone, the imagery, the symbolism, the structure and the implicit thinking in various forms of culture that have portrayed the Revolution – or, in the current jargon term, given a 'representation' of it. An unusual presupposition underlies the range of material I have brought together. If we are to examine critically the way that culture has portrayed the Revolution, we should, I maintain, consider the culture of those involved *alongside* the culture that comes after, our own included. For one thing, it would be presumptuous to assume a priori that portrayals contemporary to the Revolution reveal less of the reality of the experience than later portrayals do. What is more, contemporary culture wrestled more acutely with a problem inherent in representing history. It belonged to the history that was being made and was bound to be aware of its own relationship to the human agents who might imbibe it. For us who come after, therefore, the culture of the Revolution may naturally bear lessons about how to represent humans as historical actors.

The revolutionary festivals are only one form of culture to be examined in the first part of the book, which is devoted to contemporary representations of the Revolution. In addition, Chapter 1 analyses political rhetoric, ephemeral printing and some changes in language. Festivals appear in Chapter 2, alongside theatre and some comment on accompanying music and verse. Festivals are treated with the theatre because both involve what I call participative 'performance'. Finally, Chapter 3 completes my coverage of contemporary forms of culture, dealing with visual portrayals in prints, in fine art and in fashions, and with how contemporary politicians and writers located the Revolution in history. At first sight, it may appear forced to pair visual representations with written accounts. But, in my view, they are linked by a common concern to embody an unchanging abstract ideal in a moment in time. The moment may be an instant in a story from the ancients, a historical point of origin, or a present moment of collective renewal. A certain conception of truth can be seen at work in linking time and the ideal in the way contemporary culture did. Its internal dynamics resemble what Foucault analysed in his 'classical episteme'.[6] The tension between time and the ideal is a suitable place to end the examination of culture contemporary to the Revolution. It reflects and extends the problem which all the forms of culture had in trying to define their audience − the difficulty of conveying a realistic idea of an active, regenerative nation. The analysis of contemporary culture therefore ends with the problem of the nation's place in time.

The nature of the Revolution, and whether something like it could recur, continued to be vital issues well into the nineteenth century. But, once the Revolution itself was over, different forms of culture came into prominence in portraying it. The task was one of commentary, rather than of explicit involvement in events. The place of the Revolution in history was a natural topic. Furthermore, historical writing in the nineteenth century was much involved with the question of whether revolution could recur. Hence, the second part of this book, 'Commentaries', takes a far narrower range of cultural forms: historical writing in France, and prominent theoretical writings from different countries. The Revolution continued to be portrayed in other forms of culture, but the priority of these two areas, along with simple considerations of space, confine my attention to those scholarly portrayals. I examine them over two periods: first, I take histories written in France and broader theoretical writings from France, England and Germany up to around 1870. By that time, the immediate aftermath of the Revolution had passed. My analysis therefore breaks off at that chronological point, and moves on to consider portrayals of the Revolution in modern theories and histories (Chapter 7).

The tensions encapsulated in the contemporary cultural forms and the earliest pamphlets are to be found again in the nineteenth-century historical and the theoretical writings. They concern the relationship between the Revolution and the real social and historical existence of the people, who had originally been supposed its bedrock. Chapter 4 covers those French historians (roughly speaking, those writing from the first to the third decade of the nineteenth century) who started the practice of history writing. They located any progressive motive force for the Revolution well away from the mass of the people: in higher culture, or in the growth, spread over centuries, of the bourgeois population. Chapter 5 follows the gradual erosion of this perspective (up to the 1860s) through a romantic empathy combined with the influence of an idealist ontology about what constitutes the substance of a society's existence. By the 1860s, French historians had gone from marginalizing the people to giving them a unique, mysterious place in their ontology of historical progress.

Chapter 6 analyses various nineteenth-century theoretical writers who portrayed the Revolution in the context of a general view of social stability or transformation. The same theme is to be found: how, and on what ontological level, to conceptualize the forces which bring about a revolution, and to determine whether some good may come of it. At the end of that chapter, there is a critical assessment of the conception of human agency in the theories. It concludes, *inter alia*, that a social transformation produced from within a society can be conceived, but only if full account is taken of the potential effects and limitations of the available culture. The process and outcome will be directed and limited by how that culture can unite bodies of people into politically effective groups.

Chapter 7 considers modern historians' portrayals of the French Revolution, alongside current theories about revolution in general. Naturally, it does so in the light of the conceptual explorations of those involved and those reflecting on it during the nineteenth-century aftermath. I conclude that a portrayal of the Revolution which interprets the action of participating groups through the vicissitudes of their own self-identification in culture has three virtues: it rightly addresses a crucial feature of the Revolution; it recaptures something of the lessons of the great writers of the nineteenth century; and it is conceptually more satisfactory in itself.

THEORETICAL CONSIDERATIONS AND JUSTIFICATION

This book examines the varied and peculiar culture which portrays the French Revolution. However, it also raises a number of intriguing theoretical questions about the political existence of a modern society and about the nature of historical acts. It does this by looking at culture that is involved in society's self-conscious transformation. For those with an interest in them, I should like to state these issues, dealing first with political theory, and then with history.

The character and inherent tensions in the modern, secular polity are the primary topics of all political theory.[7] Yet, since it grounds its legitimacy in the common political identity of its members, the very existence of the modern polity depends crucially upon its culture. As Claude Nicolet has argued,[8] republicanism is the principle of political life which, more explicitly than any other, relies on the effect of words. The Revolution's way of constructing political sociability[9] therefore repays examination by the political theorist − even if you hold, with Hannah Arendt,[10] that the French Revolution merely *perverted* the political sociability necessary for freedom in the modern world. This study considers first how the culture of the Revolution was attempting to build a political sociability.

However, the analysis and argument in what follows are not exclusively about the positions of political theorists, or even the explicit theories of political writers and actors in the Revolution itself. They largely cover the style etc. of the forms of culture that portray the Revolution. They frequently analyse the understanding of the

Revolution *implicit*, rather than explicit, in such portrayals. A piece of cultural history, then? Yes, but one which also debates with the contemporary and subsequent portrayals of the Revolution, interpreting their character, appreciating their strengths and identifying their weaknesses.

How can an approach, which gives so much prominence to unwitting elements in the portrayal of a political phenomenon, make a contribution to political theory? It can do so because in political life people deploy language and devices like language: symbols, signs, and 'meanings' in general. Politics is infused with unwitting meanings, because the meanings through which the social world is perceived are essential ingredients of manipulating it, just as they are of living in it. We can, then, rightly subject politics to those techniques for the interpretation of symbols which are nowadays embraced by the term 'hermeneutics'.[11]

In the upheaval of the Revolution, the meanings present in social life — and *a fortiori* the meanings deployed in politics — were naturally put under particularly heavy strain. To make the case still more striking, politics in the Revolution embraced the idea of a fresh start for society upon an entirely new basis. New demands were made upon established meanings in politics, then, and upon the cultural forms in which they were expressed. Accordingly, those involved in the Revolution expended much effort developing and modifying meanings for what they were involved in. In the language, in the creation of symbols and in the developments in forms of culture during the Revolution, we can analyse the meanings deployed to hold together the modern polity at the moment of its inception and of their greatest strain.

Analysis of the culture of the Revolution is also of theoretical interest for history. This is not only because the Revolution was a major historical event in itself, but also because, again, the early revolutionaries had a peculiar notion of their own role in history. They believed that they were constituting themselves as immensely powerful historical agents. Because it was often directed towards this purpose, the culture of the Revolution provides an insight into the thought of people trying to perceive themselves as agents. Even though the revolutionaries were manifestly mistaken in many of their hopes, their culture is of real interest. As Peter Gay has put it, 'history is very much a study of perceptions', which commonly includes mistaken ones.[12]

We can go further. The revolutionaries' perception of themselves as historical agents touches on the very nature of human beings' historical existence. Living *in* history, human beings exercise a belief in their own power to act effectively and freely upon the temporal flow which they experience. The revolutionaries possessed in childlike excess a sense of their power to begin afresh, as free agents. Yet, this is not so much an oddity of theirs, as a stark case of a general aspect of the human historical condition.

Historiography frequently comes up against the problem of identifying homogeneous periods in historical events. The persistence of the problem arises from what Paul Ricoeur has called the 'historicity' of our condition: that is, the way that living, in itself, requires us to identify series in time in which we interpret the progress of events. Ricoeur himself has developed a hermeneutical description of the historicity of our condition. The events that occur in historical time are 'knots' from which meaning and growth (*sens* and *devenir*) irradiate.[13] In addition, for Ricoeur, human action is an irreducible level of the meaning which events have for us. At that level, we cannot but feel that we ourselves can actively *begin* series of events (though we often experience the feeling not as freedom, so much as in a constant 'battle of man the agent against the world of which he is not the author').[14] In short, the human condition entails a sense of freedom to initiate. The culture of the Revolution declared that sense, sometimes with a quite tragic defiance of objective constraints. The sole and essential condition of exercising that power on the stage of history was that the nation be united. The subsequent representations of the Revolution have struggled to incorporate or to exclude that feature of historical experience.

From these remarks, it will be seen that this study focuses on the points where what is often referred to as the 'discourses'[15] of a society face the difficulties of engaging coherently with social reality, and come up against their own limitations. They must then either break down or adapt. Analyses in terms of discourse theory often get into trouble by claiming too much ontologically. They appear to deny the existence of a 'real' world beyond discourse. They seem to claim that human discourse and thought can have no relation to a 'real' world; and that discourse is sufficient to explain what happens in the social world. Yet, where a system of meanings breaks down it manifestly may be interacting *unsuccessfully* with a 'real' world – that is to say, a world prior to description. I do not believe, therefore, that these overblown claims for discourse theory are sound, or necessary to justify the present study. Such claims appear to expose the theory to perfectly avoidable attack: on grounds of idealism,[16] of logic,[17] or even of the realities of language.[18] This does not necessarily imply, on the other hand, that the pre-descriptive world, in its turn, is causally dominant over discourse.

The present study, then, attempts to analyse the 'discourses' within and around the Revolution. It assumes that the portrayals of the Revolution contain systems of meaning with illuminating points of breakdown and evasion, which have an impact upon the thinking and action of those involved (and on us, for whom the Revolution is a significant event in our past). It supposes that the study of discourse has a peculiar importance, not that it offers ultimate truths.

APPENDICES

Although there is much history in this study, neither its methods nor its topics of interest are exclusive to students of history. To help the reader with less historical knowledge, two appendices have been included: a simple chronological chart giving dates and a brief (though possibly a tendentious) description of events; and a biographical index of contemporary figures referred to in the text. Readers new to the Revolution may wish to turn to the appendices before approaching the body of the book.

NOTES

1. These have been critically examined in R.R. Palmer, *The Improvement of Humanity: Education and the French Revolution* (Princeton, NJ: Princeton University Press, 1985).
2. Condorcet, 'Sur l'instruction publique' in *Oeuvres complètes* (Paris: 1847), vol. 9, pp. 1–24.
3. Speech of 22 Frimaire II (12 December 1793), quoted in H. Morse Stephens, *Orators of the French Revolution* (Oxford: Clarendon, 1892), p. 274.
4. Quoted in Michel de Certeau *et al.*, *Une Politique de la langue: la Révolution française et les patois* (Paris: Gallimard, 1975) p. 303.
5. Speech of 18 Floréal II (7 May 1794), quoted in Morse Stephens, op. cit., p. 410.
6. Michel Foucault, *Les Mots et les choses* (Paris: Gallimard, 1966), translated as *The Order of Things* (London: Tavistock, 1970). The term is explained more fully in Chapter 3.
7. One such theoretically interesting tension, namely that entailed in locating a sovereign unity within society itself, has recently been considered for the case of the French Revolution by Brian C.J. Singer,

Society, Theory and the French Revolution: Studies in the Revolutionary Imaginary (London: Macmillan, 1986). Singer's argument is considered again on p. 33.

8. Claude Nicolet, *L'Idée républicaine en France (1789–1924)* (Paris: Gallimard, 1982), pp. 31–4.

9. For historical studies that describe this aspect of the Revolution within the philosophical societies and the Jacobin movement, see Augustin Cochin, *Les Sociétés de pensée et la démocratie* (Paris: Plon-Nourrit, 1921; Paris: Editions Copernic, 1978); *idem, Les Sociétés de pensée et la Révolution en Bretagne (1788–89)* (Paris: H. Champion, 1925); Crane Brinton, *The Jacobins: an Essay in the New History* (New York: Macmillan, 1930); and Michael L. Kennedy, *The Jacobin Clubs in the French Revolution: the First Years* (Princeton, NJ: Princeton University Press, 1982).

10. Hannah Arendt, *On Revolution* (London: Faber & Faber, 1963), pp. 24–7, 54–5 and ch. 6 *passim*.

11. This term in its modern sense is due, of course, to Wilhelm Dilthey, *W. Dilthey: Selected Writings* (Cambridge: Cambridge University Press, 1976), pp. 228–31, who first defined it as the methods needed to understand 'the life of the mind'. Dilthey assumed an 'objective mind' where 'what is active, valuable and creative in man' is to be found all together (ibid., pp. 175–6). While using the hermeneutics' idea of the place to be given to understanding meanings in social life, I adopt the broader scope taken by the subsequent tradition of hermeneutical studies, with its focus on more diverse, often contradictory indicators of meaning.

12. Peter Gay, *Art and Act: on Causes in History* (New York: Harper and Row, 1976), p. 16.

13. Paul Ricoeur, 'Objectivité et subjectivité en histoire' in *idem, Histoire et vérité* (Paris: Seuil, 1955), esp. pp. 24–7 and 41–5.

14. Paul Ricoeur, 'L'Evénement et sens' (unpublished lecture delivered at the University of Manchester, February 1989). For a detailed exposition of precisely how this structural feature of the human condition intrudes into the *study* of history, see Paul Ricoeur, *Time and Narrative* (Chicago: Chicago University Press, 1984), translation of *Temps et récit* (Paris: Seuil, 1983), vol. 1, Part II. What Ricoeur derives for the experience of individual human beings is matched in Anthony Giddens's concept of 'structuration', as far as groups and whole societies are concerned – see Anthony Giddens, *A Contemporary Critique of Historical Materialism, Volume I: Power, Property and the State* (London: Macmillan, 1981), pp. 34–41.

15. For a purportedly Marxist presentation of discourse theory in politics, see Ernesto Laclau, *Politics and Ideology in Marxist Theory: Capitalism, Fascism and Populism* (London: New Left Books, 1977). Laclau, too, focuses on the way discourse identifies the group subject of action: '. . . what constitutes the unifying principle of an ideological discourse is the "subject" interpellated and thus constituted through this discourse' (p. 101).

16. See, for example, the polemic between Laclau and Norman Geras in *New*

Left Review, nos. 163 and 166 (1987), and no. 169 (1988).

17. See, for example, Vincent Descombes, *Objects of All Sorts* (Oxford: Basil Blackwell, 1986). Descombes expounds a distinction between 'predicamental' and 'transcendental' terms, which implies that meaning can be determined independently of the truth of a statement. It follows that a besetting breakdown of meaning simply points up 'the gap between the meaning of a statement and its truth' (p. 66).

18. This being the burden of Ricoeur's reassertion of the metaphorical, as against the metonymic, relations between language and the world in his *La Métaphore vive* (Paris: Seuil, 1975).

Part One

CONTEMPORARY CULTURE

CHAPTER ONE

Political Language: Speaking for the Revolution

'Great conspiracy against the inhabitants of the Saint-Antoine and Saint-Marceau districts' ran the 19 February 1791 headline of one of the more original popular newspapers that sprang up during the Revolution (*Le Père Duchesne*). Popular journalism, closely linked to the flowering of republican clubs, was almost an invention of the Revolution. So it is a good place to look first for the structure of revolutionary culture. The journalists knew what they were doing. Marat, perhaps the most notorious, acknowledged that he had obtained real influence through 'frightful public scandal' and 'the effusions of my soul, the outbursts of my heart, my violent denunciation of oppression, my violent attacks on the oppressors, my accents of grief, my cries of indignation, fury and despair'.[1] Journalists quickly learnt ways to sensationalize and to appear to be involved at the heart of things, which would not be out of place in modern tabloid papers.

With variations of style, though, all the journals of the period were trying to define events and place themselves at the centre. In the political effervescence of revolution, there was a hidden agenda: Where is the true national political life to be found? And what are its boundaries? Techniques to place the journalist at the heart of things implicitly answered these questions. In principle, the centre of political life was now acknowledged to be the 'nation' or the 'people'. But these are imprecise entities, marooned on an island in time. Hence, we will discover in the answers a range of characteristics attributed to the 'people': various political and moral virtues; an ability to substantiate some great political abstractions; the will to take a new, free course in history. Conversely, what lies outside the boundaries of true public life is vilified for lacking these things.

In this chapter, I will first examine political journalism, including

13

its relation to the political clubs. I will sketch out a system of concepts about the political order and history which organized the style and presentation of the journals. Having done that, I will approach the rhetoric of the spoken word and vocabulary more generally. The same system is at work in these areas. That will be the moment to consider, as well, the balance of continuity and innovation in the rhetoric of the revolutionaries. Finally, I will set out what I conceive to be the fundamental paradoxes in the structure of political language – and of political life – shared by journalists and politicians.

The strategy employed by journalists and politicians related political, 'public' life to a new, idealized focal point which epitomizes collective existence. The disputed focus of public life may be found in any number of places: from the court, to official national forums of debate and political decision, to non-official clubs or assemblies. The user of political language implicitly conveyed a model of the proper boundaries of the political and social world. What is more, he might offer himself and/or certain characteristic personal qualities as essentially identical with the core of the good social order. Political discussion then became a matter of rehearsing one's identity with, or repeatedly bearing witness to the qualities essential to the 'people'.

THE PRESS AND REPUBLICAN CLUBS

Journalism in the Revolution had a quite specific relationship to the republican clubs, which were themselves often derived from earlier ostensibly *non*-political bodies, such as literary societies, or from the organization of local militia. Their purpose was to provide the structure of political life where there had previously been none.

This is well conveyed by the very first documents of association used by the Jacobin Society of Paris to promote affiliations from the provinces. They spoke of the need 'to form so many threads which lead from all parts of the Kingdom to a common centre' and of 'the duty of good citizens . . . to form a coalition to maintain the Constitution'.[2] The threads were to be tied by correspondence between societies (on the model of literary societies). The last and most openly propagandizing of the clubs' journals, the *Journal de la Montagne*, expressed the hope that it would be a central point to which the 'purest principles of . . . true republicanism' and the surest news would converge from all of Europe.[3]

So receiving and answering correspondence formed a considerable part of the early activities of the clubs, and had a definite place in the journals which the clubs themselves set up. Clubs and journals started out with open invitations for correspondence from all good citizens. One extreme was the project of the abbé Fauchet and the politically moderate Cercle Social. Their journal, *Bouche de Fer,* had an iron mailbox in a Parisian street for all-comers to post their contributions to debate.[4] Most journals purported to be publishing correspondence from like-minded persons in various places.

The clubs' difficulties display the common ambivalence of political expressions where the proper boundaries of the political are undefined. For the clubs had no agreed criteria as to what ought to be included in their journals. The issue became progressively more contentious; and when the content did not meet expectations this was often attributed to personal shortcomings or political ambitions in the writers. Such a tension is visible in the first issue (21 November 1790) of the Jacobins' first journal, the *Journal des Amis de la Constitution.* It promised a systematic account of all of the following: the work of the National Assembly (discussed 'according to truly constitutional principles'), all decrees, all events and actions which touch the Revolution, and all attempts to undermine the constitution. But in practice, the editor enjoyed a wide discretion over what to publish, including the debates of the Paris Jacobins and the letters of other societies. The first issue ended with a section by the editor, Choderlos de Laclos, optimistically entitled 'What remains to be done', which called for the reform and a purge of public office.

As time passed the Jacobin Society found it harder to distinguish its ('true' revolutionary) line from that of its enemies. Concern over the content of its journal became more marked, and its apparatus of control was extended. Laclos himself had to be replaced when he left to join the moderates in the rival Club des Feuillants. But in fact, the history of the Jacobins and their journals is one of frequent changes of title (six between 1790 and 1793), growing awareness of the need to determine precisely the presentation of the club in its journals, and continuous tension between the embattled club and the editors (eight in the same period). Not infrequently, editors were accused from the debating floor of corruptly misrepresenting what had been said in an earlier debate. The terms contrasted in such discussions were these: on the one hand, there was the pure spirit of the public, which trusting affiliates throughout France were eager to find spelt out in the journal; on the other hand, there were the suspect activities of opponents of the club and of the Revolution. The latter could then include an egocentric editor or an agent of the club's enemies in the print shop. Attacks on the editor of the Jacobins' second journal alleged that puzzled affiliates had written to query the loyalty shown in some of the correspondence.

Let us look at the journals produced by individuals. They, too, sought to determine the proper content of politics and to be a focus of social unity. According to J.R. Censer,[5] they were able to charge extraordinarily high subscriptions, and were sometimes highly profitable for the various business arrangements which supported them. But their format, publisher, writers and even existence could change rapidly. In Censer's view, the journalists were not apart from politics in a separate profession of journalism. For them, journals were not clearly defined, long-term institutions in the political arena. Few of them had been journalists before the Revolution. Some (such as Fabre d'Eglantine, Fréron and Marat) played an active political role either during or after their careers as journalists. Journalism was an open field for the members of liberal professions such as lawyers, teachers, or doctors. Having experienced frustration, exclusion and failure before the Revolution (in an intensely status-conscious society), they created in their journals niches to participate in the Revolution, to disseminate the enlightened views characteristic of their liberal backgrounds, and to express their personal ambition. In short, they were principally political activists, with little reason for commitment to any status quo.

The journalists moved from other spheres into the fluid world of the journals. There, in the absence of any well-established political legitimacy, they could lay claim to unusual power and status. With characteristic bravura, Marat exploited this in his claim to vocation. There being a host of enemies of the Revolution in the Estates General, he wrote, he intended to check up on the Assembly, to bring its errors to light and to lead it back to good principles.[6] This was a political task comparable to that which the clubs embraced. Even if Marat is overstating his case, the openness and scope of journalism gave the journalists the chance of political sway. Thus they had a natural affinity for ideology that could justify that sway. Their shared ideology, as Censer explains,[7] was popular sovereignty.

From Censer's results, we can extrapolate the way that the journals were naturally inclined to see themselves as they would be at their strongest; namely, in a fundamental relationship with the sovereign legitimacy of the silent mass of the common people. The journals' manner of referring to the people and addressing them indicated that the people were morally sound and capable of *natural* good judgement. The people were tolerant, uncorrupted by private wealth or power.

They were committed to the support of each other, the family and the Revolution as a whole. The people combined those virtues necessary to the Revolution: steadiness, community spirit, decency and commitment — in short, the entire *moral* basis of legitimacy. Yet these virtues matched qualities that the journalist, with a background of limited success in his liberal profession, might convincingly attribute *to himself*: tolerance, articulateness, and a judgement independent of privilege and power. Via their concept of the people, journalists thus joined the 'sovereign' mass at the true heart of the new legitimate political order. Counterposed to that heart of things, were the aristocracy, which radical journalists attacked mercilessly. This was not a clear-cut category, but it certainly included all those with power and position. It could and did expand: to embrace those who were acquiring power and might be suspected of going over to the side of the powers already in place, such as lower grades of officers or of clergy.

How can we characterize the logic of this shifting view? It was that opposition to the Revolution, the people and the journals was founded on 'egotism': the tendency to turn inwards towards secretive activity, favourable to one's personal advantage. As Marat put it, 'it is the class of citizens with the least fortune that is the only one that is patriotic, just as it is the only honest one'.[8] Clearly, the journalists, whose lives before the Revolution had been on the outside of the elites and whose manner of operating relied upon publicity, would appear no more capable of this kind of activity than the powerless mass of 'the people'. In contrast, all secret discussion and action tended to be identified with the illegitimate, and the misuse of power. Before the Revolution, the normal elite order had concentrated power, privilege and all the virtues into a pyramid at the peak of society. In this representation of morals, society and politics, the pyramid was inverted: the true centre of political legitimacy was now in openness, on the *outside* of all advantaged elites and all centres of power. Evil and everything opposed to the legitimate revolutionary order was now what happened on the *inside*, behind closed doors. As another journalist-politician, Camille Desmoulins, put it: 'Those who wish to create evil look for shadows'.[9] Looked at more closely, the journals' style and the presentation of events conveyed a world to match this inverted pyramid. In that world, significant action appeared to take place *outside* the establishment of power, in the space shared by the people and the journalists.

All the journals, regardless of any plans they might announce, allowed themselves a great liberty by modern standards to arrange things without order (or sometimes even headings), according to the train of thought of the editor. Censer's careful content analysis[10] reveals very little sustained treatment of any specific events. He attributes this to the writers' previous inexperience of journalism, and notes that, even where an event does attract sufficient attention to become 'dominant', its treatment is still subordinate to the journalists' preoccupation with popular politics. However, rather than their lacking journalistic judgement, their politics could equally well be *positive* grounds for the way they presented news. We need to consider the political implications of the journalists' style more fully. In itself, arranging material according to the journalists' stream of thought made it appear as the product of an individual rather than of any institution. This style of presentation positively supported their politics. They situated legitimate power outside the established institutions; and they placed themselves at that new centre, outside all organized political elites. Political 'reality' as they saw it was portrayed in their style.

As we might imagine, the challenge to established centres of power was more marked according to the political leanings of the journal. Some were loyal to the new constitutional bodies: others were rivals. Laclos, in the earliest of the Jacobin Society journals, carefully distinguished debate on matters of opinion and criticism of functionaries who fell short of the requirements laid upon them. As editor, he would feel free to publish such things. But he would not challenge a matter settled by due legislative decision or publish a scandalous satire against agents of legitimate authority. The rationale for making such distinctions was explicitly to recall to the people 'that submission to the laws that it has made or consented to is at the same time the first virtue of the citizens and the surest safeguard of liberty'.[11] Laclos was careful to qualify his criticisms about public offices: the details can have 'no interest', he tells us, 'until the National Assembly has taken up' the reform.[12] The journal of the moderate Société de 1789 exhibits a similar ambivalence. It advanced its own title to republican virtue with an introduction in conventional rhetoric describing itself as 'united by love of country and constitution'. But it had difficulty with the story of the republican-spirited troops who had put down resistance in a provincial town. It took care to describe the outcome in terms dependent upon the neutral legal public authority to which the militia had rallied: 'the Legislature . . . called public force to the aid of public order'.[13] But, at the same time, it referred guardedly to the insurgents as 'misguided' soldiers and 'mistaken' citizens — as if not liking to exclude such ordinary people from the categories of at least potentially right-minded members of society.

The more radical, and hence populist, journals added a manner locating legitimacy and the centre of events outside the established institutions – where they also placed themselves. In his days as a deputy, Marat used his journal to defend his actions in the Assembly, with such headlines as 'A New Tactical Device Used by the People's Friend'. But this merely extended the tone he had adopted before election. From the first issue he had been 'the People's Friend', devoted single-handed to 'defending the citizen's rights, keeping a check on authority, denouncing its outrages, suppressing its malpractices'. [14]

More manifestly, a device of presentation was the imaginary folk hero, the boorish but honest 'Père Duchesne'. He was developed into a political *alter ego* by another radical political leader, Jacques Hébert. The character, whose name ('of oak') suggests stolid strength, seems to have figured in popular stories and puppet shows since at least as early as the first half of the eighteenth century. [15] But Hébert discovered 'him' while working in the theatre before the Revolution, and then established 'his' regular journal in late 1790. Issues usually had a title referring to Duchesne's state of mind: his 'Great Anger' against some action of the government; his 'Great Joy' at the arrest of counter-revolutionary leaders; his 'Great Discovery'; his 'Confession' and so forth. This puts 'his' personality centre-stage. Solid and outspoken, 'his' reactions epitomized the response of the good patriot.

On occasion, Hébert went so far as to invent a more or less plausible story. On 24 October 1790, Duchesne recounted how he had been woken late at night by the president of his *section* (the elected assembly of the quarter). He wanted to complain about dissension in sectional politics. Initially uninterested, Duchesne then thought to himself:

> This hellish rumpus in the last few days fairly makes my head spin. Damn it, liberty will be done for if that goes on. The constitution's done for. How those scoundrels of aristocrats must be laughing up their sleeves! [16]

He decided to go down to the *section* meeting (as any decent patriot clearly should do) and knock some heads together. He addressed them in his characteristic language, of course:

> Ah! you berks . . . Now I have you, you idiots! What's this! Disdaining the nation, the law and even the writings of Père Duchesne, you dare to argue in your assemblies like monks in their chapters. [17]

Needless to say, such forthright talk worked.

19

Hébert's story-telling was lively, realistic, colourful, and politically effective. For example, he details how the president staggering in was 'like a dog that had run all day without getting its teeth into a hare'.[18] Then he tells us how, having given out one shot of liquor, Duchesne closed the bottle fast for fear his unwelcome guest would drain it. The Duchesne character also permits continual humour at the expense of the elite of wealth or privilege. In the story of 13 January 1791, for example, Duchesne tells sarcastically how the conservative priest, Maury, went looking in vain for a duel with another priest opposed to him. It can be said that, in his imaginary character, Hébert portrayed the intuitive good sense and republicanism attributed to ordinary sans-culottes, and vividly painted an appealing political environment in which people like that were the legitimate and real centre of political life.

To situate the journalist in the midst of legitimate and real power redefined and reversed the political sphere. But journalists might also bring the present political moment to dramatic life by situating it at the point in history when everything was being irreversibly changed. This was a comparable reversal in the temporal sphere. Camille Desmoulins provides an example.[19] Like other radical journalists, he hovered on the fringes of official politics – through his activity in the Jacobins and the Cordelier *section* and through his association with the faction that gathered round Danton in the Assembly. His dramatic, personal style was combined with a reputation for revolutionary daring to make him a profitable journalistic investment for his backers.

As an example, I shall consider in detail a sample of Desmoulin's work. It concerns the debates (during February 1791) in the Assembly and among the Jacobins regarding the law about those leaving the country after the Revolution – possibly to join counter-revolutionaries abroad. The debate Desmoulins reports coincides with an incident in which a number of monarchists had unsuccessfully attempted to support the embattled king against the constitutional assembly. Using this background, Desmoulins manages to describe the Jacobins' meeting and the discomfiture of Mirabeau (who was opposed to a law on emigration) as if it were nothing less than the final, last-minute salvation of the Revolution itself. His unrestrained introduction announces the fact: 'How the National Assembly dishonoured the French people, how the Jacobins honoured them on the same day. That session belongs to history: but a *Tacitus* is needed to describe it.'[20] But before his readers are to be allowed to hear what happened at the 'historic' session, there is the background, in graphic terms. There had been rumours among the people and suspicious troop movements. As the most clear-seeing commentators (such as Desmoulins himself) had seen some days before, bad citizens, undissuaded by past defeats, had changed their target and were conspiring to undermine the Jacobins. But the Assembly failed to react. After *eleven* pages about his day at the Assembly, Desmoulins approaches the topic he anticipated at the start: his own personal arrival at the Jacobins. 'Now, let us go to the Jacobins, and retrace to our subscribers a session, which will be presented to posterity, as it is for ever in my memory.'[21] There, the debating hall is full. Mirabeau enters to signs of some consternation. Two speakers, whose words (reported at length) blend with Desmoulins' and who are compared in passing with Brutus and Cicero, cover the same ground as him, arguing for anti-emigrant law. Mirabeau replies, but with an offensive 'awkwardness'.[22] In the words of one of the speakers, however, 'indeed the Jacobins remain to truly know the human heart'.[23] Mirabeau is defeated, and (Desmoulins' postscript) 'Our enemies' work crumbles'.[24]

Desmoulins is not especially more wordy or disorganized than other journalists. Though his presentation is lengthy, given my account of the inversion of the political world, it is not redundantly so. He succeeds in carrying his readers with him into what appears to be the turning point of history. The story is tense and dramatic; the moment feels historic. Like other revolutionary writers, he conveyed the contemporary sense of being drunk with making history. They constantly elevated day-to-day events around them on to the level of the historic.

There were three ways of refocusing history in this way. Firstly, as above, the events could be positioned at *the* turning point in history. Secondly, there were the comparisons with great classical figures, such as we have just seen in Desmoulins. In eighteenth-century terms these would elevate those referred to to an earlier age of historical greatness. Thirdly, events could be identified with great transhistoric ideals, which were seen as the universal motivation of history. For example, the speaker (cited above) referred to the Jacobins knowing 'the human heart'. This bases their position, and his own, in a principle which apparently transcends historical time. It is entirely typical of both the speeches of the time and the writing of the journalists. It is a natural extension of that Enlightenment mode of thinking in which practical prescriptions could be derived from incontrovertible general principles available to all. In these ways, then, the plethora of events in the Revolution could be enlarged and located in time as it was conceived by the Enlightenment. History could seem to be inspired by a rational finality, with high points in the classical period and (*if* the moment is grasped) potentially in the revolutionary period, too.

The transhistorical principles at work in history were freely referred to by the journalists, as by the speakers. This is less surprising in the moderate Journal of the Société de 1789. There Enlightenment authors such as Condorcet may be found carefully developing lengthy reasoning from first principles about just taxation or the independence of state and church. The historical task of the 'enlightened men' is easily invoked at the end of such a chain of reasoning: 'Such are the principles recognized today by all enlightened men, principles that in another hemisphere [i.e. America] several wise republics have adopted.'[25] But beyond the confines of that political tendency, one finds the same link made between actions and transhistorical principles. Thus, the motto at the head of the Jacobins' *Journal de la Montagne* suggests that the armed mass of the people must fulfil the puposes of reason: 'The people's force and the force of reason are one and the same thing.' Thus Marat invokes the historical role of the people when he attacks Lafayette for 'disloyalty to the people . . . the obstacles that you have struggled to put in the way of the enterprise of citizens who have risen up . . . [and] the continual attempts you have made against the wishes of the Commune'.[26] Thus the secular battle of Revolution and counter-revolution or the morality possessed by the people (as against the aristocracy) are freely invoked by Père Duchesne. With the former, he interprets news such as that about the royal troops, allegedly searching for contraband, who fired on civilians. One reads in the issue of 25 January 1791 of the 'great anger of Père Duchesne against the young fools of hussars who wanted to mount a counter-revolution yesterday'.[27] And he invokes the morality of the people in discussing eligibility for the national guard (13 April 1791):

> In its very essence, the citizen guard is a voluntary institution, formed by love of liberty to resist oppression: the national guard formed by the Committees' plan will be a servile institution formed to consolidate ministerial despotism.[28]

The journalists invoked a historical canvas of the great principles of reason, virtue and the people's high purpose, on which all events were played out. In their accounts what *we* might consider 'the facts' about events often seem elided. In fact, their presentation is a function of a system of concepts that is redefining political reality. The writers' long-winded digressions about circumstances dramatize events in a particular way. They interpret events in terms of the realization of (or resistance to) permanent ideals, mediated through the consciousness of the people, as participants, or the journalist involved in the events. The system of concepts itself is an important new element in the message being presented. In that system, the people — who had previously been on the outside of politics — took over the centre. Their openness and their supposed virtue became the moral basis and centre of politics. Contrasted with this was the secrecy, egotism, sensuality and historic decline of what the Revolution was replacing: loosely referred to as 'aristocracy'.

POLITICAL RHETORIC

If we now broaden our view to embrace political rhetoric in general, we can extend the above analysis to a wider range of material. Once again, we will find language redefining the boundaries and focal point of the new legitimate political order. It places at the centre unity, moral superiority, timeless abstractions of nature, and a particular historical destiny, which the nation can achieve by collective action.

In this context, it is appropriate also to ask whether the characteristic rhetoric of the revolutionary period was actually different from what had gone before. Recent studies suggest that there were continuities, together with important differences, for which the rhetorical posture of Rousseau was crucial. Quite particular content appears in the rhetoric derived from Rousseau, alongside new uses for the written word. In brief, speakers employ a rhetoric which brings their own identity to the fore and equates it with that of the people, who are conceived still as the centre of political and moral right. That strategy suggests that the speaker (and those who align themselves with him) is free to fulfil a great historical destiny and realize the transhistorical principles. The structure of thought identified in the journals is therefore confirmed as innovation. In general, this makes for a most persuasive rhetoric. But, when this rhetoric is analysed critically, paradoxes also emerge in its relationship to the environment it is intended to affect.

Peter France describes the rigorous, formal training in rhetoric given in eighteenth-century French schools.[29] They taught how to analyse classical examples under a variety of headings: style, order of presentation, customary images, references, points of argument or explanation, ways of appealing to the listener, and manner of delivery.

The rationale behind this programme was, in the words of one textbook: 'to prepare them for the employments they will one day engage in: instructing, pleading causes, making a report on some matter, giving advice to a body'.[30]

Given that so many journalists and leaders in the Revolution were middle-class professionals it would be surprising if they did not make use of this training. They were constantly engaged in doing precisely those things for which rhetoric was supposed to have prepared them. It is true that many enlightenment writers were critical of phoney rhetorical skill. From the days of Descartes, argues Peter France, philosophers had idealized language as purified thought. But he finds in their writings many traces of rhetorical devices: graceful decoration, elegant terminology, elevating comparisons, and the strategy of introducing oneself to the given audience by flattering them and emphasizing one's common concern with them.

But there were changes. In particular, France finds a tendency to *deny* the use of artifice, and a new strategy of *self*-presentation in relating to one's audience, which can be credited to Rousseau. Rousseau's stated mistrust of high culture and respect for the value of the statusless people were echoed in his theory of communication. He emphasized those media which could be supposed to communicate directly from one soul to another: melody, gesture, forceful expression of feeling. We may add that much of Rousseau's public success among the revolutionaries was due to biographical writing (the *Confessions, Dialogues* and *Rêveries*), where he purported to display his heart to the reader. Taken together, this produced in Rousseau's writing a style that included *both* simplicity *and* rhetorical flourish. The writer was licensed to bring himself into the text, but only as an ostensibly simple being who speaks from the heart. The traditional self-effacing flattery to relate speaker to audience was re-cast, then. Rousseau's posture made it seem necessary to appeal to the naive feelings of one's audience in skilful professions of simplicity of heart, which denied all artifice. Rhetoric after Rousseau clearly chimes with the posture among revolutionary journalists. For them the artless people and the writer were united at the new heart of political life.

For the republicans, as Daniel Mornet pointed out,[31] Rousseau's appeal was that he 'described the people with love'. But Carole Blum has discovered the appeal of Rousseau's kind of emotionality right across the political spectrum during the Revolution. It offered a peculiar gift which must have been particularly serviceable where values were suddenly all in question: 'a world of moral superiority in which [the readers] could participate as equals with fictional characters who were . . . projected epiphenomena of the beloved author's own being'.[32] Blum traces Rousseau's rhetorical posture in the speeches and writings of Jacobin leaders during the crisis years of the Terror (especially Robespierre and Saint-Just) and in their political strategy as a whole. She argues that the rhetoric matched a belief that the political problem of the Republic was to draw out the virtue potential in the citizens.

We have already seen how the journalists portrayed themselves as the new focal point of politics, alongside the people. They often did so, in fact, with the Rousseauian rhetorical-emotional posture. Desmoulins, though rather urbane, introduced himself in a prospectus for his journal as a man guided, like Rousseau, by strong but simple passions. He tells us he was driven to follow the duty 'of a good citizen at this time' and 'gave in' to 'love of country and zeal for principle'. But, like Rousseau, he displays an ambivalent attitude to rhetorical show: criticizing political opponents for lacking it, showing it himself, and then appearing to undermine it by remarking sardonically that he will avoid it.[33] The imaginary figure of the upright Père Duchesne is, of course, central to Hébert's purpose. So he naturally appears constantly, speaking direct to the reader. Yet, by displacing the speaker of the journal into a complete persona who is distinct from the journalist, Hébert gave himself a certain freedom. Without dissolving that persona, he could insinuate another language into the voice of the artless man swearing like the common people. The interpolations preached republican virtue to the reader.[34]

But it was Marat who adopted Rousseau's motto (*vitam impendere vero* – to dedicate one's life to truth) at the head of his journal. Among the journalists, he advanced himself most explicitly as one speaking for the humble people, and speaking from the heart. In this posture, he implicitly shared the virtues of the humble. He described himself as 'the only author since Jean-Jacques who must be above all suspicion'.[35] And he argued that, though the people alone do not have the money to buy the services of corrupt advocates, they have his absolute loyalty anyway. One feels that Marat mimics Jean-Jacques at his most maudlin. Identifying himself exclusively in this way, he often puts himself forward as the sacrificial victim singled out for death by the enemies of the people.[36]

If we look at the language of those who were active in political institutions, we find the same Rousseauian discourse. The speaker placed himself at the centre of the people, who were purified of all egoism. This discourse counterposes those belonging within the people to those on the outside. It is an effective rhetoric to make the listener feel involved within a body of the good, for whom all things are possible. It makes it appear that speaker and people, newly united in a body politic, possess immediate political rectitude and a freedom to create history. But this strategy can end by defining a focal point where there is no one but the *entirely* pure people and their one *entirely* pure friend. It then collapses in upon itself. We can see this happening in the rhetoric of the revolutionary politicians.

Let us look first at a successful political speaker employing the strategy to a limited extent only. One would clearly expect that, in defending himself against charges of involvement in the disturbances of October, 1790, Mirabeau would use the rhetoric of the advocate.[37] Indeed, his approach is evidently conditioned by rhetoric. It consists of rebutting his accusers and the charges while claiming that it is neither necessary nor honourable to do so. He ingratiates himself with his audience, entrusting himself to their judgement, and making honour and reason appear as the common ground that unites him with them. No 'man of sense', he says, would believe the charges.[38] The procedure that has raised them is 'odious'[39] (hence, it is quite embarrassing to have to talk of it). Well-tempered clemency is the fitting attitude to the events as a whole, since the king and the people have now buried their differences.[40] Those supporting the proceeding are enemies of the Revolution who insinuate their own divisiveness into the 'august Assembly'.[41] This approach evokes a united political world, where the king, via the Assembly, has reached a compromise with the 'stormy' sentiments of the people.[42] Mirabeau appeals to the Assembly, then, by portraying *it* (rather than the people) as the heart of political unity and reasoned progress. (Indeed, Mirabeau held that the Assembly should 'regulate the application' of the immutable laws of nature.[43])

The rhetoric of Robespierre is strikingly different. Mirabeau identified himself before his audience by a combination of reason and personal honour. Robespierre slots the people and virtue into that central place where he identifies himself. Robespierre actually acknowledged his debt for this to the Rousseau of the *Confessions*. Rousseau, he wrote, had 'taught me to know myself'. His is, apparently, a noble, truth-loving, but isolated self. Present as the great events of the Revolution, Robespierre anticipates the need, like Rousseau, to share his self with the people by honest self-revelation. 'I shall soon owe my fellow citizens an accounting of my thoughts and of my acts', he writes.[44]

Elsewhere, Robespierre spelt out the political theory subtending this rhetoric. Since 'The People is always worth more than individuals'[45] and 'would sacrifice everything except its virtue'[46] it follows that to align oneself with the people was to join with virtue. The essential condition of the process of recognition is openness: 'publicity is the buttress of virtue, the safeguard to truth, the exterminator of crime, the scourge of intrigue'.[47] Openness implicitly holds out a further reward for joining the virtuous people. To remain outside the circle of the virtuous is to remain ignorant. Only those on the side of virtue will discover the truth of what lies hidden. Robespierre took over Rousseau's respect for the common people and his manner of adopting the role of virtue under attack. In the political situation of the Revolution, he made of those things a rhetorical posture which constantly demanded that honest intent be proclaimed and conspiracy be uncovered. It persuasively drew his listeners to support him as the natural consequence of their wish to be accepted into the political fold.

We can see this rhetoric at work in a debate at the Jacobins. In April 1792, Robespierre found himself accused of trying to fix the nomination of the member to succeed him in the revolutionary tribunal.[48] He immediately went on to the attack, claiming the right to have the agenda altered and be heard – on the grounds that the issue was not the choice of a single functionary but a general conspiracy against liberty. A matter of 'public safety' requires immediate attention. Once he had the floor, he derided his accusers and embarked upon an account of his record, interspersed with shrewd descriptions of himself. His opinion, he swears, is 'independent, isolated; neither my cause nor my principles have ever been attached, are not attached to anyone'.[49] In this way, he aligns himself with virtue and against all egoism. As he apostrophizes the people, he demonstrates his own common ground with them. He indicates that his very *lack* of success, and the mere fact that he is asking for a conspiracy to be exposed show that he shares the guileless virtue of the people.

> I understood from [when I was elected] that great moral and political truth enunciated by Jean-Jacques, that men only love those who love them; that only the people are good, just, magnanimous and that corruption and tyranny are the exclusive dress of those who disdain them . . . I can only claim the success that courage and faithfulness to rigorous duties obtain; I did not have it in me to seek that of intrigue and corruption . . .
> In vain will you seek to separate the men whom public opinion and love of the Nation have brought together . . . you outdo the calumnies

of our common enemies when you dare to accuse me of wanting to mislead and flatter the people! And how could I? I am neither a courtier, nor an advocate of caution, nor a tribune, nor a defender of the people. I am of the people myself.[50]

This passage is effective because of the way it implicitly portrays the revolutionary community, which is evoked demanding various moral qualities if one is to gain acceptance among the good. The rhetoric proffers the qualities needed to be united with them: self-revelation, adulation for the virtue of the people, and openness of spirit. Implicitly demanding that openness of his listeners, then, Robespierre appears as the exemplar of the candidness and virtue they should aspire to and the ally of the people they must wish to join. His opponents appear as the adversaries of those virtues and of the people. His audience is put on the spot. They must either join virtue, the people and openness against conspiracy, or remain ignorant of what was really going on and be excluded from all that was legitimate.

This rhetoric playing on an exclusive moral world was by no means unique to Robespierre. With the rise, after August 1792, of a more republican, and then the wartime 'revolutionary', government, it became more common. Robespierre could argue more and more in these terms: the public had to recognize its allies by their civic morality rather than by their political position.[51]

PARADOXES IN THE REVOLUTIONARIES' RHETORIC

In 1797, an opponent of the republicans produced an attack on the religious policies pursued under the Republic. It contained this telling parody of the rhetoric of exclusion.

I, who am a *philosopher*, and consequently sure to be right, I declare that my opinion is the *truth* and that all contrary opinions are *imposture*. I, who am a legislator, I declare that the *truth* and *imposture* cannot exist together on French territory; and as I and those that think like me are the *truth*, and as those who think otherwise are *imposture*, I pronounce that there must only be me and those who think like me in France.[52]

In this section, we shall see how the speaker using the rhetoric of exclusion could indeed end by leaving himself entirely isolated.

United acclamation was a common manner of taking decisions in the various political assemblies of the revolutionary period. The rhetorical posture I have outlined suited it well. It persuaded members to accept as truth whatever was being proclaimed around them. And it encouraged the good-hearted to contribute what they honestly believed to the debate, in the confident expectation of support from others. Yet it contained a number of paradoxes which will cause the strategy to break down under certain extra-discursive conditions.

The first two such paradoxes can be seen in Robespierre's case. Indeed, Robespierre's own argument for the civil religion introduced in 1794 made a vital concession. If he had had to choose between an illusion that united the people and a truth that did not, Robespierre admitted that he would choose the illusion.[53] This implies that truth and unity will not necessarily appear *together*. If that is so, then what is in effect the rhetoric's own inherent criterion of truth is undermined. How do the members of an assembly react to diversity or disagreement? They cannot then use the rhetoric's way of choosing the truth. They can no longer find the easy confidence of truth and their discourse will fall apart.

The second paradox is this. The rhetorical strategy ends by appealing for the light of open publicity to reveal the crimes of the excluded. For this appeal to fall on willing ears, the bulk of the listeners must be in a situation to feel that they themselves can be counted among the good. Where many of them feel they may be placed amongst the excluded, they will evidently resist the proposal. The speaker's opponents will not be summarily condemned; he may instead be excluded himself.

By the summer of 1794 conditions were moving against the 'revolutionary' government which Robespierre dominated. The exceptional powers put in the hands of the executive were paying off too well. The danger of military collapse was receding. But more and more of the politically active were less likely to find themselves touched by the disagreeable measures and implicated in, or even threatened by the Terror. So conditions existed for politicians to dissociate themselves from the revolutionary executive, if they got the chance. Robespierre's rhetoric offered that chance. Under those conditions, it encouraged support to fall away, rather than coalescing it.

Robespierre's last discourse to the Convention[54] aroused opposition rather than support. Politically isolated among his colleagues in the government and the Convention, he tried to present himself in the well-tried terms. He was, he said, one among the many 'friends of principle' who are without influence because others have 'thought out in the shadows, unknown to their colleagues, to take away . . . the right to defend the people, with life itself'. But, he went on in tragic tones, having seen how the defenders of liberty have always been treated, he would surrender life without regret. He appealed to the assembly: let us recall the government to its principle, throw light on the hidden abuses, denounce the traitors. It has often been asked why Robespierre failed to say *whom* he wanted proscribed. For this aroused fears in *all* his listeners. But silence on that point was usual and natural to his rhetoric and to his view of the Revolution. He sought to establish an implicit confidence between himself and those in the audience who felt themselves to be on the side of the people and the good. To specify could undermine that sense of understanding. But this time the majority felt themselves linked together *to the exclusion of Robespierre*. His entire image of the Revolution failed him at that moment.

The speeches of Saint-Just, who was an ally of Robespierre in the government, display a similar system of concepts. But, as a speaker, Saint-Just was more concerned to place himself in time: at the historical moment when freedom is about to be realized in the community of the virtuous people. This led to a tragic posture. For Saint-Just, the Republic, in whose name he spoke, would re-establish the open, trustful association natural to humankind, or die. Saint-Just's early *L'Esprit de la Révolution et la Constitution de la France*, linked his own identity, the people and the freedom that can be achieved through virtue. 'As a member of the sovereign I wanted to know if I was free', he wrote.[55] He concluded that laws might be framed by which 'I would be obeying only my own virtue'.

The system of exclusion which makes the people the focal point of legitimacy and virtue is apparent in the speech that first attracted attention to him: at the king's trial before the Convention. Saint-Just's implicit position is that an exclusive social compact is formed by the association of virtuous citizens. This logic excludes the king on two grounds. As he is the government, he cannot be embraced by the social compact. And he has excluded himself, *as would any other member*, by his criminal deeds: 'As soon as a man is guilty, he quits the city'.[56] But as he speaks, Saint-Just also invokes a notion of the history in which the Revolution is realizing the community founded on virtue. Routine classical references compare the situation of Louis to that of Caesar, stabbed without legal ceremony by Brutus himself. But Saint-Just situates that comparison in an imagined historical *advance* beyond the level of liberty achieved by the Romans:

One day, people will be amazed that in the Eighteenth Century, we

30

were less advanced than in Caesar's day. . . . A certain uncertainty has arisen. . . . Each [of you] sees the king's trial with his own particular view. . . . We seek liberty and make ourselves the slaves of each other! . . . What republic do you want to establish in the midst of individual combats and collective weaknesses?[57]

Rhetorically, the implied historical situation of the Convention possesses considerable force. The people, for whom Saint-Just speaks, appear as the unique repository of social virtue, ascending through history. So Saint-Just can contrast the chaos of egotistical voices in the Convention. Then he can invite the Convention to embrace the role of the community and the course of history itself.[58]

When he spoke in the Convention debate on the 1793 constitution, Saint-Just evoked the same terms. The sovereign assembly elected by the people acts as one united body, he argued. He presupposed that the citizens are virtuous and politically conscious. But that permitted a persuasive promise to the constitution-writers: that they can 'order the future'[59] and construct the harmonious nation that is required by the historical moment.

Europe will demand peace of you the day you give a Constitution to the French people.

On that very day, divisions will cease, defeated factions will stoop beneath the yoke of liberty; citizens will return to their workshops, to their tasks, and the peace that reigns in the Republic will make monarchs tremble.[60]

In following through his rhetorical stance, however, Saint-Just's longing for a seamless fraternity leads him on to a wish for death rather than compromise with the human reality of vice and dissension. In the speech he wanted to make to the Convention the day before his execution, Saint-Just's hope for transparent harmony is transposed into pathetic appeals to another, transcendent public opinion beyond the assembly. According to the text of his speech, his enemies' deceiving words at the meeting of the government the previous night 'blighted'[61] his heart and 'made it tremble'. His sole hope, as one isolated man, was to call upon Providence and public opinion.[62] Thus he appears tragically alone, the only virtuous and honest one in a welter of conspiracy. He adopts the attitude of the classical suicide:

I resolved, therefore, to trample over all cowardly considerations, and to open up [the] affair immediately before [the Convention] . . . The situation I find myself in would have seemed delicate to anyone with anything to reproach himself with; . . . but, for sure, it would be a small thing to quit a life in which one must be either the accomplice or the silent witness of evil.[63]

That version of the Revolution which saw it expelling from the inner sanctum all of the previous political values and personnel reaches its ultimate point. Saint-Just rejects *all* the given reality of political power and abandons life itself for the abstract value of the harmonious people.

The general character of political *vocabulary* in the revolutionary period to some extent backs up the impression gained in my analysis of the *use* made of language. Language was being used to redefine the focal point and the periphery of legitimate politics and situate the speaker at the centre where virtue, destiny in historical time and the freedom to weld history were located. So vocabulary was extended to encompass more easily abstract ideals of community and to distinguish political deeds in keeping with the new legitimacy from those opposed to it.

In his glossary of revolutionary political language, Max Frey,[64] examined the devices to extend the vocabulary. Suffixes attached to a large number of proper or common names generated terms for a more or less abstract movement, or deed. *'Robespierrisme'*, *'dantonisme'*, *'rolandisme'*, *'fréronisme'* (together with their adjectives: *'robespierriste'*, etc.) are the most obvious cases. They elevate the political personage to the status of a political current or ideal. Other new terms made political symbols out of what is ordinary: thus a *'carémiste'* is one who willingly goes without for the good of the Republic. Because ordinary deeds acquired political significance, many new verbs were formed out of the names of individuals or historical occasions: *'septembriser'* (to summarily execute by rioting crowds), *'juillettiser'* (to inspire with the revolutionary enthusiasm of July 1789), *'monsieuriser'* (to address someone as *'monsieur'* in spite of official pressure to use only the status-neutral 'citizen'), *'ministérialiser'* (to convert to support the government as against the people or the legislature).[65] Suffixes and prefixes achieved a similar purpose. They enabled the speaker to give actions a broad political character: *'liberticide'* (the crime of trying to destroy liberty by acting in the wrong political direction); *'clubinomanie'* (the obsessive frequentation of political clubs); *'lèse-nation'* or *'lèse-société'* (the crime of acting in a way that loosens fraternal ties in society); and *'stratocratie'* (rule from above).

The analysis in this chapter has shown how political language tried to effect and convey a conceptual restructuring of the political-social world. It portrayed the Revolution's new political world: defining what belonged inside the legitimate collective processes of politics and what was excluded. The users of political language naturally located themselves inside the new common territory. They defined it in terms of sovereign right, virtue, unity, purity, openness, historic strength born of political activity, and knowledge born of openness. Yet the new centre of communal life was unstable; it showed a tendency under pressure to dissolve into vacuousness or self-defeat.

Were the dissolution of unity or the collapse into abstraction the *inevitable* outcome of redrawing the boundaries of political right around the people? I think not. But various critics argue along these lines.[66] Blum argues for this conclusion.[67] According to her, Robespierre and Saint-Just were caught in a spiral that progressively narrowed the circle of the politically virtuous until, in effect, the political leader found himself alone with no strategy but to die for his ideal. Another version of the argument can be found in the analysis of Brian Singer.[68] Singer's thesis is that, by constituting society as its own self-referring legitimation, secular post-Enlightenment ideas could only identify the nation and 'its' representation so closely as to render all opposition or division treasonable. Consequently, the Revolution had to wrestle with the difficulty inherent in the belief that pure truth is immanent within society itself. That is to say, the new political order had to suppress signs of internal division or power relations. Yet another, most suggestive version of this argument can be found in a short essay by Paul Chanier.[69] Chanier argues that the revolutionaries are frequently guilty of the 'sophism of self-reference'; that is, the belief that a proposition can validate its own truth. Through this prism, Chanier identifies widespread aspects of the revolutionary mentality: the view that innocent error is impossible because the truly virtuous heart divines the truth; the feeling that normal human sympathy for those whom the self-validating sovereign executes was irrational; and the expectation of an absolute, universal authority which needs no force to obtain obedience. All are incoherent for the same, logical reason. Self-reference cannot be enough to establish truth; there have to be some distinct rules of decision prior to decisions themselves.

These critical analyses offer different explanations of why the new organization of collective politics was liable to collapse. The anticipated virtue cannot be found (Blum). The all-encompassing unity is cross-cut by differences of view, interest and purpose, and those who are open suspect some veiled opposition (Singer). The new institutions and their pronouncements fall into the contradiction of self-reference (Chanier). The latter two analyses are particularly instructive. For they pare down a revolutionary habit of mind to a step in the logic of the system of concepts: the system's enclosure upon itself. The revolutionaries usually sought self-referential totalities: abstract, seamless and exclusive.

Logical analyses confront the problem of the collapse of the revolutionaries' way of determining the new political and social order in its most general, logical *form*. But, revealing as they are, logical accounts serve poorly as terms in an *explanation*. Chanier, for example, explains the logic in the revolutionaries' thinking as the effect of inertia: it merely carried on a logical error found widely in the eighteenth century. My analysis, on the other hand, has drawn attention instead to a cultural *process* going on *within* the Revolution: the attempt to define a new political-social-moral world, with a new centre and new exclusions. This process was a pressing necessity for those involved. Without a new understanding for the social world in which they were operating, they would flounder. In my perspective, then, the logical form of the system of concepts adopted can hardly be looked upon as the deep *origin* of its tendency to collapse. Logic merely sums it up.

Instead, it is necessary to attend to the connection *between* the cultural process and what it tried to represent. We can then ask: Was the cultural process *intended* to encompass social reality in its representation of the new political-social order? The answer must be yes. Still focusing on the cultural process, the next question must be whether the process managed to connect with reality. Not for long, it appears. It sought to determine a solid political community of the good, and failed. Abstraction needs to be seen as the outcome of failing in the effort to discover virtue or seamless unity. These were evidently risky categories to adopt, because they were likely to prove empty. But then, why did the culture adopt them, and how close did they come to managing to sustain them? We need to look at further attempts to identify the new centre by other cultural means and media. This I shall do in the following chapters.

NOTES

1. Meeting with Robespierre on 13 May 1792, quoted in Norman Hampson, *Will and Circumstance: Montesquieu, Rousseau and the French Revolution* (London: Duckworth, 1983), p. 202.
2. Michael J. Kennedy, *The Jacobin Clubs in the French Revolution: the First Years* (Princeton, NJ: Princeton University Press, 1982), pp. 13 and 19,

and see ch. 1, *passim*. Compare the following description of the Société de 1789: 'une compagnie des hommes . . . et agents du commerce des vérités sociales' (*Journal de la Société de 1789*, 5 June 1790, p. 3).

3. See Michael Phillip Carter, 'Prolegomena to a Study of Revolutionary Discourse: The Jacobins Club of Paris in the Year II', unpublished Ph.D. dissertation, Stanford University, 1973, ch. II, esp. pp. 41 and 51.

4. See Ruth Graham, 'The Revolutionary Bishop and the *Philosophes*', *Eighteenth-century Studies*, 16, 1983.

5. Jack Richard Censer, *Prelude to Power: the Parisian Radical Press, 1789–91* (Baltimore, MD and London: Johns Hopkins University Press, 1976).

6. J.P Marat, *Appel à la Nation*, in A. Vermorel (ed.), *Oeuvres de J.P. Marat* (Paris: 1869), p. 48: 'La manière dont les états généraux avaient été composés . . . m'avait fait sentir la nécessité de surveiller avec sollicitude l'Assemblée Nationale, de relever ses erreurs, de la ramener aux bons principes'.

7. Censer, op. cit., Chapter 3.

8. 'c'est que la classe de citoyens infortunés est la seule qui soit patriote, comme elle est la seule qui soit honnête' (*Ami du Peuple*, 6 September 1790, quoted in J.M. Roberts (ed.), *French Revolutionary Documents*, vol. 1 (Oxford: Blackwell, 1966), pp. 268–9.

9. Desmoulins, *Révolutions de France et de Brabant* (Paris: n.d.), no. 23, 3 May 1790, quoted in Censer, op. cit., p. 54.

10. Censer, op. cit., Chapter 4.

11. 'la soumission aux lois qu'il a faites ou consenties est à la fois la première vertu des Citoyens et la sauvegarde la plus sûre de la liberté' (*Journal des Amis de la Constitution*, 21 November 1790, p. 3).

12. 'jusqu'à ce que l'Assemblée Nationale s'occupe de cette réform désirée' (ibid., p. 33).

13. 'Toutefois le législateur . . . appelle la force publique au secours de l'ordre publique' (*Mémoires de la Société de 1789*, 15 September 1790, pp. 1–8).

14. 'Nouveau tour de tactique employé par l'Ami du Peuple' in *L'Ami du Peuple*, no. 132, 24 February 1793. '. . . défendre les droits du citoyen, de contrôler l'autorité, de réclamer contre leurs attentats, de réprimer leurs malversations' *Appel à la Nation*, in *Oeuvres*, op. cit., p. 49.

15. See F. Braesch (ed.), *Le Père Duchesne d'Hébert* (Paris: Société de l'Histoire de la Révolution Française and Rieder, 1922), vol. 1, pp. 31ff.

16. Ibid., p. 283.

17. Ibid., p. 285.

18. Ibid., p. 281.

19. *Révolutions de France et de Brabant* (Paris: n.d.), vols 6–7, no. 67, pp. 49–96.

20. Ibid., p. 49.

21. Ibid., p. 60.

22. Ibid., pp. 74–5.

23. Ibid., p. 82.

24. Ibid., p. 96.

25. 'Tels sont les principes aujourd'hui reconnus par tous les hommes éclairés, principes que dans un autre hémisphère plusieurs sages républiques ont adoptés' (*Journal de la Société de 1789*, no. II, 12 June 1790).
26. *L'Ami du Peuple*, 28 June 1790 (quoted in Roberts, op. cit., p. 264): 'déloyauté pour le peuple . . . les obstacles que vous vous êtes efforcé de mettre à l'entreprise des citoyens soulevés . . . les tentatives continuelles que vous ne cessez de faire contre le voeu de la Commune'.
27. Braesch, op. cit., vol. 1, p. 541.
28. Braesch, op. cit., vol. 2.
29. Peter France, *Rhetoric and Truth in France: Descartes to Diderot* (Oxford: Clarendon, 1972).
30. 'de les préparer aux emplois qu'ils doivent un jour exercer: instruire, plaider, faire un rapport d'une affaire, dire son avis à une compagnie' (C. Rollin, *De la Manière d'enseigner et d'étudier les belles-lettres* (Paris: 1726, 1775); quoted in France, op. cit., p. 7).
31. Daniel Mornet, *Origines intellectuelles de la Révolution française* (Paris: Armand Colin, 1933), p. 297.
32. Carole Blum, *Rousseau and the Republic of Virtue: The Language of Politics in the French Revolution* (Ithaca, NY and London: Cornell University Press, 1986), p. 140.
33. 'You imagine, dear Reader, that I am going to continue in this manner, and wear myself out with such long tirades?' ('Vous imaginez, mon cher Lecteur, que je vais continuer sur ce ton, et épuiser mon haleine par de si longues tirades?') Desmoulins, op. cit., no. 1, p. 9.
34. For a detailed structural analysis of Duchesne's bipolar vocabulary, dividing political forces into those adding to and those opposing the popular legitimacy, see J. Guilhaumou, 'L'Idéologie du Père Duchesne: Les forces adjuvantes', in Régine Robin, *Langues et idéologies: le discours comme objet de l'histoire* (Paris: Editions Sociales, 1974) pp. 81–116. Guilhaumou concludes that Père Duchesne 'as a Jacobin ideology . . . functioned not only to occlude the exploitative relations at the heart of the Third Estate, but also to circulate among the sansculottes masses a bourgeois conception of democracy, with the help of a process that camouflaged the content at the level of the form' (p. 115).
35. 'le seul auteur depuis Jean-Jacques qui dût être à l'abri de tout soupçon' (Marat, in Vermorel, op. cit., p. 44, also p. 45).
36. 'Je sais tous les dangers auxquels je m'expose en m'élevant contre vous [i.e. Lafayette]. Mais n'espérez point à me réduire au silence: je vous voue une haine éternelle, tant que vous machinerez contre la liberté.' *L'Ami du Peuple*, 28 June 1790, quoted in Roberts, op. cit., p. 265.
37. Mirabeau, *Discours*, ed. F. Furet (Paris: Gallimard, 1973), pp. 276–88.
38. Ibid., p. 277.
39. Ibid., p. 278.
40. Ibid., p. 277.
41. Ibid., p. 278.
42. Ibid., p. 277.
43. Ibid., p. 396.

44. 'Dedication to Jean-Jacques Rousseau', quoted in Blum, op. cit., pp. 156–7, q.v. for discussion of the document's authenticity.
45. Robespierre, *Oeuvres complètes*, vol. 5, ed. G. Laurent (Gap: Louis Jean, 1961), p. 209.
46. Ibid., vol. 10, ed. M. Bouloiseau and A. Soboul (Paris: Presses Universitaires de France, 1967), p. 560.
47. Robespierre, *Textes choisis*, ed. J. Poperen (Paris: Editions Sociales, 1974) vol. 2, p. 155.
48. Robespierre, *Oeuvres complètes*, vol. 8, ed. M. Bouloiseau, G. Lefèbvre and A. Soboul (Paris: PUF, 1954), pp. 303ff.
49. Ibid., p. 306.
50. Ibid., pp. 308–11.
51. Ibid., vol. 5, ed. G. Laurent (Gap: Louis Jean, 1961), pp. 17–19.
52. Jean-François La Harpe, *Du Fanatisme dans la langue révolutionnaire* (Paris: 1797), pp. 93–4.
53. 'quiconque renonce, par cupidité, même à une erreur qu'il regarde comme un vérité, est déjà corrompu.' (Robespierre, *Oeuvres complètes*, vol. 5, pp. 117–19).
54. 8 Thermidor II, references are from Robespierre, *Textes choisis*, pp. 185–93.
55. Saint-Just, *Oeuvres complètes*, ed. C. Vellay (Paris: Charpentier et Fasquelle, 1908), vol. 1, p. 251, quoted in Blum, op. cit., p. 163.
56. A. Soboul (ed.), *Saint-Just: Discours et rapports* (Paris: Editions Sociales, 1970), p. 67.
57. Ibid., pp. 63–4.
58. Ibid., p. 65.
59. Ibid., p. 99.
60. Ibid., p. 95.
61. Ibid., p. 202.
62. Ibid., pp. 213 and 214.
63. Ibid., pp. 203–4.
64. Max Frey, *Les Transformations du vocabulaire français à l'époque de la Révolution* (Paris: Presses Universitaires de France, 1925).
65. Desmoulins, op. cit., no. 67, p. 77, for example, asserted that the Jacobins would never be 'ministerialized'.
66. François Furet, who is considered in detail in Chapter 7, must also be counted among these.
67. Blum, op. cit., esp. Chapter 10.
68. Brian C.J. Singer, *Society, Theory and the French Revolution: Studies in the Revolutionary Imaginary* (London: Macmillan, 1986).
69. Paul Chanier, 'Si Robespierre avait lu Tarski: antinomie et discours révolutionnaires' in A. Tosel (ed.), *Philosophies de la Révolution française* (Paris: Vrin, 1984), pp. 271–84.

CHAPTER TWO

Theatre and Festivals: Performing the Revolution

We have seen in the previous chapter how the political language of the Revolution manifested a frustrated need to define a new focal point of social and political life: the sovereign public. Suppose a different form of culture working with the representations of the new political-social order. We might also find that attempts to resolve this problem in the culture involve some kind of performance by people. Some writers were very confident of the possibilities of the theatre, for example:

> Citizens, just think back to how, in the old days, the most respectable classes of the sovereign people were vilified, degraded, unworthily ridiculed, to give a laugh to kings and their flunkies at court. I thought it was high time to pay them back in their own coin, and to amuse ourselves in our turn. [1]

In this chapter, I shall analyse four areas of what I call 'performing': the theatre, festivals and, to a limited extent, songs and language.

It will be seen immediately that I am using the term 'performing' in a particular, though not a unique sense. For example, I shall argue that, by virtue of the manners and stagecraft of the time, the theatre produced a sort of participation in shared feelings of belonging to an active collectivity. Shows in the theatre at the time produced behaviour and emotions in the auditorium which encouraged members of the audience to feel that they belonged together. My interest is not, then, the performance by the actors, but that by the audience. Attending and responding together to the actors was a 'performance' by them of a role as members of the public that had been newly turned into a republican collectivity. Members of the audience engaged in a 'performance', in the sense of a pattern of behaviour appropriate to fostering their involvement in their position in the new social-political order.

The participants in the communal events known variously as *fêtes*, 'festivals' or 'carnivals' perform a participatory act in the same sense as the audience in the theatre. More explicitly than theatre, in the revolutionary period, their performance imparted a sense of the content of the new centre of the political-social world.[2] And, both within the *fêtes* and beyond, performing music was a further way, during this period, in which people fostered involvement in their own new position.

In this chapter, then, I shall analyse the effects sought in the performances in the theatre, festival and music of the Revolution, in their efforts to lend substance to the new system of concepts around social-political life. There is a considerable body of theoretical writing on the anthropology of the carnival, both in general and in the Revolution. Using this to understand the cultural processes in performance, I can assess how near the media I consider came to overcoming the difficulties discovered in those looked at in Chapter 1.

THE THEATRE: PARTICIPATION AND SENTIMENT

Before looking closely at some political pieces that were played on the Paris stage during the revolutionary years, we need to see them in context. Beatrice Hyslop's study of what was performed[3] has shown that the most obviously political plays were not the most successful ones. But, on the other hand, the spectacles that were well received did show a politically significant inflection in their subject matter and values. Furthermore, we can find both innovations and continuities in a variety of theatrical experiences that would give substance to the new conceptual system of legitimacy.

An evolutionary process extended changes going on for some decades before the Revolution. The traditional theatre was characterized by lengthy verse speeches and the static manner of classical tragedy. Even before the Revolution, it had branched out to accommodate a new audience, offer new sorts of entertainment, and treat new themes. In Paris, the theatre had come to attract largely middle-class audiences, mostly for comedy. Tragedy (including historical drama such as de Belloy's play about the siege of Calais) and fantasies (personifying gods, moral qualities, etc.) came a poor second in popularity. Music played a prominent role and new combinations of the accepted genres were

39

being tried all the time. In addition, an increasing number of less reputable playhouses were coming into existence. There, in an attempt to attract clientele, livelier productions were put on including fantasy spectacles with sensational tricks such as lighting a pyre on stage.[4] In sum, while the themes and characters of theatrical performance in the latter half of the eighteenth century were broadening a little, stagecraft was changing a lot.

It has been argued[5] that drama in the late eighteenth-century mainstream theatres reflected essentially middle-class experience and values. Comedies, which were very strait-laced by modern standards, rehearsed certain well-tried formulas such as star-crossed lovers, the reuniting of divided families and relations between masters and servants. The subject matter and the dewy-eyed modesty of the treatment suited steady middle-class citizens. Politically sensitive themes, which might have reflected enlightened views, were outlawed apparently by both public taste and official censorship. So were the lives of the lower orders — except in the shape of stage rustics invested with pastoral wisdom, and fishwives, who were spoofed in one of a new type of play known as *poissardes*.

However, though the middle classes may have dominated the theatres numerically, their values (as John Lough has argued)[6] did not oust those of others. When 'middle-class' situations were portrayed, it was in the lives of socially elevated characters. (Where immoral behaviour was portrayed, this was usually in the person of an even more elevated, though dissolute, aristocrat). The *social* atmosphere of the theatre was dominated by rank. Stage seats, where aristocrats would settle themselves to a respectful greeting from audience *and company*, had disappeared in mid-century. But the stratification between the pit and the different rows of boxes in the theatre remained. That, and the habit of keeping house lights up, made a visit to the theatre very much a social occasion. In the status-ridden society of the *ancien régime*, the middle classes continued to share a high regard for the value of social elevation. Accordingly, the social experience of the theatre did not become middle-class just because the audiences were.

Socially, theatre goers were united by a feeling of what sentiments should be experienced in the theatre. This way of sharing feeling was to be passed on to the post-revolutionary theatre. Visible expression of sympathy, pity and joy at the predicament of the characters was as common in the auditorium as on stage. Spectators responded freely to the customary sentimental style of acting (known as 'breathless') and to the succession of passionate exchanges played out before them. Music

40

occupied a vital role in the emotional effect of productions – as it appears to have done in the theatre of almost all ages but our own.[7]

The activity of the audience was very much more prominent in the late eighteenth-century theatre than today. The manner of production matched this. Plays were put on with little preparation, alternated with each other and freely changed. The theatre was a *social*, in a very real sense a *public* occasion. Members of the audience greated each other, chatted freely, showed their approval or disapproval, and commentated on what was on stage – even interrupting the dialogue. Applause and encores of particularly well-liked speeches were common. Productions must have resembled a modern poetry reading or a folk concert, in which each speech, scene or song was treated like an individual number performed for the audience. The shared reactions of the audience was given prominence in the theatre, then. It was the stigma of rowdy behaviour rather than a respect for the play as an integrated whole which constrained the audience to silence, where they gave it.

In sum, in the late eighteenth century the audience brought its social existence *visibly* into the theatre. As a form of culture, theatre gave great space to the social relations of acquaintance or of hierarchical differentiation between the members of the audience, and validated certain shared emotions.

The upheaval of the Revolution offered a moment of opportunity as well as risk for the theatre. Though the top stratum of the audiences fell away, or left the country, the core of the theatre-going public remained constant, and there was some influx from the poorer classes. On the other hand, there was much public and official enthusiasm for theatrical spectacles expressing the new ideas and sentiments. The new authorities were keen to offer money and expropriated buildings (churches, the halls of aristocrats' *hôtels*) for shows directed at the newly recognised people. For their part, theatre groups involved themselves in patriotic public festivals and/or replayed them afterwards on stage. Theatres enlivened the evening's entertainment by leading the audience in patriotic songs. Rather ghoulishly (to us from another age), they even read out lists of traitors executed that day.

Plays and spectacles on new, patriotic subjects had been advocated in some quarters since the middle of the century.[8] The removal of censorship – though it only lasted until 1794 – opened the way to spectacles on new subjects. The effort to adapt was, on the other hand, politically hazardous, and some enthusiasts for the new order found themselves persecuted by those they had tried to support.[9] Overall, rather than overhauling its forms, the theatre after the Revolution seems to have modulated its range of subject matter and emotions around new themes. Whatever the shade of revolutionary politics represented, however, it can be seen to have been conveying the experience of the new moral identity and unity of the public, with its sense of altering the shape of history.

Many plays from before the Revolution continued in the repertoire. But the new political ideas appeared in both the inherited programme and in successful new works. The latter showed a new attention to the lower orders. Old and new plays and operas about military heroism, love of country, and the fight for national freedom were well received. Both an old and a new version of the William Tell story were successful, for example. And newly written tragedies depicting struggles for the Roman republic shared success with pre-revolutionary works on the same theme, notably Voltaire's *Brutus*,[10] which will be looked at more closely later in the next section. The characters and language of comedy retained the decency noted above. The writers of comedy simply adapted their range of basic situations by inserting sansculotte families into them, changing the social position of the characters and giving a new prominence to their political values. Tensions now arose — only to be happily resolved — over such matters as whether the family should read French history or accounts of contemporary civic dutifulness. Lovers were now separated or reunited over their love of country versus the call of military duty, or over suspicions of a lack of *civisme* or of counter-revolution (as in *L'Ami des lois*, which I will examine shortly). The most successful fantasy production in the early 1790s was *Nicodème dans la lune*. A fairly traditional theatrical peasant is transferred to the society on the moon, where his unflattering comparisons with the old regime inspire a peaceful revolution. More vindictively, *Le Jugement dernier des rois* (also to be examined later) imagines the Pope plus all the monarchs of Europe banished to a volcanic island, there to be consumed by fire.

Two new forms of production should be mentioned, however. Melodrama was not shaped into a regular form until Pixérécourt's work in the late 1790s. Yet already the practice of expressing a silent character's emotion with accompanying music (the original meaning of melodrama, due to Rousseau) was established. Other elements, such as stock characters and spectacular dénouements were also to be seen. So, we can say that the mood of melodrama, if not its explicit form, was present in the theatre in the revolutionary period. One other form, with strong and explicit political connections, must be noted. The *pièce de circonstance* re-enacted events such as national victories in the war, or national celebrations at the great festivals. One of the most successful of these, Gossec and Cardel's *Offrande à la liberté* (performed approximately 100 times) imitated the music, cannons and pageantry of the *fête de Notre Dame.*

We know little directly of audience reactions during the revolutionary period. Incidents occurred right across the country when radical patriots clashed with others in the audience. Disputes broke out over such matters as whether the republican red cap could be worn during a performance, or whether a given play took a just view of the nation, the government or the people. In these episodes, communes, revolutionary committees and/or republican clubs often intervened to maintain order and 'proper' patriotism in what was performed. It is hard to say whether the authorities were more troubled by the threat of riot or by lack of patriotism. They probably reasoned that the dignity of true patriotism would discourage the disorder. As a place of assembly, however, the theatre clearly became a site for *political* expression in the audience.[11] Given the considerable similarity of material and form, it seems right to suppose that overall reactions continued to be *emotional* and *dramatically similar*, while the social and political content of the public response changed.

Hyslop's findings suggest that it was still theatrical, rather than political qualities that brought success. Spectacle, humour or songs (which the audience joined in with) must have contributed much to the popularity of a successful play like *Nicodème*. The longest-running production of all (called *La Journée des capucins aux frontières*) was described as a '*ballet-pantomime-parlant*', indicating the continuing appeal of music in theatrical spectacles. Hyslop concludes that, though political content became common, it reflected imprecise political positions, and was certainly not slavishly close to the regime in power.

But the changes were significant, especially in terms of the themes I have been tracing. Simply to present serious political sentiments must have been a stunning innovation to members of the older generation. Beaumarchais, for example, requested that the hostess of a private play-reading exclude 'worn-out hearts' and 'dried-up souls', who were 'only good for talking revolution'.[12] But the target of the theatres was still emotional warmth, and sensation, even though it was now adapted to a new thematic and emotional content in plays or productions. That is to say, productions aimed at the same emotional response in a medium which retained its public, social character. They continued to portray similar upright virtues of honesty, fidelity, loyalty or heroism. But these were now linked to love of country etc., and located in a lower — though still respectable — social class, rather a stage version of the poor. In this way, productions could encourage their audiences to experience a sense of belonging to the public, which was now the focus of legitimacy.

SOME PLAYS

We can now see this at work in some specific examples and follow the evolution of themes and their treatment. Though it dated from 1730, Voltaire's *Brutus* was often produced in the years after the Revolution. It situated in classical history a tragic conflict between duty towards the public good and private passion and ambition. No more need be said about how the comparison with the classical era elevated modern history. The point would hardly be lost on the audiences of the 1790s. The figure of Brutus dominates the play from the start. He proclaims to the Senate (assembled on stage) that virtue and law are their gods, and that they must teach monarchs to pay due respect to the republic, its free people and their rights. The tragedy arises because, unbeknown to Brutus, the deposed king and his allies are enlisting the support of Brutus's own passionate, ambitious son in a conspiracy against the republic. In its own day, Voltaire's play clearly steered a narrow political line towards some kind of constitutional restraint on the monarchy. In the early 1790s, the parallel between the situation of Rome and of France (also surrounded by hostile monarchies) can only have reinforced its effectiveness and elevated the contemporary battles on to the level of transhistorical pursuit of freedom under law.

But, given Voltaire's strict adherence to classical unities and rules of staging, the play does this by evoking emotions and ideals in its poetry. Brutus's expression of commitment to the republic as he refuses all consolation after the execution of his son (which he himself had ordered) is chillingly awesome:

> Vous connaissez Brutus et l'osez consoler!
> Songez qu'on nous prépare une attaque nouvelle:
> Rome seule a mes soins: mon coeur ne connaît qu'elle. [13]

His son's admission of a moment's fatal weakness might, on the other hand, evoke sympathetic condemnation.

> Mon coeur encore surpris de son égarement,
> Emporté loin de soi, fut coupable un moment:
> Ce moment m'a couvert d'une honte éternelle,
> A mon pays que j'aime il m'a fait infidèle:[14]

This suggests an entirely undramatic presentation by modern standards. But we may grasp its effectiveness if we take the contemporary theatrical ethos into account. With an emphasis on the heartfelt delivery of passages of poetry, the contemporary audience would respond openly together to the poetic evocation of these apposite patriotic sentiments and of the lower human emotions in conflict with them. *Brutus* could enable the revolutionary tragedy audience to rehearse collectively the sentiments felt to be necessary for the citizen of the new France.

Marie-Joseph Chénier's *Charles IX* was written in the build-up to the Revolution and first performed in the midst of a public furore in 1789. It successfully employed the same classical tragedy approach as the means to present progressive ideas. Yet the ideas, and hence the emotional import, are significantly different. Voltaire had counterposed two *principles* (public good as opposed to private passion and ambition) in the thoughts of a small number of notable characters. Chénier portrays two morally contrasted social types. One of them plainly includes the people as a moral point of reference. Overall, the play seems intended to evoke hope for the future of France grounded in progressive constitutional principles of respect for law, sound government and, most notably, the integrity of the people.

Chénier adopted a tactical version of the history of France. It had already been used in Voltaire's epic poem the *Henriade*. He 'recalled' the principles of good government to the present-day regime and public by going back to the moment in French history when the first of the Bourbons was about to ascend the throne. He thus associated those principles with the royal family of his day. The target of criticism in the play, the character of *court* life as a whole, is more pointed than that of *Brutus*, however. Whereas in *Brutus* tyranny is merely camped on the banks of the Tiber outside the city, in Chénier's play corruption is all around us. It may have been the progressive principles that caused the furore about *Charles IX*. Or it may have been the portrayal of a corrupt court dominated by a woman (Catherine de Medici) – too much like Louis XVI's court was rumoured to be. But Chénier's play portrays the survival of the good in spite of all-enveloping evil in the government. Its effect, therefore, is to evince gloom and hatred of courtly government at the same time as hope.

Its handling of this history is dramatically freer, more powerful and emotionally more immediate than Voltaire's. Scenes change faster and build up to an emotional atmosphere quite absent in the earlier play. This style is probably the product of late eighteenth-century pre-romantic trends (including the gradual acceptance of Shakespeare). However that may be, it allows a radically different *political* experience in the play. One after another the audience meets the heroic admiral who will in time be murdered by decision of the king; the conspiring cardinal with the ambitious, haughty contender he wants to see on the throne; the devious queen mother (with whom they are in untrusting alliance); and the indecisive king, tottering between the advice of one and the other. The scheming ends with the king ordering the massacre that actually took place on St Bartholomew's Day 1572. Yet within an all-enveloping, murderous world, there is a political alternative and a beam of hope. It is felt in the young Bourbon, Henri IV (plain-speaking and unaffected by court life), and in the incorruptible chancellor.

The contrast between the two social types in the play is defined by personal qualities linked to political attitudes towards the people. On one side, the cardinal urges his protégé (who is jealous of the popularity of the young Henri IV) to 'become more popular; bend in order to govern; you are admired, you must please people'. [15] But the ambitious duke disdains the public: 'Let's forget this public, this inconstant mob, the tumultuous echo of fables of its own invention.'[16] And the queen mother commends rule 'by discord' and division. [17] On the other side, there is the martial admiral, and Henri, who harks back to the plain decency and 'rough virtue' of his military life: 'In stead of servants subject to my orders, I saw around me equals, friends.'[18] And at his side the chancellor, forthright 'citizen of France', is secured by his faith in principles of tolerance, reason and law. Respect for the people is continually on his lips: 'night', he tells the audience in the very first scene, 'surrounds the sacred rights of the people and the duties of the throne'. [19] It is these last two characters who survive at the end, to fight unscathed for the future; while King Charles himself is ineffectually smitten with remorse over the St Bartholomew murders.

What would be the net emotional effect of *Charles IX?* The play requires a serious, not to say highly literate audience. But the atmosphere is powerful and tragic. The play's insertion into history and the allusion to the people are vital. In contrast to the moral limitations of the court, the future King Henri IV and the chancellor value and respect the people. Seeing it at this time, the spectators must have felt that the future belonged to that progressive, peace-loving party. The audience is encouraged to share a heroic faith straddling history: that history may be rebuilt beyond the limitations of an enclosed monarchical government disdainful of the people. The good heart and respect for the people portrayed in this second group of characters define a response for Chénier's audience.

After two works in the fairly elevated tragic genre, let us now look at a later play, a comedy with melodramatic elements and a quite explicitly political plot. In 'Citoyen' Laya's *L'Ami des lois* (1793), M. (formerly marquis) de Forlis – upright philosophical citizen of the new republic, agent of M. (formerly baron) Versac and suitor for his daughter – is threatened by an accusation put secretly before the revolutionary tribunal. The evildoers are his rival for the girl, one M. Nomophage, and a journalist associate, M. Duricrane. But good does triumph: M. de Forlis's accusers are exposed, he is exonerated to public as well as private rejoicing, and the way is clear for a happy ending.

The artificial sounding names (especially for the bad characters) add to the melodramatic effect of the play, and make it difficult to believe the author's denials that this is an anti-Jacobin satire. Take, for example, the evil 'Nomophage', whose name hints at some flesh-consuming disease. He secretly lusts for power, wealth and the former aristocrat's daughter. He is trying to win over her mother with plans to obtain money corruptly out of revolutionary expropriations. Take his fellow conspirator, 'Duricrane', whose name suggests ruthless hard-headedness. These are easy characters to hate. We can only suppose that the emotionally frank audiences of the time took the hint: weeping at the prospect of the lovers happily united and jeering at remarks such as this from Duricrane:

> I was born an informer: spying is my destiny. When I don't know of about a plot, I always guess about it.[20]

Political barbs such as this were likely to make the audience jeer.[21] But in responding to the sentimentality, they would have absorbed other feelings. They could sense a world in which virtuous people are distinguished by goodness of heart and public spirit. Forlis indicates that the name of 'patriot' is gained by dint of virtue,[22] and that virtue is *visible*. He observes to a contrite friend in the final, happy scene: 'I have read into your heart, it is sound.'[23] The spirit of the post-revolutionary social order is evoked as an open-hearted union of the various social classes around shared respect for virtue and benign

47

principles of philosophy and law. Laya was deploying the responses of comedy and melodrama to generate a feeling of this order as he saw it. The warm, shared response in the contemporary audience could enable its members to feel that they were part of a new and emotionally united people.

Though we are told of a public reception accorded his hero after he is freed by the tribunal, Laya did not attempt to bring 'the people' as such into the staging of his story. Sylvain Maréchal's *Le Jugement dernier des rois* (also from 1793), which inventively worked in fantasy-spectacle, does bring the people on stage. All the action takes place on a desert island (a customary setting for fantasy plays) dominated by a spitting volcano – which erupts at the end! By then, the Pope and the crowned heads of Europe have appeared on stage, banished to the island. The stage fills up gradually, however. We meet a number of symbolic characters. First, there is an old man banished there himself long ago by the arbitrary power of the French king. Then, there are a 'large number' of sansculottes from all the nations of Europe, plus a family of primitives. The unseated monarchs and the Pope, all resplendently dressed, are then led on with mock dignity one by one – in what appears to be their order of loathsomeness to the French public at war (Austrian, British and so on). The old man and the primitives listen as their crimes against the people of Europe are rehearsed by the sansculottes. Then they are left to their own devices – to live from nature (as, we are given to understand, all men should). They are clearly intended to make a pretty ragged bunch. They scrap amongst themselves, disgrace themselves in response to Tsarina Catherine's sexual advances, and generally abandon both their dignity and their religion at the drop of a hat.

This is clearly a wartime play. Some of the republicans' favourite ideas about the war are stated: that monarchical government is the origin of all mankind's ills; and that the war is being fought because of a 'handful of cowardly brigands'.[24] The wartime public must have enjoyed the fantasy resolution of the war, brought about by the union of all the common people of Europe under the leadership of France. But much of the play's manner of evoking responses in the theatre is more complex than the mere pronouncement of sympathetically received political messages such as this.

It must have resembled nothing in modern theatre so much as a pantomime. Against the sensational volcano backdrop, France's enemies are seen trounced. The author's publicity notice[25] invited people to come and jeer at the parody of enemy monarchs. Their

48

fighting over a crust of bread must have filled the bill. The effect of their jeering can well be imagined: to lighten apprehension and impart a sense of power to citizens of Paris weak and threatened by the defeats of war. But more is conveyed by the multiple identification which the audience is offered through characters on the stage. These act to represent a common response in the audience – and no doubt led one.

Perhaps Daniel Hamiche goes too far when he writes that Maréchal found the means to represent 'the most positive features of the sansculottes' mentality'.[26] But three types of 'ordinary' people are assembled on the stage to respond to the indictments of the monarchs: the old man (wise from painful experience of the arbitrary ways of absolute monarchs); 'sansculottes' from each of the countries of Europe; and the primitives. The stories behind each of these three make fables for the audience. The old man evokes the oppressiveness of kings. He responds on behalf of all sufferers under monarchy when he is told that the kings are merely being banished: 'It would have been more practical to hang them all, under the gateways of their palaces'.[27] The sansculottes express the hope of harmony and collective action. The primitives ('our elders in liberty')[28] portray the 'natural' life. As they listen, they make 'silent gestures of surprise and indignation' at the indictments.[29] Their generosity to the old man in his struggle to survive bears the message that harmonious co-operation is possible among people of humble demands. By contrast, the monarchs immediately argue over who is to serve the little bread they have. The Pope then explains that their dissension is due to the presence of schismatics![30] At the climax, all three groups of ordinary people are on stage responding on the audience's behalf. The assembled sansculottes swear in unison (very much in the manner of oath-taking ceremonies at the festival) never to speak well of kings again:

We swear it! . . . long live liberty! long live the republic![31]

Where this play works in the theatre, its audience would experience an ingenious two-way transference of feeling. The burlesque humour against common enemies in authority would have encouraged both laughter (with the comfort and belonging associated with it), and a sense of confidence *vis-à-vis* the enemy and authority. Talkative in any case by the virtue of the manners of the theatre at that time, those in the audience who had not already expressed their feelings are invited to do so in this climax, and provided with words to speak by a range of characters whom they may identify with. The characters in the play speak for them; they find their own shared political sentiments in the words on stage. This is quite explicitly a performance in the sense that I defined it at the start of this chapter.

Yet, *Le Jugement dernier* is merely the most clear-cut of the four plays I have examined in doing this. With different manners of presentation, emotional responses and politics, all the plays have encouraged the audience to witness and to rehearse together virtues and emotions deemed to characterize the new legitimate public. Each encouraged a sense that history was manageable and hence that, together, the members of the new polity were free agents in history. They could achieve this either by the force of courage and faith in principle, or by love of liberty, or by the unity of ordinary people. Some portrayed serious sentiments of the dreadful necessity for virtue. Others invited humour, breaking down barriers, encouraging the audience to look afresh at the familiar, imbuing a sense of freedom by their playfulness and ability to make light of what might seem overwhelming. In each case, the audience could come together to share feelings, and 'perform' their role as members of the new public.

FÊTES AND FESTIVALS

Perhaps the post-revolutionary period's only truly original cultural form, the revolutionary festival encouraged vast numbers of people to participate in a kind of performance of the revolutionary order in the open air. This was quite explicitly an attempt to form the sovereign public through a cultural event. In his plans for it, the painter David described the festival of 10 August 1793 thus:

> They will get under way . . . At the head the popular societies, then the Convention, the commissioners of the primary [electoral] assemblies of the eighty-six departments . . . the mass of the sovereign [people] all mixed up together, the mayor beside the hewers of wood and the masons . . .[32]

The interest of historians in the role of the crowd in the Revolution[33] has come together with the interests of anthropology, so that there is now a distinct literature on the revolutionary festival.[34] The anthropologists' attention is caught by the variety of pre-existing *fêtes* and by what is revealed in their modification during the revolutionary period. As Bronislaw Baczko put it:

How can we characterize the social imagination at work in a revolution at a moment when it is transforming itself? I believe that the *fête* is a privileged event which brings to light the dynamic and the specific language of that imagination.[35]

Figure 2.1 Sergent-Marceau, *Festival of Liberty in a Village* (© Photos Archives Editions Arthaud, Paris; photo: John Rylands University Library of Manchester)

On the other hand, many crucial historical moments in the Revolution were the action of crowds. And rural disorders of the late 1780s and early 1790s were commonly accompanied by *fête* elements such as dancing or planting a may tree (a threat of collective action against the chosen victim). The organized festivals arose in this context. They were in part an attempt to substitute orderly crowd activity for the riot; though they could, in any case, turn into a political debate or a riot, which would lead to the ceremonial burning of legal documents. So, the festival seems to have been a crucial phenomenon, indicating quite particular social and cultural processes intimately related to the character of the Revolution.

It is a promising cultural form to examine in an enquiry about how culture could handle the conceptual system of the new revolutionary political order. As we shall see, it is a highly adaptable form. It allows large numbers to experience participation and a kind of freedom. To a degree, it straddles the limitations of history and time as experienced by ordinary people. That is part of the reason why it was both widely embraced by ordinary people and deliberately cultivated by political leaders.

What happened in the festivals and *fêtes*? We can divide them roughly into four types, which grew up in a rough chronological order.

1. The traditional *fête* flourished under the *ancien régime*. In towns, their frequency is astounding: 32 per year in Paris; 60 in Marseilles.[36] In villages (see Figure 2.1), they were a major element in the calendar. Days or weeks of preparation would precede the day. In the morning, under the patronage of the local notables and the priest, open-air music dedicated to the patron saint would be followed by mass and a procession, led by the 'joy' (a torch decorated with symbolic objects) and conveying the relics and a statuette associated with the saint and the village, perhaps to a shrine outside the village. The afternoon and evening saw sports competitions; the award of prizes; music; dancing (including the *farandole*); gambling; sometimes the acting-out of scenes from the history of the village or of ancient magical significance; the blessing of items important to the life of the village (tools, cattle); and finally a communal feast. By the end of the day, the priest and the notables might have been uneasy about some of the goings-on: gambling, flirtation, even ritualized violence.[37]

In towns, the same elements were found, but separated and spread over different days of the year. Ceremonies and processions, with religious blessing, were held for saints' days and occasional celebrations by corporations of different trades, lay orders of 'penitents', or different categories of dignitary. The city as a whole could hold a *fête*, too: as it did in Marseilles, where the city's pagan origins were evoked and its ships (the key to its prosperity) blessed as the climax of the combined procession.

2. As the anniversary of the Bastille in July 1790 approached, a movement in the provinces developed (without official prompting) to gather representatives of the National Guard militia from across the whole of France in a ceremony in Paris. Perhaps as many as 300,000 soldiers and national guardsmen travelled to Paris for this first 'Festival of the Federation' (see Figures 3.13 and 3.14 on page 98). A grand ceremony was organized by the municipality at the Champs de Mars, where an oath of loyalty to king and constitution was administered at the same moment in Paris as in cities and towns across the country.

Some traditional elements did appear in the festivals of the Federation: processions of the different segments of the community; reference to saints and myths; communal meals; dancing; freelance celebrations as dawn broke and after the main event. But new elements appeared also: open-air altars; the simultaneous oaths; a procession of citizens without regard to any corporation; new symbols of the regenerated nation (tricolours, red bonnets — which had been adopted by the sansculottes; images of broken chairs; classical allusions such as the ceremonial wagon drawn by animals).

The central ceremonial of the Paris event was rather limited: a strictly military procession marched, bearing regimental and departmental flags, from the Champ de Mars, round the city and back to take the oath in the specially constructed amphitheatre. The vast oath-taking ceremony was the most telling innovation. It directed attention to the idea of the nation, and it brought the feel of religious ceremony out from the churches to a space dominated by open sky and the classically inspired columns and obelisks. The pressure for further innovation still was evident from the suggestions which the authorities felt it best to turn down:[38] a procession of women, floats portraying the destruction of the aristocratic enemies of the new France, and so on. Outside Paris, there was an unselfconscious *mélange* of elements, all counting towards the new, loyal, non-aristocratic France. Tricolours, the traditional may trees, lighted torches, processions of the old and the young, saints' and corporation days, and heterodox oaths[39] were mixed together.

3. During 1792–3, more diverse public festivals and *fêtes* were organized centrally or locally by more or less official groups. They commemorated various moments deemed significant for the Revolu-

tion: the fall of the Bastille or the fall of the monarchy, for example. They served as memorials for significant people: figures as different as Voltaire, Lasowski (who led the attack of 10 August), the journalist Marat, Lepelletier (a deputy assassinated by a royalist just before the execution of the king), and Bara (teenage victim of the anti-republican Vendée rebels). The sentiments of the festival were thus fused with those of a funeral or of canonization. A cult of various dead heroes or 'martyrs' grew up. Finally, the festivals were occasions for somewhat disorderly collective jubilation.

In this period, the festivals were increasingly organized from above. The symbolism used was extended and joined by high art. The first schemes for *systems* of festivals appeared: the Convention actually approved Robespierre's (derived from a text by Lepelletier). They looked to the atmosphere of the festival, as Condorcet put it, to 'breathe liberty, the sentiment of humanity and love of country'.[40] Robespierre's case for the festivals (in his speech of 7 March 1794) stressed the political value of bringing people together, and likened his projects to the practices of the ancients.

This was also the period when the new republican calendar was introduced (in November 1793). It took the declaration of the Republic as its starting date (as against the birth of Christ), and divided the year into months and subdivisions of ten days, called '*décades*'. It deliberately ran across the old periodizations. The aim of the calendar and the schemes of festivals was to punctuate the year as Sundays, traditional religious festivals and saints' days had done: to bring the values of Revolution right into the pattern of time experienced by ordinary people. So, in Robespierre's scheme, there were days to celebrate liberty (10 August), equality (21 January, the date of the king's execution), and so on.

The festival also became the means to promote various political aims more specific than the simple search for unification.[41] 'Official' celebrations always put forward a carefully constructed account of events. The execution of the king was marked allusively by an annual event to celebrate the 'end of tyranny' and the 'martyrdom' of Lepelletier. The fall of the monarchy (10 August 1792) was marked, a year later, by a festival of 'unity and indivisibility' — at the very moment when a 'federalist' uprising threatened unity itself. This was a quite theatrically staged event. The procession covered a route with five stations. The first, at the Place de la Bastille, was decorated with a statue of Nature, whose breasts formed a fountain 'of regeneration'. The Boulevard Poissonière boasted a triumphal arch erected to the women of Paris, to celebrate their march to Versailles (on 5 October 1789) to bring back the king. At the Place de la Révolution (now the Place de la Concorde) symbols of the monarchy were burnt before a statue of liberty bearing republican symbols. Then, at Les Invalides, the crowd saw a statue of the French people hacking down aristocracy. Finally, there was an oath-taking ceremony (to 'liberty, equality, fraternity or death') at the Champs de Mars, followed by a simple communal meal. The event cost 1.2 million livres,[42] and engaged the services of the painter David as principal director, the composer Gossec, and the poet Chénier (author of *Charles IX*), who wrote words to accompany the music.

Alongside the official events, others were organized or arose spontaneously to put forward alternative versions of things. From the Festival of the Federation on, more radical views were pushing for an airing. For example, progressive citizens organized their own event on 15 April 1792, with help from the Paris municipality. In a self-consciously non-elitist style, they commemorated the persecution of the Swiss guards of Chateauvieux (who had been punished by the crown for disobeying orders). The procession at this festival[43] was a loosely organized crowd mixing militia and civilians, which broke off frequently to dance the popular *farandole* or sing the republican song, 'Ça ira'. It moved off after a reading of the Declaration of the Rights of Man, which was also inscribed in tablets they bore with them, and followed a float of commemorative objects (the chains of the martyrs, a model of the galley they had been condemned to) carried shoulder-high. In the procession were: busts of Voltaire, Rousseau, Sydney and Franklin; two sarcophagi; a statue of Louis XVI wearing the red cap of liberty; a float drawn by 20 horses (decorated by David with images of Brutus and William Tell, plus a statue of liberty carrying a club); and finally a charger ridden by a joker (symbol of the stupidity and superstition of the past).

Such non-official events could, of course, be put up by contending sides. A few weeks later, militia and Parisian citizens from a more conservative section mounted a *fête* dedicated to Simoneau, the mayor of Estampes who had been murdered in a peasant riot in May 1792. They built it round the theme of respect for law, under the mottoes: 'Truly free men are slaves of the law' and 'liberty, equality, property'. Their procession comprised gendarmerie units, officers of the *sections*, soldiers, national guardsmen, floats bearing symbols of the law (such as an open book), a statue of the law, relics and a bust of the deceased (borne by figures in pseudo-monastic garb), departmental administrators and members of the Convention. It was a quieter, more respectable ceremony than the Chateauvieux festival: the murderers of Simoneau were portrayed as pike-bearing republicans. Spectators (some apparently shouting republican slogans) were held back.

4. A distinctive religiosity in festivals had already appeared by 1793. The funeral pageants of that year colonized a preserve of religion, incorporating 'cults' and taking over the processions of the church year with those of republican 'saints'. At the funeral of Marat, who was murdered in July 1793, his writings took the place of sacred books. A 'dechristianizing' movement was getting under way: in the provinces, crowds led by radicals were attacking churches. The festivals reflected both this pressure from militants and the authorities' wish to contain it.

The most famous of the dechristianizing festivals was the 'Festival of Reason',[44] mounted on 10 November 1793 at the cathedral of Notre Dame, with the hesitant involvement of the Convention. The Paris commune and departmental authorities, which had largely organized the event, led a procession into the nave, dominated by a mock ceremonial hill with a round Greek temple on it (see Figure 2.2). The words 'To philosophy' and an altar, where a torch of truth was burning,

Figure 2.2 Festival of Reason, Paris, November 1793 (from *Révolutions de Paris* No. 215, John Rylands University Library of Manchester)

adorned the temple. Watched by busts of Voltaire, Rousseau, Franklin and Montesquieu, two lines of torch-bearing young girls filed past the altar, bowing. Then a singer from the Paris Opéra, personifying liberty, descended from the temple to greet the crowd, who were singing a hymn:

> Come down, oh Liberty, daughter of nature; the people has reconquered its immortal power: they re-erect your altar on the pompous ruins of antique imposture.

The procession then filed off to the Convention, where their 'Liberty' shared the podium with the president, later returning to the church to rerun the event.

During this period, festivals were both impromptu local events and ceremonies which had been meticulously organized by the authorities. On the one hand, to represent the death of superstition, the local popular club at Tulle organized a *farandole* dance and a procession. It sported a coffin (which was decked out with a missal, clerical hat and donkey ears), ornaments stolen from the cathedral, and effigies of the saints.[45] On the other hand, the official 'Festival of the Supreme Being' (of 7 June 1794) was carefully scripted as a deistic reply to the atheism of the dechristianizers. A crowd made up of a group from each of the Paris *sections* listened to harangues by the president of the Convention (Robespierre). Differentiated by sex and age, each category bore its symbol: young girls, baskets of flowers for youth; mothers, roses for grace; men, oak branches for strength and liberty, and so on. Robespierre spoke of the end of tyranny, the dangers of atheism, and the satisfaction felt by the Author of Nature at the growth of republican virtue. He defined the purpose of the gathering: to acknowledge that the Supreme Being 'has created the universe to show his power'.[46] The Supreme Being placed 'calm and pride in the heart of the oppressed innocent' and engraved there the code of justice. 'He sees this day', Robespierre continued, 'an entire nation locked in battle with the oppressors of the human race.' An enormous effigy of atheism was then burned, revealing, behind it, a statue of wisdom. The procession, led by members of the Convention, then moved off to the Champs de Mars (see Figure 2.3), accompanied by a classical float, which was drawn by oxen and bore a statue of liberty and an oak tree sheltering symbols of industry and agriculture. Once there, the groups disposed themselves around an artificial hill, sang patriotic hymns and swore loyalty to the Republic, throwing their flowers to the wind or waving their swords in the air.

Figure 2.3 Ceremonial float from Festival of Supreme Being, Paris, June 1793 (Musée Carnavalet; photo: Musées de la Ville de Paris © SPADEM 1989)

Having seen the variety and the themes in the festivals, we can now make some preliminary observations about their scope. Their changing materials and their manner are striking, as is their use of words and music. On the other hand, their most striking feature as cultural events is to embrace the experience of participants and spectators in a performance.

The traditional *fête* had succeeded in a number of functions. It brought the community together, evoking both the different parts and the unity of the whole. It reran the history and looked to the future life of the community. It brought the higher-level blessing of religion to various day-to-day secular activities. It was a medium for the symbolism that was important in people's lives. Via the music, singing and dancing that were a normal part, it offered a more or less contained outlet for romance, high spirits and other, wilder inclinations.

SONGS IN THE FESTIVALS AND THE THEATRE

For the Festival of the Federation, Chénier and Gossec composed a hymn. As a musical form, the hymn was explicitly designed to come to the aid of rhetoric, by sharpening and emphasizing the inflections of speech, so that it can communicate in large assemblies.[47] Chénier's hymn duly reflected the link with transhistorical principles which the event was trying to make:

> God of the people and of kings, of cities and the countryside, of Luther, of Calvin, of the children of Israel . . . here are assembled beneath your immense gaze the sons and the supporters of the French empire, equal in your eyes as in their own, celebrating before you their happiness, just beginning.[48]

In fact, from the start, we may find music integrated into the festival, extending its impact. Before making a fuller assessment of the festivals, let us look briefly at the place of music — though it could merit a chapter all to itself.[49] In using music, the festival clearly pursued emotional impact along the same lines as a spectacle such as the melodrama in the theatre. Both theatre and festivals existed alongside a culture of popular songs outside. By adopting music, either written for the event or already established in the public mind, both kinds of theatrical spectacle could enhance the emotional impact of the performance that their participants engaged in, and find a place in a broader day-to-day currency of popular songs. If the participants went away with appropriate songs on their minds, that would sustain the feelings evoked by the event for long afterwards. This was clearly the intention behind the finale of the popular comedy about a young man going off to serve in the forces, *Au Retour*, which ends neatly evoking its own title:

> *Rois et tyrans, nobles et prêtres,*
> *Que tout ça tombe dans un jour.*
> *Et si chez nous restent de traîtres,*
> *Vous n'en trouverez plus au retour.*[50]

The songs operated with the same system of representations as we have discovered in the other forms of culture. They identified the 'people' and ascribed certain qualities to them. They encouraged people to join in. They celebrated the qualities of the people or great events in which the people had taken a part, which figured as turning points in the making of history. Take, for example, the *Carmagnole des royalistes*, sung to a tune of unknown origin and (by its title) intended for dancing hand-in-hand. The words rehearsed the embarrassment of the king and queen after the flight to Varennes. 'Monsieur' and 'Madame Véto' had

59

been hoping to use their constitutional powers against the people: now they cannot. It then identified the true friends of the patriot: 'The patriot has all the good people of the country for friends.'[51] At the other end of the political scale, *Lous Paisans* (*The Peasants*), an anonymous peasant song in the dialect of the Limousin region, described how the peasant, having tilled the soil while others lie in bed, is then called up to serve under the republican flag and 'make the earth tremble'.[52] On the other hand, *Le Salpêtre républicain,* from early 1794, used a sense of making history to galvanize miners with a sense of higher, patriotic duty. At the same time, it even taught them lessons about the process:

> Let us go down into the earth, Liberty invites us there, Republicans, she speaks with the voice of the nation. Wash the soil in a barrel, evaporate the water: soon the nitrate will appear . . . The spirit of our ancestors lies in the soil of our caverns; they buried the black pain of having masters under their barrels . . .[53]

The composition and diffusion of songs like this resembled that of popular news-sheets and journals. Indeed, Hébert himself published a song, called 'The Dream of Père Duchesne' to encourage patriots to enlist. There was a vigorous trade in song lyrics to be sung to familiar tunes. The trade adapted quickly to a new market for popular songs to celebrate revolutionary events. From the early days of the Revolution, songs appeared addressed to the Third Estate or celebrating the Bastille.

Simple songs, written in short rhyming lines and preferably needing no accompaniment, could be rapidly on the lips of ordinary people and infuse their everyday activities and meetings with a particular spirit. The 'Marseillaise', which was composed in 1792 and achieved fame almost immediately, is the classic case of new words and a new melody matching the requirements of popularity.[54] But most songs that caught on in the revolutionary period were to be sung to familiar tunes. A song such as the famous 'Ça ira' (with its four line stanzas, of which two repeated the words 'ça ira', while only the last was required to rhyme) could quickly take on extra lines and verses to express new or different moods. Finally, as I have already noted, the crowds at festivals often danced. Shared moods could be performed in dancing and singing. Songs were written with that in mind. Readers may even be able to *feel* the dance rhythm, at three beats to the line, in this little egalitarian sample from 1794:

Il faut raccourcir les géants
Et rendre les petits plus grands.
Tous à la même hauteur,
Voilà le vrai bonheur.[55]

THE ORIGINALITY AND SUCCESS OF THE FESTIVALS (AND LANGUAGE AGAIN)

What can we say about the festivals as a cultural process in the post-revolutionary set-up? More clearly than the theatre, they constituted a performance adapted to the conceptual system outlined in Chapter 1. We can first examine their evolution and their mechanism and then explain their peculiar strength.

The Festival of the Federation and its ilk contained significant innovations as compared with traditional *fêtes*: open-air oath-taking and revolutionary icons of unity, law and the freedom of the nation. Jean Starobinski has argued[56] that this *form* of oath matched the profound innovation entailed in a secular nation: it is *self*-created, not given by God through the intermediary of a king. Hence, the people creates itself by an oath outside the church, and under the open sky where it can feel itself to be taking its place, without mediation, in the very universe of the sky. We can characterize the evolution of the festivals by their search for appropriate symbolism. In the period of politically competing festivals, the language of symbols developed further, with considerable efforts to involve ordinary people. The pseudo-religious festival of the period from 1793 goes still further in the breadth of symbolic space that it embraces, explicitly invading the transcendent level claimed by established religion. Albert Soboul[57] cites still surviving cases to support the view that, for their followers, republican martyrs took on the supernatural power (which had been attributed traditionally to Christian saints) to give practical aid in life. In short, the festivals gradually extended the symbolic levels by which they sought to involve their participants in a performance adapted to the post-revolutionary political-social order.

Symbolic as it was, though, the festival elided the line between social-political life and its cultural representation. The 'Festival of Reason', for example, took its procession to the Convention (imitating the frequent marches of petitioning crowds), so as to form out of the participants a party in the current political conflict. This was days after the bishop and the clergy of Paris had resigned their Catholic priestly functions to the sovereign people (in the form of the Convention), and

61

agreed that 'there should no longer be any other public religion than that of liberty and sacred equality'.[58] Here, then, was a symbolic surrogate for them, confirming the wish and the victory of the 'sovereign people'. In turning into an active political body, the festival merely carried over a feature that seemed to come naturally to less highly organized *fêtes*. Peasant villagers had often combined dancing the *farandole* with attacking the local château to burn legal documents. Again, in Paris itself (on 27 January 1793) a ceremony to plant a liberty tree had spontaneously moved off to the Palais Royale gardens (then an equivalent of Hyde Park Corner) to root out *émigrés*, spies, deserters and supposed royalist agents. This disposition to direct action was gorily extended in September 1792, when mobs defended the city from the Prussian invaders by massacring thousands of politically suspect inmates of the Paris prisons.

Why this capacity to cross the boundary between art and life? It was easy for the festival to the extent that the political conflicts of the time were, by modern standards, symbolic. The organization of symbolism in society was an explicit political issue. The pseudo-religious festival echoed a political victory over religion, which had been fought for in the Convention, in the Paris commune and in the political clubs. More broadly, the secular funeral festivals belonged to the long-term secularization of social symbolism in the latter half of the eighteenth century.[59]

None the less, the power of the festivals to import the experience of the Revolution into the experience of individuals does seem to be quite particular: contemporaries on all sides in the political struggle believed in it. Various theories account for it. Rousseau's evocation of festivals in the *Considerations on the Government of Poland* (1770–2) may have been the first. It was influential in establishing a romantic faith in festivals and *fêtes* even before the Revolution.[60] Modern views to account for the strength of the *fêtes* and carnivals can be situated between two poles of thought. There are those that see the *fête* as a more or less effective device for integrating a community. And those that see in it a sort of chink in the fabric of society through which are glimpsed forces too powerful to be contained or too dire to be acknowledged explicitly.

Rousseau's is the classic of the first type. He recommended public 'ceremonials' to bring the people together to share common pleasures that would encourage patriotic virtue 'by passion' rather than by cold duty or self-interest. Since that attitude was an influence at the time, some historians view the festivals principally as part of a conscious politics of religion intended to propagandize a political line (though they differ as to the reality or otherwise of popular religious sentiments to echo those promoted from above).[61]

Vovelle's examination of festivals in Provence over a 50-year period took off from the opposite pole of thought. Far from manufacturing them politically, the Jacobins in power had to rein in the popular sentiments and forms of communal enjoyment. The explosion of revolutionary festivities tilted at the church or celebrated, and sometimes hastened the defeat of, authority.[62] Mona Ozouf's seminal study goes further, making the festivals a movement quite independent of any political campaign such as the conflict over religion. Her view embraces integrative and disruptive tendencies in the festival. It was a unique post-Enlightenment social institution. It adapted tradition to express the new existence of France as a secular state constituted out of 'nature' by the collective will of the people. Only in the festival could the singular agent of this act of constitution (the people) rehearse its founding act in the setting of nature. Hence, in the language of one contemporary account, the Festival of the Federation was 'several thousand armed men . . . going to form a nation'. However, the festival was itself a site for conflict: between political factions; between the state and its own militants (whom it tried to regiment); between the state and ordinary citizens. May trees and spontaneous gatherings were often too close to traditional religion or improvised violence for the liking of the secular post-Enlightenment state. Yet the festival straddled the tension between these sectors and tendencies in society, symbolically brought together as one. It also straddled the tension of timeless abstract verities with the desire to represent social reality in the events.[63] Lynn Hunt describes the festivals as one 'symbolic form of political practice' with real influence on the minds of the people. It was, however, a particularly powerful form. It squared the once-for-all transparency sought by the Revolution with rapid changes in ideological position. And it moved easily between the 'generic plots' by which the revolutionaries understood their position (comedy, romance or tragedy).[64]

An alternative modern view of the revolutionary festivals regards them as failures. They might *aim* for social unification along the lines described above; but they could not achieve it. Yves-Marie Bercé attributes a fuller integrity to fifteenth- and sixteenth-century popular *fêtes* and carnivals than the revolutionary festivals. For him, the festivals of the Revolution belong to the forces of modernity *suppressing* that older culture: the post-Reformation church, the centralizing state,

Enlightenment secularization. The pre-existing *fêtes* had a far greater impact on the life of the people.[65] A Marxist interpreter, on the other hand, finds that the integrative purpose of the festival is frustrated wherever class conflict is not overcome in a truly communist society. Given the attachment of the Jacobins to bourgeois values, the *fêtes* they invented to sustain their power ideologically could not but have a 'moralizing vacuousness or abstract idealism'.[66]

A balanced assessment can gain from general theories which identify, in *fête* or carnival, a creative safety valve for profounder forces running through human existence. In a classic essay of 1949, John Huizinga argued, for example, that all forms of carnival are 'play': moments of creative rapture which sustain civilisation.[67] Robert Duvignaud also draws in carnival phenomena from many times and places to argue that, in the carnival, human groups can 'step outside themselves and face . . . that universe without rule or form', beyond the givens of their society. It follows that the carnival serves profoundly to aid us assimilate certain givens of life: birth, death and change over time. When society is confronted by breakdown and change to a new order, carnival's role is greater still. This was the case over the entire baroque period, and, more acutely still, during the years of the Revolution.[68] Nicolas Wagner[69] also related carnival to what is fearful – though as a rather more sinister 'shock of lucidity', which reminds us of the feebleness of culture's victory over nature.

Finally, Mikhail Bakhtin, who himself witnessed revolution in Russia, offers an influential theory that links profound, transcendent tensions of existence with class tensions. When the carnival temporarily subverts the safe regularity of the world, it subverts social hierarchy as well. Not only is carnival 'the feast of becoming, change and renewal . . . hostile to all that was immortalised and complete'; it also 'celebrates temporary liberation from the prevailing truth of the established order'.[70]

These safety-valve theories leave considerable scope to judge whether the *fêtes* express a fruitful creative leap or irresolvable tension in the society of the Revolution. From the debate about it, the festival appears to be an ambivalent cultural form. It both oversteps and contains tensions. In so far as the *fêtes* and festivals deployed the capacities of carnival, they might, however, be a peculiarly appropriate cultural form. Flexibility and power to straddle tensions in symbolism and play were needed to master the paradoxes in the culture of the revolutionary period. I have already identified these in Chapter 1. They appeared in the logic of exclusion from the new legitimate collectivity, which tends to abstraction as real humans and real human qualities are placed on the outside.

The *fête* seems, then, to have the following strengths and weaknesses as a cultural process in the revolutionary period. It was a strong, heterodox form of established popular culture, already evolving innovation in its symbolism.[71] It was already a way in which the community actually came together physically. Now, the people could be gathered together symbolically conscious of their own unity and identity as the new legitimate focal point of political and social life. The adaptation of the traditional may tree illustrates the flexibility of symbolism in the *fête*. It served as an accompaniment to burning the local noble's records, and yet could then be turned into the 'liberty tree' favoured by peasants and Jacobins alike.

Politically, the *fête*, through its carnival nature, can invert the usual relationship between the given order and inclinations at odds with normality (especially in ordinary people). But this did not need to entail a permanent launch into the unknown. Because it evokes the possibility of an alternative state of affairs, the *fête* had a natural political tinge. It directed the thoughts of the participants beyond the given social reality to an imagined or desired alternative. That is why the carnival atmosphere could be joined to more or less direct political action to change an aspect of social life, such as the authority of the local noble's land title. What better than the *fête* or festival, then, to embody the hope of *permanent* transformation from the *ancien régime* structure of social life, with its older focal points and exclusions? Little wonder that politicians of the central state in Paris should vie with each other, and with militants in the towns and villages, to try in the festival to convey the meaning of the revolutionary upheaval, its new order, and the hope and excitement it brought.

This assessment of the festivals and *fêtes* is not undermined by the tension between the opposed impulses expressed in them: fear versus hope, order from above versus anarchy from below. The *fête* was inherently *different* from what went before and what came after. It was naturally heterodox. The central government attempted to regularize the festivals in a clear, rational scheme. Their enlightened functionaries expressed distaste for the crude tradition and tasteless invention they found in the provinces. On the other hand (as both Ozouf and Bercé have emphasized), carnival violence released popular opposition to a normality experienced as arbitrary. These are the tensions the *fêtes* might naturally embrace.

Historical change undertaken by the people was a component of the new political-social order that the Revolution was trying to portray. Given the insights of Duvignaud and Baczko, it appears that the *fête* offered the real possibility of handling the paradoxes under this heading. Traditionally the *fête* referred to the history of the community. Some elements, such as rededication or the planting of may trees, constituted a sort of contract between past, present and future generations.[72] The *fête* rehearsed a self-image for the community, bringing it to life and domesticating it within the awareness of ordinary people. Subtler still, as an event, the *fête* belonged both to real life and to a world in which barely imaginable historic changes may be realized – or, for that matter, faced. The collective elevation of spirit, the comedy or the ribaldry at the expense of authority are corollaries of that peculiar level of reality which the carnival possesses. It takes the participants out of the given routine of life and into an activity that is both normal (because traditional) and abnormal (because irregular and bizarre). It is both real (because it actively engages participation) and abstract (because it addresses mysteries beyond the normal). It makes safe what otherwise feels (or perhaps is) dangerous – notably dramatic changes in the given order, which are made to seem manageable or bearable. The *fête* recalls the historical existence of the community, epitomizes its freedom to it, and suggests the possibility of change. Festivals exploited this complex link with history when they staged historical moments from the founding of the new republic. The new appeared as both significant past and ideal future.

Though I have examined the use of language in Chapter 1, some further uses can now be brought into the analysis. The festival required a number of acts achieved through the power of language. Dedication or rededication of sacred objects, or objects central to communal life, and of members of the community to their place: these were all traditional high-points of the *fête*. These are 'perlocutionary' acts; that is, acts constituted by the use of some specific formulas in language.[73] The revolutionary period added other dedications. And it added other types of perlocutionary act, such as an oath of loyalty to the abstract body of the nation represented only by the assembly taking the oath itself.

Far beyond the confines of the festival, the revolutionary culture also mimicked the performative language of religion. The cult of the Supreme Being, for example, provoked 'credos'. A typical sample addressed the 'Father of light, eternal power who causes the sun to proceed before liberty to illuminate its august labours'.[74] The range of beliefs affirmed in this credo embraced both the new political-social order and its hoped-for history.

I believe in the new French Republic, one and indivisible, in its laws and in the sacred rights of man, which the French people have received from the sacred mountain of the Convention which created them.

The hopes expressed included short-term developments in the war, such as

that the European people, leaving their culpable lethargy, will recognize the rights of man, for which the true children of France have sworn to live and die.

Alongside the many credos, catechisms were produced by republican writers, such as Maréchal (author of *Le Jugement dernier des rois*) and Volney (who is considered at length in Chapter 3). These set out an accessible, systematic justification from first principles for fundamental beliefs, such as the rights of man or the laws of nature.

The classic perlocutionary act, naming, was also employed where symbols for abstract notions, or for real persons and things were identified by simply placing writing on them. Examples of this are legion – from the habitual designation of statues of 'the People', 'Liberty', and so forth,[75] to the ironic words 'the final settlement of all rents', hung upon the may tree which was planted after burning down the local château. It is true that this freedom to name symbolic objects would be essential to making signs with the crude technological means available at the time. However, late eighteenth-century culture clearly was one where objects were readily viewed as signs. It was a culture still susceptible to the allegorical vision, and the *fête* knew how to bring that into play. Free creativity may be felt more in the ability to generate language than in any other aspect of human life. In using language to stipulate the reality of what transpired, the *fête* embodied the community's sense of freedom to create its realm of action.

CONCLUSION

As matters stood at the end of Chapter 1, it appeared that journalism and rhetoric left the new focal point of the post-revolutionary order abstract and unstable. How has the analysis of the theatre and the festival altered this picture of the cultural processes representing the Revolution? Both theatre and festival evoked behaviour which (by images, stereotypes, self-identification or symbolism) enabled participants to experience some membership and moral content for the new

67

public. Furthermore, in both forms, the shape of historical time was redefined into a purportedly benign direction. What I have called 'performance' – a pattern of behaviour appropriate to a role evoked in a form of culture – has, I claim, given substance to the notion of the new boundaries and centre of social-political life. There are differences between the media, of course. The theatre (as Enlightenment thinking believed) is more cut off from the ordinary reality outside the spectacle. Conversely, its more detailed action and ease in using language allows it to identify more fully the meaning of its symbolism. But both forms could and did adapt familiar meanings in order to promote 'performance' in the public. In 'performing', these forms of culture held the new order together in a portrayal better than the journals or political rhetoric.

There remain tensions in these forms, however. It is delicate to maintain a relationship with both the actual world and the possible historical worlds. As Ozouf argues,[76] the systems of festivals had frequently to undertake the difficult task of *altering* the pattern they were designed to ascribe to history. They resituated the start of the new era, for example, so as to play down the role of violent popular upheaval or of particular political figures. The problem is not simply a corollary of *political* manipulation of the conception of the past. The nub of it is that once a society has structured historical time to suit its self-image, the society itself moves on through time. It then adds to or destroys the historical past it needs to regard as a significant given. Both the *fête* and the theatre are good at straddling this difficult relationship between actual and possible; but it cannot be avoided altogether. As Gaignebet and Florentin have pointed out,[77] the celebration in carnivals must *either* rehearse a given order in time *or* break out of it. *Fêtes* and theatre try to do both at once.

Comedy might be expected to come to the rescue in this sort of difficulty. And so it did in both theatre and festival; but only to a limited extent. It was a major component in a play such as *Le Jugement dernier*, and was frequently present in the traditional tilting at order in the *fête*. But that was in cases where it was directed *against* an external order. In principle, comedy might (in the new theatrical comedies of the period) offer a sentimental portrayal of ironies in the new order: for example, the confusion between patriotic and family duty – though, in this case the tone was that of gentle concern rather than comedy proper. In looking at portrayals of themselves, the revolutionaries judged what they saw straightforwardly in terms of whether the image matched up to what they literally thought themselves to be like.[78] As Richard Cobb has pointed out in considering the mentality of the militant revolutionaries,[79] in general they were humourless and naive. Republican comic perception seems, in fact, to have been limited to the social order they were destroying. There was no humour in their view of what they themselves were, or what they were creating. Both ordinary people and those in power shared a tendency to fix their vision upon the literal truth or falsity, as they supposed it, of any portrayal of the revolutionary order.

More broadly, failure to perceive in the comic mode would seriously limit the power of the culture to keep in mind both the actual and the possible. Where the view of cultural representations is too literal-minded, it excludes the flexibility needed for history to be both firmly established and a field for change. In the Revolution, literal-mindedness like that reintroduced tensions over the content of culture, making the authorities awkward and oppressive even towards participants in the *fête* or artists in theatre who were fundamentally in sympathy with the Revolution. It informed the authorities' efforts to impose a strict, rational order on the fête. In consequence, the alien order of the state was opposed to the disorderly sentiments of ordinary people. The final judgement upon the festivals and the theatre has to be that, where they were not organized according to a rigid scheme at odds with diversity, invention and change across time, they were powerful cultural means to resolve the tensions of the new order's identity and history.

NOTES

1. 'Citoyens, rappelez-vous donc comment, au temps passé, sur tous les théâtres on avilissait, on dégradait, on ridiculisait indignement les classes les plus respectables du peuple-souverain, pour faire rire les rois et les valets de cour. J'ai pensé qu'il était bien temps de leur rendre la pareille, et de nous amuser à notre tour' (*Journal des Révolutions de Paris*, quoted in M. Louis Moland (ed.), *Théâtre de la Révolution* (Paris: Garnier, 1877), p. 302).

2. The late eighteenth century separated sharply the 'imitation' attempted in the confined space of the theatre and a 'real' experience that might be had on the outside, such as in the public festival. There is therefore a problem, theoretically, in analysing the theatre and the festival in the same terms. However, the 'performance' of the audience is not concerned with imitation. So the distinction between imitation and real experience has no bearing on my line of argument.

69

3. Beatrice Hyslop, 'The Theater during a Crisis: the Parisian Theater during the Reign of Terror', *Journal of Modern History*, vol. XVII, December 1945, pp. 333–55. According to Hyslop's information, *Le Jugement dernier des rois*, which I analyse below, was offered to the Parisian public only 25 times.
4. Pierre Larthomas, *Le Théâtre en France au XVIII siècle* (Paris: Presses Universitaires de France, 1980), pp. 41ff.
5. See ibid., pp. 98–105.
6. John Lough, *Paris Theatre Audiences in the 17th and 18th Centuries* (Oxford: Oxford University Press, 1957), esp. pp. 227ff.
7. See David Mayer, 'The Music of Melodrama' in D. Bradby, L. James and B. Sharratt (eds), *Performance and Politics in Popular Drama* (Cambridge: Cambridge University Press, 1980), p. 51: 'music is an affecting and effecting device to underline and emphasise the emotional content of a play's action, to further concentration, very probably masking the improbabilities that we so often recognise in melodrama, and maintaining the momentum of the play's headlong rush from sensation to sensation'.
8. See Anne Boës, *La Lanterne magique de l'histoire: essai sur le théâtre historique en France de 1750 à 1789* (Oxford: Voltaire Foundation, 1982).
9. See Paul d'Estrée, *Le Théâtre sous la Terreur* (Paris: Emile-Paul, 1913), esp. pp. 69–115 and pp. 292–4.
10. See Hyslop, op. cit., pp. 342–3.
11. See d'Estrée, op. cit., pp. 95 and 105–7.
12. Letter to the comtesse d'Albany, quoted in Larthomas, op. cit., p. 113: Beaumarchais wished to exclude 'les coeurs usés, les âmes désséchées', who were 'bons qu'à parler révolution', and asked instead for 'quelques femmes sensibles, des hommes pour qui le coeur n'est pas un chimère, et puis pleurons à plein canal'.
13. 'You know Brutus and you dare to console him!/Call to mind that a new attack is being prepared:/Rome alone is my concern; my heart knows only her' (Voltaire, *Brutus*, Act V, scene 8, taken from *Théâtre de Voltaire* (Paris: Garnier, 1874)).
14. 'My heart, still taken aback by its wanderings,/Carried far from its own way, was guilty for a moment:/That moment has covered me with eternal shame;/It made me unfaithful to my country whom I love' (*Brutus*, Act V, scene 7).
15. Chénier, *Charles IX*, Act I, scene 4: 'Deviens plus populaire;/Fléchis pour gouverner: on t'admire; il faut plaire' (quoted in Moland, op. cit.).
16. *Charles IX*, Act I, scene 4: 'Laissons-là ce public; cette foule inconstante,/ Echo tumultueux des fables qu'elle invente.'
17. *Charles IX*, Act II, scene 1: 'régner par la discorde, et diviser sans cesse'.
18. *Charles IX*, Act I, scene 2: 'Au lieu de serviteurs à mes ordres soumis,/Je voyais près de moi de égaux, des amis.'
19. *Charles IX*, Act I, scene 1: 'la nuit environne/Les droits sacrés du peuple et les devoirs du trône.'
20. Laya, *L'Ami des lois*, Act II, scene 4: 'J'étais né délateur: épier est mon

lot./Quand j'ignore un complot, toujours je le devine.' (quoted in Moland, op. cit.)

21. Another example, from *L'Ami*, Act I, scene 4, is aimed at direct democracy: 'Ces Solons nés hier, enfants réformateurs/Qui redigeant en lois leurs rêves destructeurs,/Pour se le partager voudraient mettre à la gêne/Cette immense pays rétréci comme Athènes.' ('These Solons, born yesterday, reforming children, who, translating their destructive dreams into laws, would, in order to divide it among themselves, like to torment this country shrunk to the size of Athens.').

22. *L'Ami*, Act I, scene 4: 'Patriotes! ce titre est saint et respecté,/A force de vertus veut être mérité' ('Patriots! this title is both sacred and respected, [and] wants to be gained by dint of virtue').

23. *L'Ami*, Act V, scene 6: 'J'ai lu dans votre âme,/Elle est droite.'

24. Maréchal, *Le Jugement dernier des rois*, scene 5, p. 319: 'C'est pour le service de cette poignée de lâches brigands . . . que le sang d'un million . . . d'hommes, dont le pire valait mieux qu'eux tous, a été versé sur presque tous les points du continent'.

25. See note 1.

26. Daniel Hamiche, *Le Théâtre de la Révolution* (Paris: Union Générale d'Edition, 1973), pp. 183–4.

27. *Le Jugement*, scene 3, p. 312: 'Il eût été plus expédient de les pendre tous, sous le portique de leurs palais.' Yet the emotion is not all cruel: In a penultimate scene, the sansculottes return briefly to the stage to give the prisoners food to help them until they can fend for themselves.

28. *Le Jugement*, scene 4, p. 314.

29. *Le Jugement*, scene 5, p. 317.

30. *Le Jugement*, scene 6, pp. 320–3.

31. *Le Jugement*, scene 5, p. 320: 'Nous le jurons! . . . vive la liberté! vive la république!'

32. Quoted in Serge Bianchi, *La Révolution culturelle en l'An II: Elites et peuples, 1789–1799* (Paris: Aubier, 1982), p. 183.

33. See, especially, Georges Rudé, *The Crowd in the French Revolution* (Oxford: Oxford University Press, 1959); and Georges Lefèbvre, *La Grande Peur* (Paris: Colin, 1932) translated as *The Great Fear* (London: New Left Books, 1973), and *idem* 'Les Foules révolutionnaires' in *idem, Etudes sur la Révolution* (Paris: 1954).

34. See, notably, Maurice Agulhon, *Marianne au combat: l'imagerie et le symbolique de 1789 à 1880* (Paris: Flammarion, 1979), translated as *Marianne into Battle* (Cambridge: Cambridge University Press, 1981); Yves-Marie Bercé, *Fête et révolte: des mentalités populaires de XVIme au XVIIIme siècle* (Paris: Hachette, 1976); Jean Erhard and Paul Vialleneix, *Les Fêtes de la Révolution* (Paris: Société des Etudes Robespierristes, 1977); Mona Ozouf, *La Fête révolutionnaire* (Paris: Gallimard, 1976), translated as *Festivals and the French Revolution* (Cambridge, MA and London: Harvard University Press, 1988); Michel Vovelle, *Les Métamorphoses de la Fête en Provence de 1750 à 1820* (Paris: Aubier/Flammarion, 1976).

35. In Erhard and Vialleneix, op. cit., p. 642.

36. Ozouf, op. cit., p. 7; Vovelle, op. cit., p. 68.
37. Vovelle, op. cit., ch. 5.
38. Ozouf, op. cit., pp. 58–60.
39. See ibid., p. 61.
40. Condorcet, *Oeuvres* (Paris: 1847) vol. 9, p. 288.
41. H.T. Parker, *The Cult of Antiquity and the French Revolutionaries* (New York: Octagon, 1965) argues that the campaign for hearts and minds became paramount when institutional reform had to be shelved to get on with winning the war.
42. Bianchi, op. cit., p. 204.
43. See D.L. Dowd, *Pageant Master of the Republic: Jacques-Louis David and the French Revolution* (New York: Books for Libraries Press, 1948), ch. 3.
44. See Alphonse Aulard, *Le Culte de la raison et le culte de l'Etre Suprême* (Paris: 1892), pp. 53–9.
45. Ozouf, op. cit., p. 107.
46. Aulard, op. cit., pp. 312–15.
47. For an extensive catalogue, see C. Pierre, *Les Hymnes et chansons de la Révolution française* (Paris: Imprimerie Nationale, 1904); or G. Marty and G. Marty, *Dictionnaire des chansons de la Révolution, 1787–1799* (Paris: Tallandier, 1987).
48.

> Dieu du peuple et des rois, des cités, des campagnes,
> De Luther, de Calvin, des enfants d'Israël, . . .
> Ici sont rassemblés sous ton regard immense
> De l'empire français les fils et les soutiens,
> Célébrant devant toi leur bonheur qui commence,
>   Egaux à leurs yeux comme aux tiens.

Quoted in R. Brécy, 'La Chanson révolutionnaire de 1789 à 1799', *Annales historiques de la Révolution française*, no. 244 (1981), p. 286.
49. See J.-L. Jam, 'La Fonction des hymes révolutionnaires' in Erhard and Vialleneix, op. cit., pp. 433–42.
50. 'Kings and tyrants, nobles and priests,/Let all that fall in a day./And if there are still traitors at home,/You won't find any when you return', quoted in Hyslop, op. cit., p. 337.
51. 'Le patriote a pour amis/Tous les bonnes gens du pays,/ . . . nous nous souviendrons toujours/Des sans-culottes des faubourgs,/A leur santé buvons', quoted in Brécy, op. cit., p. 293.
52. Ibid., pp. 296–7.
53. 'Descendons dans nos souterrains,/La liberté nous y convie,/Elle parle,/Républicains,/Et c'est la voix de la patrie,/Lavez la terre dans un tonneau/ En faisant évaporer l'eau:/Bientôt le nitre va paraître./ . . . C'est dans le sol de nos caveaux/Que gît l'esprit de nos ancêtres;/Ils enterraient sous leurs tonneaux/Le noir chagrin d'avoir des maîtres', quoted in ibid., p. 299.
54. See the discussion in Jam, op. cit., pp. 438–42.
55. 'We must shorten the tall/And make the small ones larger./Have

everyone at the same height,/That's how to be truly happy', quoted in J. Furet and D. Richet, *The French Revolution*, trans. S. Hardman (London: Weidenfeld and Nicolson), 1970.

56. Jean Starobinski, *Les Emblêmes de la raison* (Milan: Instituto Editoriale, 1973; Paris: Flammarion, 1979) pp. 65f.

57. Albert Soboul, 'Religious Sentiments and Popular Cults during the Revolution' in J. Kaplan (ed.), *New Perspectives on the French Revolution* (New York: Wiley, 1965), originally published in *Annales historiques de la Révolution française*, 1957, pp. 195–213.

58. Aulard, op. cit., p. 43.

59. See John McManners, *Death and the Enlightenment: Changing Attitudes to Death in 18th-century France* (Oxford: Clarendon, 1981; Oxford: Oxford University Press, 1985) ch. 10, esp. pp. 353–67; also Michel Vovelle, *Mourir autrefois* (Paris: Gallimard, 1973); and *idem*, *La Mort et l'Occident de 1300 à nos jours* (Paris: Gallimard, 1983).

60. J.-J. Rousseau, *Considérations sur le gouvernement de Pologne*, in *idem*, *Oeuvres complètes*, ed. Bernard Gagnebin and Marcel Raymond, vol. III (Paris: Gallimard, 1964), pp. 959–65. Though, before the Revolution itself, the romantic impulse from Rousseau was more directed towards an idyllic, rural event of a non-political character. On this issue, see, B. Didier, 'La Fête champêtre dans quelques romans de la fin du XVIIIme siècle' in Erhard and Vialleneix, op. cit.

61. Aulard, op. cit.; and Albert Mathiez, *Les Origines des cultes révolutionnaires* (Paris: 1904; Geneva: Slatkine, 1977). Though the argument between these two is nominally about the dechristianizing campaign rather than about the festivals as such, both use notions of the religious which, by equating it with the sacred rituals of a society, encompass the festivals as the centre-piece of dechristianization.

62. See Vovelle, op. cit., esp. chs 6–8.

63. Ozouf, op. cit., *passim* and pp. 153–4 for quotation. See also Ozouf's essays, 'La Fête révolutionnaire et le renouvellement de l'imaginaire collectif' and 'Le Simulacre et la fête révolutionnaire' in Erhard and Vialleneix, op. cit., pp. 303–322 and 323–53, respectively. Emmanuel Le Roy Ladurie's *Le Carnaval à Romans* (Paris: Gallimard, 1979; trans. Feeney, *Carnival at Romans*, London: Penguin, 1981) is a classic analysis of a specific case of social tensions integrated into and then spilling over in a traditional festival (see N. Parker, 'The Anthropology of Anarchy', *Radical Philosophy* no. 31, (1982), pp. 32–3).

64. Lynn Hunt, *Politics, Culture and Class in the French Revolution* (Berkeley: University of California Press, 1984), esp. chs 1 and 2.

65. Yves-Marie Bercé, *Fête et révolte: des mentalités populaires du XVIme au XVIIIme siècle* (Paris: Hachette, 1976), esp. pp. 88–9, 119–21 and 189–90.

66. Claude Mazauric, 'La Fête révolutionnaire: manifestation de la politique jacobine: Rouen, 1793' in Erhard and Vialleneix, op. cit., p. 190: 'vigueur, précision, et réalisme des objectifs politiques assignés à la fête . . . mais vacuité moralisante ou idéalisme abstrait de ses justifications'.

See also D. Mascolo, *Le Communisme: Révolution et communication ou dialectique des valeurs et des besoins* (Paris: 1953), p. 146.

67. John Huizinga, *Homo Ludens: a Study of the Play Element in Culture* (London: Routledge and Kegan Paul, 1949; London: Paladin, 1970).

68. Robert Duvignaud, *Fêtes et civilisations* (Geneva: Weber, 1973) esp. pp. 72–8, 92–116 and 178.

69. Nicholas Wagner, 'Fête et dissolution sociale: à propos de quelques notices du *Journal de Paris*', in Erhard and Vialleneix, op. cit., pp. 525–36, esp. p. 535.

70. Mikhail Bakhtin, *Rabelais and his World*, trans. H. Iswolsky (Cambridge, MA: MIT Press, 1968), p. 109.

71. This accounts for what Soboul, op. cit., p. 342, refers to as the 'syncretism' of the new revolutionary cults and the traditional forms of worship.

72. See Ozouf, op. cit., pp. 294ff.

73. The terminology used is due to J.L. Austin, 'Performative Utterances' in J.O. Urmston and G.J. Warnock (eds), *Philosophical Papers* (Oxford: Oxford University Press, 1979), pp. 233–52.

74. 'O Père de lumière! éternelle puissance, toi qui fais marcher le soleil devant la liberté, pour éclairer ses augustes travaux . . . Je crois a la nouvelle République française, une et indivisible, à ses loix et aux droits sacrés de l'homme, que le peuple français ont reçus de la Montagne sacrée de la Convention qui les a créés . . . Que le peuple Européen, sortant de sa léthargie coupable, reconnoisse les droits de l'homme, pour lesquels les vrais enfants de la France ont juré de vivre et mourir' (quoted in Jean Massin, *Almanach de la Révolution française* (Paris: Club français du livre, 1963).

75. See J.-E. Schlanger, 'Le Peuple au front gravé' in Erhard and Vialleneix, op. cit., pp. 377–95.

76. See Ozouf, op. cit., esp. ch. 7. One is reminded of the difficulty of the Soviet encyclopedia from which certain key actors in the Revolution had to be removed according as their political stature in Stalin's Russia was altered, or indeed of the job Orwell's hero in *1984* does for a living: correcting the historical record.

77. Claude Gaignebet and Marie-Claude Florentin, *Le Carnaval* (Paris: Payot, 1979), pp. 153f.

78. D'Estrée, op. cit., p. 155, quotes a typical comment on a jolly comedy about enlisting: 'L'auteur aurait pu prêter un peu plus de chaleur et d'héroïsme à ses ouvriers patriotes'.

79. Richard Cobb, 'Some Aspects of the Revolutionary Mentality' in Kaplan, op. cit.

CHAPTER THREE

Pictures, Fashions, History: Locating the Revolution

The contemporary system of concepts tried to portray the revolutionary order in relation to the new public. However, the task has proved hard for the cultural processes I have examined. The scheme of boundaries, exclusions and content defining the public's identity could be portrayed in language and in 'performances' with varying degrees of success. Tensions appeared in its representation, however. They show up at points where the culture is trying to determine the public too closely or locate it within a confined point in historical time – though the carnival's flexibility could overcome much of the difficulty. In this chapter, I will examine other cultural processes, which are particularly well under the control of their creator: paintings, prints, the implicit historiography of descriptions in writing.

The examination of visual portrayals is swung towards high art by the preponderance of established study and available examples. Though such art may be elevated, however, its internal workings are more explicit. It therefore grapples more specifically with the tensions involved in its enterprise. In particular, so-called 'neo-classicism' attempted to address the issue of the new public.

These areas bring out explicitly an issue which has been under the surface in the spoken and performed types of culture. How can the new revolutionary order be located within history? By adding to the previous material on the public's moral character an account of how the new public appeared in the temporal dimension, this examination will complete my analysis of cultural processes in the revolutionary period.

NEW DIRECTIONS AND THE REORGANIZATION OF ART

The central place in the course of art in the late eighteenth century belongs to the rise of 'neo-classicism'. The seminal, though not the sole expression of the attempt to encompass revolutionary themes in art can also be found in neo-classicism, notably that of David. But neo-classical is no easily defined, clear-cut category. It describes as much an imprecise aspiration shared by artists and critics as a type of art. Though it is the core trend, the characteristic developments in the visual arts do not only appear in the neo-classical. But in spite of these strictures, it is nevertheless essential to adopt the idea of the neo-classical in my analysis.

Commentaries[1] apply the term 'neo-classicism' to three trends in art which gradually intertwined during the second half of the century. The archaeology of the classical world was rediscovered in Italy. A new public and a new type of critic demanded greater moral seriousness in art. And the supposed sparseness and severity of classical art, architecture and décor came to be accepted as an aesthetic model. These tendencies came together in a desire for art embodying austere moral virtues in a severe manner, supposedly reproducing a classical aesthetic style: 'noble simplicity and quiet grandeur', as Winckelmann put it in the 1750s. The reality was often somewhat different. Rococo elements were subtly introduced into reproductions of rediscovered classical models. Classical subjects were interpreted with a pre-romantic taste for sublime terror or gothic horror. Moral subjects in painting often did not owe their meaning to classical references.

In parallel with these tendencies in art, anti-establishment French critics and pamphleteers were creating a stir. La Font de Saint-Yenne as early as 1747, Diderot in the 1760s, then Carmontelle and Mercier in the 1780s, all contributed to this trend before the Revolution. Others were to become journalists and politicians during the Revolution itself: Marat, Brissot, Carra and Gorsas. These critics condemned the voluptuous, private taste of the *ancien régime* aristocracy, and the power of the art hierarchy in the Academy. They called for painting to be 'a school of morals'. It should portray models of morality such as

> the heroic and virtuous actions of great men, examples of the human spirit, of generosity, of courage, of scorn for danger or even for life, of passionate zeal for the honour and the safety of [the] fatherland, and above all of defence of religion.[2]

In the later decades of the century, this morality of devotion to *public* duty (arguably of a peculiarly callous kind)[3] was increasingly called for. Private virtues, such as loyalty or gentleness among family and friends,

Figure 3.1 Antoine Vestier, *Latude showing the demolishers of the Bastille* (Musée Carnavalet; photo: Musées de la Ville de Paris © SPADEM 1989)

went out of favour. The officialdom of art came to accept these values, too. They set subjects and awarded prizes for stories from the classical era — particularly in the most prestigious category, 'history' painting.

Neo-classicism as such did not embrace the whole of the trend towards new, austere public morality or a particular politics.[4] When the above trends were successfully combined, it was with formal qualities from earlier post-Renaissance sources (such as Poussin and Caravaggio) overlaying the style of Christian genres (like the *pietà*). Yet, neo-classicism is a most revealing 'facet of a broader, more embracing transformation that pervades eighteenth-century experience'.[5] It represents, as Kenneth Clarke argues,[6] the moment when classical and romantic elements in art came into tension. Yet, the conflict between them was important. Whatever its limitations as a category, neo-classicism has to be central to my analysis. It throws light on the struggle for meaning within pictorial art in late eighteenth-century France.

When the Revolution happened, the art world was turned upside down, like everything else. It too had had its rigid, status-ridden hierarchy, centred in the Academy in Paris and numerous provincial replicas. The inevitable corollary had been a large group of disgruntled artists of low status, who felt they were denied artistic expression, a decent income, and the recognition they deserved. Like others, this pre-existing hierarchy was overturned, and the up-and-coming artists threw themselves enthusiastically into the revolutionary cause. As the influence of the old guard withered, the rising trend in subjects and style rapidly became dominant. Newer styles, purportedly appropriate to the new era, were put forward by a newly articulate majority of artists, who whole-heartedly supported the broad aims of the Revolution.[7]

The atmosphere of the revolutionary period was favourable to painting with a serious purpose likely to foster public morality. The annual showcase *salon* of 1789 saw some portrayals of the events or of leading political figures in the Revolution so far: the Estates General, Necker, and a one-time prisoner of the Bastille, Latude. Yet there was no easy accord about how to treat revolutionary subjects in paint: Latude (Figure 3.1) is finely dressed and pictured, quite conventionally, in a sprightly pose that points to something associated with him. The symbolic object has to be a picturesque Bastille, slipped uncomfortably into the edge of the frame, where workmen are demolishing it.

People in the art world naturally expected a renewal in art to accompany that in society. As one critic wrote: 'Prejudices will evaporate, virtue and the arts will be re-born'. In the early 1790s, there was a new demand: for allegories of the cosmic basis of the new order;

for images of events in the Revolution; and for busts of revolutionary heroes or classical heroes such as Brutus, who symbolized those virtues sought by loyal members of the Republic. These were to adorn the legislative building, the halls of political clubs and the private homes of activists. The *salons* of the years after 1789 did refer to the Revolution. But they did so without departing from the pre-existing conventions regarding style and subject matter. Thus Gauffier's *Generosity of Roman Women* (1797 – Figure 3.2) took the same story from Plutarch as a work by Brenet, exhibited in 1785: wealthy Roman women giving their jewellery to the state. There are stylistic innovations: the composition is bolder, with solider figures and physical objects; and there is a concentration of light on the leading women and on the area where the representatives of the Republic sit. But an extraneous factor had increased the political significance of the story. In September 1789, some wealthy women, following the example set by Mme David and the wives of other artists, had taken to donating their jewellery to the state.

Meanwhile David, already successful as a portraitist and an

Figure 3.2 Louis Gauffier, *Generosity of Roman Women* (Musée de Sainte-Croix de Poitiers; photo: Musée de Poitiers – Christian Vignaud)

iconoclastic history painter, had quickly gathered the support of the numerous lower-status 'agréés' of the French Academy. He and the more republican of the anti-establishment artists formed the Société Populaire et Républicaine des Arts. It petitioned successfully against the privileges of the Academy, and in favour of commissioning portrayals of civic virtue for public display. By 1794, all the institutions of art under the *ancien régime* had been replaced. A 'commune' and a national jury of artists awarded prizes. A new conservatory supervised teaching. A 'Commission' of the arts granted honours, supervised the national art assets and generally co-ordinated policy on art. The prizes, if not all the content of the annual *salon*, were largely under the sway of the new guard in the art world.

All the new institutions were under the direction of David, who also pursued a full political career.[8] What is more, it was he, of course, who was stage-managing most of the major festivals in Paris. But, though David is the exemplary figure at the focal point of art and revolutionary politics, neither his politics nor his art represent the full range. There were other artists in the Convention, in other clubs of various political colours and in other political-artistic enterprises. Quatremère de Quincy, critic and designer, was on the Committee of Public Instruction with David. He stage-managed the conservative Simoneau festival,[9] and organized the refurbishment of the new secular 'Panthéon' for the remains of the dead heroes of the nation. Prieur was a history painter and member of the revolutionary tribunal. Yet other artists were further to the left than David: two, Topino-Lebrun and Hennequin, ended up on trial in connection with the radical Conspiracy of Equals of 1806.[10]

The politicians of the new national institutions kept pace with the enthusiasm for art in the service of the Revolution among the art public and the artists themselves.[11] The revolutionary legislatures commissioned Quatremère and approved the new art institutions. And they treated certain images – much like certain speeches – as worth wide publication. David was commissioned to prepare a series of prints 'which would arouse public feeling and make people aware of how hateful and ridiculous are the enemies of the Revolution'.[12] Barère proposed that an engraving of Bara, the child martyr, be made for display in all primary schools. The Committee of Public Safety commissioned prints of Fabre, representative of the government who was killed fighting with the army in the Pyrenees,[13] and a printed version of Caresme's painting of the adult republican hero, Chalier. In the picture (Figure 3.3), we see Chalier pronouncing his last defiant

Figure 3.3 Jacques-Philippe Caresme, *Last Words of Joseph Chalier* (Département des Estampes, Bibliothèque Nationale; photo: Bibl. Nat. Paris)

words before being taken off to execution in the counter-revolutionary uprising at Lyons.

All sides in the relationship between the state, the artists and the public agreed broadly on the role and effect of art. That agreement simply extended the rising moralism from before the Revolution. The aesthetic of gravity, exemplary morality and elevation was the same. But that view became dominant, and the schemes to put it into practice became grander. In 1793, Barère spoke to the Convention, as a representative of the government, of 'a vast plan of regeneration, the result of which will be to banish from the Republic in one step immorality, prejudices, superstition and atheism'.[14] The Convention wanted art to 'immortalize virtuous actions . . . linked to morality, enlarged like the souls' of men in this 'century of liberty'.[15] This is what the critics from earlier in the century had wanted, and the painters were offering to provide.

Figure 3.4 Jacques-Louis David, *Tennis Court Oath* (Musée Carnavalet; photo: Musées de la Ville de Paris © SPADEM 1989)

Yet only a small proportion of the projected republican art was actually produced. We have many sketches and outlines for unfinished works. Not the least are two massive projects by David: *Tennis Court Oath* (Figure 3.4) and *The Triumph of the French People*. Why the failures? Might they tell us anything about the enterprise of portraying the Revolution in paint? The problems were partly practical. Many prizes and grants were awarded for sketches and schemes that were time-consuming, vulnerable to shifts rendering their content politically ambiguous, and too expensive for a bankrupt state at war. But there were unresolved aesthetic dilemmas, as well. In 1793, the jury had difficulty in reaching agreement on a winner; and in 1794, it was quite unable to do so. The winners who were chosen in 1795 mostly failed to produce a work on the subject they had originally offered, reverting instead to subjects from classical history.[16] The mixture of styles in the works that actually were produced shows the difficulty of settling the matter of which qualities were appropriate to the agreed political and moral purposes. Artists, who were freshly liberated from the dead hand of the Academy's rules and arguing among themselves about aesthetic means, were being asked to reach agreement with political militants over the worth of specific works. The actual output

Figure 3.5 Louis Léopold Boilly, *The Triumph of Marat* (Lille, Musée des Beaux-Arts)

thus shows no aesthetic accord. It ranges from the portrait of Latude, to the Greuze-like moralism of gesture and dingy setting of Caresme's *Chalier*, to the jubilant activity of *The Triumph of Marat* (Figure 3.5) by one-time rococo artist, Boilly. The Société Populaire found this last attempt frivolous. David's voice stands out aesthetically, as well as politically. From his very success in giving pictorial form to austere republican morality, we may identify those limits to what was aesthetically possible which weighed on the artists as a whole.

NEO-CLASSICISM AND THE IDEAL IN THE REVOLUTION

David himself said this to the Convention:

> The arts . . . are the imitation of nature in its most beautiful and its
> most perfect aspects; a sentiment natural to man attracts him toward the
> same object. It is not only by charming the eyes that the monuments of
> art have fulfilled this end; it is by penetrating the soul, it is by making
> on the mind a profound impression, similar to reality. It is thus that the
> traits of heroism, and of civic virtues offered to the regard of the people,

Figure 3.6 Jacques-Louis David, *The Oath of the Horatii* (Musée du Louvre; photo: John Rylands University Library of Manchester)

will electrify its soul and will cause to germinate in it all the passions of glory, of devotion to the welfare of the fatherland. [17]

In this speech, David was rehearsing the agreed moral and political needs of the new Republic. He then claimed them as the natural territory of his neo-classicism. What is meant by the cultural needs of the Republic is familiar enough (not least from my first two chapters). They are to convey to the public, with its new central role, an effective impression of the qualities that the new political-social order needs it to possess. According to David, those virtues belong to nature in its ideal, 'most perfect' form. The power of visual art is to capture that ideal in a manner which provokes the public's natural attachment to it. We can begin to judge how a visual portrayal fulfilling the needs of post-revolutionary society might be achievable, if we examine David's execution of his aims in the history painting. Three examples are reproduced: *The Oath of the Horatii* of 1784 (Figure 3.6), the uncompleted *Tennis Court Oath* of 1791 (Figure 3.4), and *Death of Marat* (Figure 3.7) of 1793.

84

Figure 3.7 Jacques-Louis David, *Death of Marat* (Musée Royal des Beaux-Arts, Brussels)

The original neo-classical project was to revive the classical aesthetic for the sake of its supposed seriousness in conveying a public morality. But the trade marks of David's neo-classicism were inventiveness over subject matter, vivid realism, and a flexibility in the use of allusion, gesture, space and background. These are necessary in order to *subvert*

85

the original neo-classical project. To a significant degree, David's personal success was bought at the cost of modifying all the letter of neo-classicism in order to live up to his republican enterprise.

The paradigm of neo-classical genres was the history painting. It is a genre that works with both the ideal and time. The ideal is projected into time — just as, in other forms of revolutionary culture, the idealized people were situated in history. The genre works by dramatizing just one point in time as *the* moment in the story. It is a 'moment' both in the sense of an instant in time and in the sense of a crucial, deciding point, when a course of action is taken and a direction set. The story is already known and understood by the spectators. Thus the artist finds room to manoeuvre in the choice of moment to portray and how to present it.

Detailed research[18] has shown how David carefully defined the moral meaning that he wanted to impart in the story of the Horatii. It allows us to witness David working his chosen ideal into a moment captured in a visual image. The story concerns three Roman brothers, two of whom die in combat with three brothers on the enemy side. It had an ambiguous sequel, which appeared in Livy and in Corneille's tragedy, *Horace*. The one surviving brother murders one of his sisters in a fit of temper when she presumes to grieve over one of the dead enemies, who had been betrothed to her. But then he is let off his crime by the Senate. The story of the Horatii is rich with the passionate commitment to the national good which characterizes the revolutionary period. In working with this story, David eschewed from the start the Corneille version, which relies on the intercession of royal authority. He then toyed with a republican vision of the moral conflict in the sequel: Horace senior (father of the murdered girl) appealing to the Senate for clemency towards his son. The sketches for this version are still in existence: they set the guilty son on the sidelines, and focus attention instead on the painful sentiments of the old man, shown in his passionate gestures.

But, in the end, David abandoned this and settled on a much earlier moment in the story, from a completely different classical writer, Dionysius of Halicarnassus. The final picture shows all three of the brothers, united with their father, in an energetic upward-reaching gesture. They are simply taking an oath to save Rome or die. By his choice of moment, David has lifted the risks of death and emotional distress in what they are doing. That is portrayed instead in the vague, symmetrical grace of the sisters' gesture as they swoon in apprehension in the right-hand segment of the picture. What David has done is to select, and then envision, a moment when any potential conflicts and ambivalences in the brothers' commitment to the Roman republic are only dimly felt. This permits the inspiration of commitment to a common ideal to be conveyed cleanly. It is shared by the four male figures, and implicitly by the whole of the republic. The tragedy inherent in a commitment of that kind is portrayed alongside, in a sad, but not overwhelming way. David's is not a narrow-minded representation of nationalist commitment, but the aesthetic means have been carefully tailored to a censored moral content.

In general, David's history paintings show this kind of inventiveness with the historical story, in pursuit of a level of generality uncluttered by specifics or ambivalences. That was needed, I would argue, to convey the abstracted public virtue he wished to represent in his works. His version of Brutus (the same Brutus as in Voltaire's play) also takes the same tragic conflict of public duty and family loyalty, but in a moment David himself invented. Brutus's wife and daughters start up in shock as his traitor sons' bodies are brought home for burial; Brutus himself, lost in pained, stoical thought, turns distractedly in the shadows on the far side of the picture. In him, the distress and conflict entailed in public duty is almost calmed. The *Tennis Court Oath* captures the countless members of the Third Estate, united in an upward gesture comparable to that of the Horatii. Once again, David chose a symbolic moment outside the real action. It is the first moment that the Third Estate took on the role of a national assembly, representative of the sovereign people. They are united in an abstracted, historic gesture. But the variety and energy of David's figures succeed perhaps in bringing them to life in spite of the abstraction in the moment he has envisioned.

David also constructed around his scenes a space designed to convey his abstract ideal. The geometrical grandeur of a stone setting lends classical greatness, pared down to austere essentials. The upward opening of space, for example, above the two oaths (the Horatii and the Tennis Court) connects their gesture to a higher abstraction. The abstraction is thus grounded in a historical reality. The virtue of early Rome is in the simple columns of the two Roman paintings: commitment to the public good is contained in the space above. The public itself gazes in on the Tennis Court from the real world, whence a dramatic breeze lifts the curtains. By the time of *Death of Marat*, however, David has moved on to another level in the use of space surrounding the scene. Once again, he chooses a moment outside the historic action. Marat appears as a hero of classical grandeur, but in the present day. He is portrayed where he has been murdered, at home in his bath, in the very act of responding with charity to his murderer's begging letter. Classical stonework is replaced by a supernaturally darkened space. This ousts the detail of Marat's room, but lends a more immediate and open-ended greatness than could be possessed by any figure located in a classically defined space. The scene is domestic, but transcendent. The intangible openness of the space, offset by the few revered personal belongings conveyed with *trompe-l'oeil* realism, gives the martyr a mysterious greatness transcending time. In Kenneth Clarke's phrase, David manages to 'strike a perfect balance with the ideal'[19] by giving the impression that some absolute truth is present *within* the scene.

But David's flexibility has fundamentally modified his neo-classicism so as to achieve the priorities he had in adopting it in the first place. The pose of the dead figure is far closer to the traditional Christ lifted down from the Cross than it is to anything classically noble. The compromises with neo-classical principles enable David to achieve his moral purpose in paint: a vision of compassionate, intimate love of the people in the contemporary, post-revolutionary world. The strategy modifies almost out of recognition the neo-classical rules of background and geometry in the setting. But, given the choice between the rules and the purpose David sought through them, David chose to sacrifice the rules.

Looking back over David's words and the paintings, we can now see how the cultural purpose which neo-classicism offered to fulfil for the new social-political order met its limits in his work. The speech to the Convention argued two points: that the arts 'imitated nature' in a 'perfect' form which attracts people to it; and that the 'profound impression' they could make would foster a love of that ideal virtue. In the history pictures, David constructed scenes which conveyed virtue as a higher-level 'nature' of moral-political ideals. The choice of an encapsulating historical moment in itself caused David great difficulty, as he tried to distance the republican ideal from the dissension or grief it might involve. With the growing sense that the Revolution had its own status as 'history', David broke with scenes from the historical past, but only in the direction of another abstraction.

But there is still a problem in locating the ideal in an abstract nature. David's realism can make it seem that ultimate truth inheres in the image by the very brilliance and solidity of figures and objects. But he finds great difficulty in envisioning the ideal in a contemporary social reality. In principle, the ideal was located in the people, which was the ultimate foundation of the new social order. Theoretically, their united action constituted them, and made history. That is why David took up the festivals. He understood that in a festival the people could actually be gathered together, united and active. 'National festivals are instituted for the people;' he said,[20] 'it is fitting that they play the principal role in them.' He did master the art of arranging organized movement for vast numbers of people over the length of a day. But in the pictures, which outlast that space of time, the people in whom the ideal is grounded appear only because David stretches the possibilities of allusion. In the pre-revolutionary painting the republic can be represented by its distinguished servants (the Horatii or Brutus), rather than the people as such. The revolutionary system of concepts made allusion to the past less acceptable. But even in the post-revolutionary *Tennis Court Oath*, the people can only be seen on the edges. In *Death of Marat* (and in David's other pictures of martyrs: Bara, Le Pelletier), the ideal is still *alluded* to, via an unmistakably Christian symbolism and via a single individual in a darkened space — and a dead individual at that. The still figure in death has to represent the ideal in commitment to the people.

In neo-classicism, David adopted the classical past as a myth of the ideal. But that distanced the ideal he wished to convey to the public. It was removed along two axes: one tending towards an unrealizable abstraction; and one going back through historical time. During the early years of the Revolution, David was able to recover the ideal from the past so as to locate it in a transcendent space in the present, and potentially in the future. He abandoned the historicism of neo-classicism to improve its focus on the ideal. But that does not pull the ideal back from abstraction, though the persistent force of his realism on the canvas counters that tendency. On the other hand, his attempts to portray the sovereign public in action on canvas, or to bring them together as a living body of people, were left short-lived or incomplete. David's development of neo-classicism could go far, then. But it could not completely negate the vacant points in its enterprise: the ideal of the people creating open-ended history.

Having said that about David's brilliant attempt to use them, we can grasp neo-classicism's strengths and difficulties. It is a movement to represent a rationalistic species of order and virtue: 'noble simplicity and quiet grandeur'. The ideal is epitomized in classical example. Roman civic virtue could be seized upon for images to envision the new legitimate public. Neo-classical ways of constructing a pictorial image in geometrical form are intended to translate the figures, and their

Figure 3.8 Anne-Louis Girodet, Drawing for *Hippocrates refusing the gifts of Artaxerxes* (Musée Bonnat, Bayonne; photo: Arch. Phot. Paris/SPADEM)

actions, on to an abstract level of symmetry that can be felt as an ideal of humanity. We can see this in the preparatory *Drawing for Hippocrates refusing the gifts of Artaxerxes* by Girodet, a pupil of David (Figure 3.8). Neo-classicism provided inspiring, emotionally appealing images of what citizens could be. Because it eschewed voluptuousness and made reference to the abstract ideal and the historical past, it was equipped to convey a transcendent truth to a 'public' in the process of formation.

By ending his study of painters from the 1740s onwards with David's hugely successful launch of the *Horatii* at the 1785 *salon*, Thomas Crow tends to confirm a favourable impression of neo-classicism. Art critics and the changing clientele had been trying to identify a kind of art addressed to an ideal public, which was counterposed to the absolutist state or the enclosed, 'decadent' aristocracy predominant in *ancien régime* society. The painters had apparently tailored their art to these demands for a new public life. By the mid-1780s, writes Crow, 'any piece of art had to declare itself in this way, had to declare that it belonged, like David's art, to the special language of truth'.[21] Starobinski's wide-ranging analysis of dominant images in *Les Emblêmes de la raison* also confirms the strength

90

of neo-classicism's project. It sought a return to the lost direction of humankind, deemed present in original nature yet beyond the reach of memory. Neo-classicism is a visual art tailored to the task that post-revolutionary society needed done: to develop the new public by translating and conveying abstract ideals to it. Art could provide the emblems of this ungraspable other reality of reason.

But Starobinski also identifies the dilemma for the revolutionary spirit. It was impossible to ground pronouncements of high principle in anything firmer or more public than the personality of the individual making the pronouncements. But that was inherently suspect. [22] The other side of the coin for neo-classicism is seen after the Revolution, when the neo-classical programme can be put into practice. Artists committed to the cause of the Revolution undertook works to envision those ideals, and then failed to complete the commissions. We might say that they simply reverted to choosing images from more familiar classical territory. Certainly, *reality* did make it hard for them. One claimed embodiment of the ideal was replaced so rapidly by another. As Crow points out, David was hampered in executing the *Tennis Court Oath* by the fall from political grace of so many of the figures even as he painted them in.

It is not, however, merely that the given real public or a real political stance did not match an unspecified ideal. [23] That certainly is a dimension of the problem. Yet the neo-classical enterprise of envisioning ideals does not in itself require that particular period of past history. And these were artists politically committed to the Revolution's own historical present. It is as if, in their present historical reality, the artists could not identify aesthetically the ideal, or the actual public. By portraying dead martyrs enveloped in mysterious, hospitable voids, David only reached the ideal in the stillness of death. The ideal is still wrapped in a moment. Another moment of living and change would risk qualifying and losing it. We need to consider more closely the way the ideal is conceived in this neo-classical project.

The ideal as conceived in neo-classicism had always been limited in this way. It was embodied in precisely *one* point of time; it was sensed in a moment; it was not fit for change and hence for reality. Neo-classicism was offering the Revolution a profoundly abstracted kind of ideal. It was excluding from its ideal much of what is necessary for any kind of realization. The emotional feel of David's work was a quite peculiar, and unsustainable combination of features to evoke the ideal as real. Clarke points out that the evocation broke down anyway in

David's later years.[24] Though the work may be intended to inspire an emotional commitment in the spectator, neo-classical severity excluded living emotion, as Starobinski's commentary argues. The portrayal of paradigmatic moments and acts led to a sort of self-absorbed lethargy in the subjects.[25] Though neo-classicism sought to embody an ideal and convey it to the public of real people, it had enormous difficulty in giving convincing reality both to the ideal and to the spectator. What is more, to portray individual heroes as embodiments of the ideal must have the effect of differentiating the bearer of the ideal from the observer and, hence, from the public. As is shown by another recent commentary, the neo-classical period's fascination with self-absorbed figures produced images calculated to *exclude* the spectator from the ideal world of the picture.[26]

In sum, neo-classicism was defining an ideal for the new legitimate public in terms that necessarily rejected the reality of that same public. It was an ideal calling upon an emotionality it implicitly condemned. Hence, it is glimpsed frozen in an instant and shorn of existence in time. It was located in an alien, fixed, self-referring world, usually that of the classical past — hence, it was located more easily in the individual hero than in any body of people.

FASHIONS, POPULAR IMAGES AND HEROES

How much might this kind of problem in fine art have impeded visual art for a wider public? Analogous problems are certainly present. Two manifestations of visible imagery come to mind: popular fashions and printed images. Fashions in dress can be seen pursuing the same directions as revolutionary neo-classicism. They try to identify the public and relate it to history. Over the decade following the Revolution this impulse from above meets an impulse towards other fashions from below.[27] The styles of printed images reveal a tension analogous to that in neo-classicism between abstraction and the difficult choice of individuals who can serve as emblems.

The most famous popular fashion, of course, was the red cap of liberty. It seems to have appeared first in the provincial festivals of 1790 as a neo-classical allusion to the practice of freed Roman slaves.[28] It then caught on rapidly among ordinary people. Yet, renowned as it is, it is something of an exception: a classical style accepted by and largely confined to the lower orders. Most styles worn by the common

Figure 3.9 Drawing of a revolutionary fashion for women (1791)
(Bibliothèque Nationale, Paris; photo: John Rylands University Library of
Manchester)

people which acquired political significance were drawn directly from
immediate experience and pre-existing habits of dress with a clear
practical basis. This is true of the loose-fitting *pantalon*, short
carmagnole jacket and clogs, though the wollen cap was also, of course,

a practical garment. To these items of clothing we should add the pike, widely carried both as symbol and, of course, with the intention of perhaps using it for political purposes. Not surprisingly, what seems to have happened in the dress of the poorer classes is that they continued to wear what they would have worn anyway, but more insistently and with more political meaning.

Dress is a conscious mark of one's social position and group. So by their dress ordinary people could not but show themselves to be humble. But ordinary republicans now proclaimed that they were good citizens of the republic *because* they were humble. Hence, the militants' own term for themselves: *sansculottes*. Those not able to dress in fine, fitted trousers claimed equal status with each other and with the wealthy. Fashions in clothing reflected a desire among all classes to display a common identity as equal members of the same respected public. In the same spirit, the wealthy embraced the dress styles of the poor – though only to a very limited extent. Some bourgeois republicans, such as Madame Roland, set fashions in simple peasant bonnets. (One can be seen worn by ladies in the foreground of Boilly's *The Triumph of Marat*.) The symbolism of dress remained class- and gender-bound, however. Professional creators of fashions mimicked the dress of the poor in designs which are manifestly for the well-off (Figure 3.9). The attempts often seem fairly naive. Even sansculotte women never got into the habit of wearing the red cap. So real differences of class, wealth and gender limited the impact of these directions in fashion.

The meaning of dress for the shared identity of a body of equal citizens was evident to leaders of the Revolution as well. David's Société Populaire et Républicaine des Arts was in the forefront of suggestions for central reform of dress habits to reflect equality and a shared sense of exclusive identity. National costume, a member of the society argued, 'would announce to everyone immediately one's citizenship and prevent the French people being confused with people of other nations still branded by the shackles of servitude'.[29] Over and above his designs for use in festivals, David himself produced various designs in more or less classical style for citizens and state officials. Though they did have some influence on later Napoleonic uniforms, in the end they were not taken up. Perhaps this is not surprising; for the society's reflections also seem limited by naivety. They largely missed the practical and economic aspects of dress – and hence its class aspects, too. Costume, they thought, should be 'dictated by reason and good sense'. In such timeless categories, they saw not so much the realities of everyday social life, but a peculiar unity between classical taste, aesthetic priorities and the historical greatness of the Revolution. Altered styles of dress would help the artists to record the Revolution because their materials would no longer be 'paralysed by the ingratitude of a costume which causes the cloth to groan, which resists the chisel'.[30] In sum, in spite of its natural capacity to advance a common identity, fashion was caught in the tension of alluding to an ideal in the historical past. Too often this was divorced from the reality of social life where the creators sought to realize those values.

Lynn Hunt has argued that the established trade in popular prints was better able to respond to the Revolution than was fine art. It was accustomed to retailing images quickly to the public at large.[31] According to Hunt, the considerable output of the trade evolved through a series of different emphases, each one suggesting a different conception of the Revolution. First, there was satire directed against the powerful and wealthy of the past. Then, scenes of mass action introduced the active people into the image. Allegorical images of the republic as a young girl or of civic virtues removed the people again. Then came satire against the post-revolutionary republic (after the fall of the Jacobin government in 1794), and, in the later years of the revolutionary decade, images of republican soldiers and generals. The allegorical images of the republic evolved, too: towards more and more sedate and abstract figures. Hunt draws the convincing conclusion that these changes reflect the changing political climate, structure and propaganda strategies. On the one hand, the revolutionary crowd became a source of fear. On the other, the values of the Republic were gradually relocated towards abstractions and the increasingly powerful republican army. Looking exclusively at both visual and verbal allegories for the republic, Maurice Agulhon has traced a similar development of the common people's image of the republic over the century following 1789.[32] He finds that the emblem that evolved among them is in tension with the abstractions offered from above. Their folk-symbol, Marianne, is an altogether different figure from the official allegories of Reason.

If we accept the thesis that prints directly reflected changes in political orientation, we need to attend to their style and organization to understand how the reflection was articulated. One thing is clear: the predominant style in prints was manifestly not *neo*-classical.[33] Yet we can see from samples what continuities (some of them classical) defined the options for artists in working out how to respond to the Revolution's demands. There are basically two strategies of representa-

95

tion available: realism or emblematic reference. I shall consider each in turn.

Continuity in the training of draughtsmen employed by the print-makers ensured that a respect for balance, form and architecture is apparent in realist prints throughout the period. Even in the cruder realist portrayals, historical events are framed in perspective lines of walls (see Figure 3.10 or Figure 3.11 of a republican intervening to save church monuments). Where the image is technically better, it normally uses more of the conventional devices found in painting. Columns and arches set the action as if on stage (see Figure 3.12, the Tuileries, or Figures 3.13 and 3.14 where perspective and an arch of almost Piranesi-like picturesqueness dominate the event). Plumes of smoke and turbulent cloud traverse open-air scenes (see Figure 3.15). Individual figures are cast in stylized gestures (see Figures 3.10, 3.11 and 3.16). In general, then, the realist strategy tends to import the aesthetic of geometry and classical reference, even if not in a neo-classical manner.

But, because of their looser professional organization and more demanding pattern of work, the engravers were unwittingly open to aesthetic and ideological currents both from the world of high culture and from further afield in society at large. As one commentator put it,

Figure 3.10 Print of massacre of prisoners, September 1793 (Mansell Collection)

96

Figure 3.11 Print of destruction of religious relics (© Photos Archives Editions Arthaud, Paris; photo: John Rylands University Library of Manchester)

Figure 3.12 Print of invasion of the Tuileries (Wayland Publishers Ltd)

Figure 3.13 Print of the Festival of the Federation, 1790 (Wayland Publishers Ltd)

Figure 3.14 Print of the Festival of the Federation, 1790 (Mansell Collection)

Figure 3.15 Print of the massacre at the Champs de Mars (Wayland Publishers Ltd)

the engravers, whose principal tools had changed little since ancient times, discreetly insinuated an old, rustic foundation into the scale of values appearing with the rise of the Bourgeoisie . . . the current from the masses, far from turning away from the dominant one, aimed to join with it as well as possible . . .[34]

Hence, where the prints move away from realism (as in Figure 3.17), we find expressions of a more marginal culture. In this context, direct reference can be called on comfortably to interpret what is portrayed. So emblematic reference, requiring very limited technical means, carried on from a pre-revolutionary language of religious images and cartoons. Figure 3.17, for example, represents the hoped-for accord between the different Estates of 1789 by simple references to dress and an emblematic tree.

There was still greater freedom in caricature, where language was used ironically to accompany the visual as it was in popular festivals.

At that time there was an image civilization, with . . . a 'grammar of images'. Caricature answered a need for expression, as invective does in certain countries with an oral tradition. Hence the frequent dislocation [of the image] with the text accompanying it.[35]

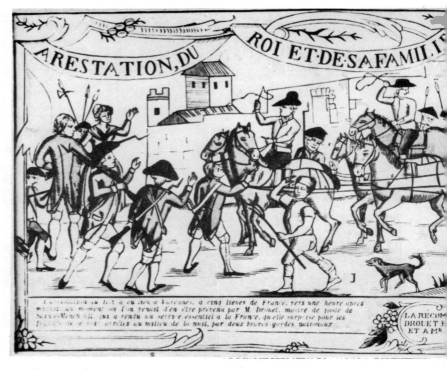

Figure 3.16 Print of the king's arrest at Varennes (Wayland Publishers Ltd)

Figure 3.17 Print of bishop, commoner and aristocrat playing music together
(Wayland Publishers Ltd: photo: John Rylands University Library of Manchester)

Combined with the power of direct reference to specify what is present with words, cartoons permitted derision through crude, unflattering comparisons. (See, for example, Figure 3.18 portraying the royal family being led away to gaol, in which the queen has a bare bosom and snakes in her hair.)

But this emblematic iconography still exhibits the tensions between classes that we saw in the language of clothes. Emblems of the true core of the nation were sites of conflict between different ranks and different political tendencies. Though the aesthetic and practical parameters are different, the problems of portraying the Revolution in prints are therefore embedded in the same paradoxes as the paintings. The realistic strategy reduced individual subjects to the abstraction of conventional gesture and the people as a mass to figures within an abstract geometry. This dehistoricizes and detracts from the reality it is intended to portray. It is the same tension as we found in neo-classicism. The alternative strategy refers to the people by picturing

101

Figure 3.18 Caricature of the royal family being brought back from Varennes
(Mansell Collection)

single individuals. But this relies upon iconography and popular sentiment that are bound to be disputed. Michel Vovelle has demonstrated this for a particularly telling case. Vovelle shows how the countryside and the peasants, who practised no visual art to portray themselves, were co-opted to a place in the iconography of urban political perceptions. In the early phase of the Revolution, for example, the peasant figured in prints as the victim of abuses that the bourgeoisie was complaining about. Later, the courageous peasant woman appeared as the victim of anti-republican rebels.[36] The heroes of the dominant groups, on the other hand, are the abstracted, idealized figures of neo-classical painting.

In rhetoric and political language, in theatrical and carnival performance, we found the frustration of complex strategies pursued by cultural processes to identify and portray the new public. Often, their difficulties were as much extraneous to them as internal: to do with their insertion into the society of the day. The strategy in visual art is epitomized in neo-classicism, where we have seen its tendency to become self-enclosed. The analogous problem appears in popular prints, with a more evident extraneous context. For the benefit of the new social-political order the public has to be represented to itself as real and active in historical time, not excluded by the ideal (be it in purified forms or in ambivalent heroism). But it proved most difficult to find forms or an effective language of signs to do this.

THE REVOLUTION AS A HISTORICAL MOMENT

A powerful theme in the forms of culture examined in this chapter has been the relation of the ideal to time. Neo-classicism aimed to fix on a narrow moment in time which contains the abstracted ideal of the action or virtue. Its difficulties arise crucially from this way of containing the ideal. It removed the ideal evoked from evolving historical reality. Likewise, prints employed classical form to impart the grandeur of the classical past. Fashions sought to relive the present political moment as a recovery of past time.

Yet historical time, and locating of the present revolutionary order in it, was also a recurring strand in other cultural forms. The journalist tried to place himself with the people, in a present, crucial turning point of events. Similarly, the political speaker tried to identify the present as the moment for the people to renew itself and start afresh. The festivals evoked, reiterated and (in carnival spirit) broke from the historical moment they commemorated. There are persistent, if ambivalent ways in which various cultural forms identify time and situate the sovereign French people in it. We should complete this analysis of culture within the Revolution, then, by examining how contemporaries conceptualized the Revolution's location in history.

The neo-classical version of this problem about time can be stated schematically thus: to evoke the ideal it is located in a moment so narrow as to be abstracted from the real movement of time or from real existence in time. The theme of time in previous chapters could be stated in similar terms. This conception of the ideal has been traced by Michel Foucault, using his concept of the classical system of concepts, or, in Foucault's terminology the 'classical episteme'. Even if Foucault's actual account of the growth and decline of his classical episteme is disputable, it is possible to show that a 'classical' discourse, with its limitations, is at work here. In either case, Foucault's analysis and critique throw light upon the problems that have been revealed in the contemporary notion of the Revolution's place in history.

Foucault identifies a cast of mind which holds that the objects of knowledge belong to a self-substantive 'order of things', which can be directly present to the mind with neither intermediaries nor the mind's positive intervention. Language, for example, merely *reproduces* the categories existing in the real world: 'the order of things'. This conception of language elides the positive reality of the human mind. Human language is taken to be a reflection, term for term, of the universal order, objective to actual human minds. Neither the activity nor the evolution of the human minds creating or expressing language can properly be a factor within language.

The classical 'episteme' as defined by Foucault excludes both the human mind's real existence and the possibility of its existing and changing in historical time. 'The classical order', Foucault writes,

> distributed in a permanent space non-quantitative identities and differences which separated and united things: it was this order which reigned supreme . . . over the discourse of men, the pattern of natural beings and the exchange of wealth.[37]

Because, as Hugh Silverman has argued, in the classical episteme, the essence of a thing is independent and unalterable, its moment of origin in time is the natural focus of attention.[38] For its essential character is that which it has at the moment of its temporal origin.

This logic of unalterable essence and its origin is at work in the attempts to realize and portray the ideal as a legitimation of the Revolution. As Renaud Barral puts it in discussing how the Jacobins thought of the Revolution in history:

> If men such as Condorcet and Saint-Just were able to agree on a political programme, with the other Jacobins occupying all the positions in between theirs, that is because in spite of antithetic convictions they both referred politics to nature, be it in pursuit of its transcendence or of a return to its origins.[39]

In the logic of the classical episteme, the basis of the Revolution is drawn towards an abstraction without a history, usually referred to as nature and often located in a distant historical point of reference. It sets aside the positivity of historically real people, existing and evolving. The very idea of the people as a legitimation of this type is incompatible with their being real, historically evolving human beings. In its visual representation, then, whatever lies behind the Revolution (virtue, the unity, commitment or character of the people, etc.) has, following the terms of the classical view, to be an ideal, self-substantive entity. It is therefore to be contrasted with the empirical real and not subject to historical change. True reality, or nature, does not exist in historical time.

In contemporary accounts of the Revolution, the notions of history and historical change wrestle with the problem of locating legitimacy outside and yet also within history. A variety of positions were adopted. Some described the historical events of the Revolution as though, exceptionally, some extra-historical principle had irrupted into history. Others attempted to discover a fresh kind of historicity in which the present and the future are both historical and guided by principle. All are engaged in the dialectic of history and abstract, ideal principle, or nature.

As outlined by Barral, the Jacobins in general believed that, if there was a historical cause for the outbreak of the Revolution, it was the growing power of enlightenment in people's minds. This had over-turned the long reign of prejudice. Appearances notwithstanding, this is really a profoundly anti-historical conception. For the Jacobin clubs' propaganda, by extending reasoned moral awareness among the people, was trying to 'attach the abstract universalism of political speculations to concrete reality'.[40] The few years of the Revolution take on a quite exceptional historical character. During that period alone the ideal principle of reason is politically dominant, and the people are empowered, by negating the pre-existing political order, to bypass the confusion of real historical institutions and beliefs.[41] Three revolutionary politicians – Sieyès, Robespierre and Saint-Just – illustrate the strategy adopted to give principle a place in history.

From the time of his crucial *What is the Third Estate?* in 1789, Sieyès defined the nation as the principle underlying political life. He explicitly disputed the rightness of whatever has already come about in history (notably the English example), on the grounds that it is merely 'the product of chance and circumstance'. Any 'ideal model of society' can be known as well directly as by example.[42] As a recent study explains, for Sieyès, the nation has to slough off its 'adventitious historical structures' and, 'free of any procedures', form 'an equal union of individuals' who agree on the terms of their union and on the manner it is to be represented.[43] In chapter 5 of the pamphlet, therefore, Sieyès constructs a *speculative* history of the phases necessary for the nation to constitute itself. What this implies is that the citizens should act according to the principles that are inherent in the existence of a nation as such. Reason could intervene against the whole current of history. Accordingly, in a draft decree to the Assembly, he wrote that 'the Revolution which is taking place bears no resemblance to any other . . . because it has as its first and true cause the progress of reason'.[44]

Robespierre and Saint-Just pursue the same structure of thought in a rather different way. Robespierre argued that the emergency wartime regime (the so-called 'revolutionary government') was without precedent in historical example or political writing. But for him it was the people, with their moral purity, that underpinned the Republic. So the government should bypass constitutional rules so as to 'direct the *moral and physical forces of the nation towards the goal of its foundation*'.[45] The mechanisms of government have shifted, yet it is still pure extra-historical principle that is supposed to intervene to create the nation or win the war for the Revolution. The same may be said of Saint-Just. His argument for the 1793 constitution, for example, was deduced from the existence of a social order morally prior to any political constitution. The success or otherwise of the nation's political action depended primarily upon its honesty and political virtue.[46]

Alongside those views, other currents of thinking were trying to relate the Revolution's historical existence to something other than an extra-historical principle of origin. These were to lead, in due course, to the more evolutionist and materialist conceptions of historical processes which arose after the Revolution, and which I examine in Part II. Two representatives of this current, Volney and Condorcet, belong in the pre-history of the so-called *idéologues* movement.[47]

Volney's popular *Les Ruines: méditations sur les révolutions des empires* (1791) constructed an image in a pre-romantic spirit turning the historical symbolism of the early years of the Revolution towards a scientific analysis of the growth of socially cohesive ideas.[48] The book is a long fantasy in which the writer meditates, before a ruined Egyptian city, on how great civilizations collapse and disappear. A 'fantom' appears to him and explains how, in spite of the human potential for unity, *all* past societies have ended in cupidity and tyranny.[49] In an elaborate vision,[50] the writer then sees 'all the labouring and learned professions',[51] followed by all the nations, assembling to face the oppressing classes identified by the Revolution: the nobility and the clergy. A 'legislator' figure explains to them the 'universal basis of all right and all law',[52] and how to avoid the differences over religion that divide them.

Up to this point, Volney's vision has preserved the notion of an extra-historical reference point. Historical time is overturned.[53] The long history of ignorance and corruption is brought to an end by a union of all the world's useful, thinking people. But the new world in Volney's vision does not end history. The legislator explains to the assembled super-nation that it is the creation of a historical process; namely, a programme of 'ideological' analysis to establish the power and limits of human knowledge in a more or less deistic mould.

The cause of your disagreements does not inhere in the objects themselves but in your minds, in the way you perceive or you judge . . . To establish unanimity of opinion, we must first establish a firm certainty, and confirm that the pictures which the mind paints for itself exactly resemble their models.[54]

The idea of the programme amends the classical conception of how extra-historical principles may intervene, by including within history a sensationalist process of learning. Human beings' grasp of the principles (though not their truth) can evolve via the positive, conscious intervention of the mind. *Les Ruines* manipulates both theoretical and aesthetic elements of the classical view. It exploits the late eighteenth-century taste for meditations upon graves and monuments.[55] It evokes the *iconography* beloved by the organizers of the revolutionary festivals, but re-forms it in a different image of history. It also suggests a theoretical account of past corruption linked to a scientific and educational programme. Though its vision resembles an enormous Festival of the Federation, the assembled people do not *revive* the classical republics or *repeat* the acts of the Revolution. *Les Ruines* interposes a programme[56] of development between ideals located in the past and the prospect of future success.

Condorcet's *Sketch for a Historical Picture of the Progress of the Human Mind* (written in 1794) also introduces historical growth into the classical view. Condorcet places the Revolution in a long-term *historical* progress of enlightenment and science. In this longer history, one sees the effect of 'human reason slowly forming through the natural progress of civilization'.[57] The best corrupting and oppressive efforts of superstition and despotism had merely retarded it. Condorcet's is a speculative history of a very eighteenth-century materialist kind, which puts historical flesh on the intervention of principle into human perfectibility. He argues that the advance and practical application of the sciences is bound to resolve the imbalance between men's needs and their capacity to satisfy them. This will permit national and international political unity. Whatever shortcomings the Revolution might display, then, it belonged in an overall progress towards improvement.

Condorcet's conception of history is another half-way house from the classical view. Though humanity evolves in history, what it discovers as it does so is self-substantive truth. Progress for Condorcet is a 'scientific' fact:

The sole basis of belief in the natural sciences is this idea: that general laws . . . are necessary and constant; and how could this be thought less true for the intellectual and moral faculties of man than for the other operations of nature?[58]

The Revolution is made historical by its insertion into another history:[59] it asserts rational, transhistorical principles discovered in the eighteenth century and the American Revolution.

The moderate Jacobin politician Barnave's *Introduction à la Révolution française* (written in 1792–3) offers another way to relate the abstract ideal to historically evolving human lives. In its use of Montesquieu-style geographical and economic explanations, and its references to ancient and modern European states, the book reads like the proto-sociological histories produced by the Scottish Enlightenment. According to Barnave, geographical-economic causes account for a Europe-wide evolution towards democracy. The key link is that between democracy and commerce (as against aristocratic, landed property). Feudalism has impoverished the majority and suppressed their political aspirations. But, commercial society 'enriches the industrious class of the people, impoverishes the great landed proprietors, and brings the classes closer together in wealth'. At the same time, 'the progress of education mutually assimilates their morals, and recalls . . . the primitive idea of equality'.[60] Initially, this breaks down the feudal distribution of power and gives it either to the people (in small republics) or to a monarch, acting with their support. But the gradually more despotic military power of the monarchies, particularly in land-locked states, then brings it into conflict with the democratic pressure from an increasingly enlightened commercial society. In France, this long-term conflict combined with the effects of military defeat and economic shortage to bring on the Revolution.

Barnave's version of history acknowledged the classical conception of an ahistorical point of reference, but set it aside. He keeps it in the background: 'the gradual influence of nature always prevails in the long run'. But direct insight into nature belongs to the classical era of the past; it is no longer accessible for modern Europe:

> When we began [to see] that nature was the true model, we no longer had the youth that can perceive and paint her. Genius and taste, which among the Greeks existed together, have been successive among us . . . we wasted in false knowledge and feeble imitations the period destined for perceiving and depicting nature: precious age which, like the passions of youth, once past never returns.[61]

In the modern era, however, the Revolution does not appear as the irruption of an abstract ideal into history. 'Natural' principles of democracy and equality surface, to be put into practice through material causes affecting human minds. The outcomes – a revolution and its precise evolution in practice – then depend upon the positive construction of those involved. Hence, the abstract principle is not mapped directly on to history. Barnave has advanced some way towards identifying an evolving public placed in real historical movement.

In contemporary views of the Revolution as a historical movement we can observe an unresolved tension between the idea of principles that could be directly present to the mind and the positive evolution of historically real human minds. Volnay, Condorcet and Barnave indicate routes to escape. One point Barnave certainly did not grasp, on the other hand, was that his 'industrious class' could itself be riven by conflict.[62] Conflict within the real public contrasts with Barnave's theoretical position just as it undermined the political strategy pursued by him and the Jacobins more generally. We have seen that the revolutionaries tried with difficulty to portray, involve and place the people in both moral and historical dimensions. Finally, however, the people were a disappointment to the Jacobins – as, no doubt, was the Revolution to the people. Thus, when historical portrayal was taken up again, after the Revolution, it started from the presumption that the spirit of reason and the historical origin of the Revolution were to be located well away from the people, as they had been in the Revolution.

NOTES

1. See Hugh Honour, *Neo-Classicism* (Harmondsworth: Penguin, 1968); Kenneth Clarke, *The Romantic Rebellion: Romantic versus Classical Art* (London: Murray, 1973); Robert Rosenblum *Transformations in Late Eighteenth-century Art* (Princeton, NJ: Princeton University Press, 1967).
2. 'les actions vertueuses et héroïques de grands hommes, les exemples d'humanité, de générosité, de mépris des dangers et même de la vie, d'un zèle passioné pour l'honneur et le salut de sa Patrie, et surtout de défense de la religion.' (La Font de Saint-Yenne, *Réflexions sur quelques causes de l'état de la peinture en France* (The Hague: 1747), quoted in Rosenblum, op. cit., pp. 55–6).
3. Rosenblum, op. cit., pp. 62–6.
4. Honour, op. cit., ch. 3.
5. Rosenblum, op. cit., p. 28
6. Clarke, op. cit., pp. 17–18.
7. For a detailed survey of the majority of painters' diverse pro-revolutionary political affiliations and activities, and a (generally favourable) assessment of the sincerity of their commitment to the cause of the Revolution, see

D.L. Dowd, 'The French Revolution and the Painters', *French Historical Studies* (1959) vol. 1, no. 2, pp. 127–48.

8. For details of David's activities in the republican politics of art, see D.L. Dowd, *Pageant Master of the Republic: Jacques-Louis David and the French Revolution* (New York: Books for Libraries Press, 1948), esp. ch. 4.

9. See Chapter 2, pp. 55–6.

10. See Dowd, 'The French Revolution and the Painters', pp. 138–9.

11. For a detailed account of the revolutionary state's injunctions and contracts with artists, see James A. Leith, *The Idea of Art as Propaganda* (Toronto: University of Toronto Press, 1965), esp. ch. 5. Unfortunately, the usefulness of the book as a whole is limited by its uncritical use, not to say fear, of 'totalitarianism', which, in particular, blinds it to the fact that, corresponding to the state's wish to use art, there was a real, albeit perhaps miguided, desire among artists to make themselves useful.

12. Lynn Hunt, 'Engraving the Republic: Print and Propaganda in the French Revolution', *History Today*, no. 30, October 1980, pp. 11–17.

13. Leith, op. cit., pp. 107 and 121–2.

14. Quoted in ibid., pp. 119–120.

15. '. . . un programme ...e concours entre tous les artistes pour immortaliser les actions vertueuses et tout ce qui peut développer l'amour de la liberté et de l'égalité', Thuriot, 18 January 1792, quoted in Leith, op. cit., p. 114; ' . . . mais dans le siècle de la liberté, les arts liés à la morale, agrandis comme les âmes, ont une destination plus relevée, une utilité plus générale' (7 Messidor II, quoted in ibid., p. 121).

16. Ibid., pp. 115, 117 and 126–7.

17. 15 November 1793, quoted in Dowd, *Pageant Master*, p. 79.

18. See L.D. Ettlinger, 'Jacques-Louis David and Roman Virtue', *Journal of the Royal Society of Arts*, vol. 115 (1966–7), pp. 105–23.

19. Clarke, op. cit., p. 32.

20. Quoted in Dowd, *Pageant Master*, p. 66.

21. Thomas E. Crow, *Painters and the Public Life in Eighteenth-century Paris* (New Haven, CT and London: Yale University Press, 1985).

22. Jean Starobinski, *Les Emblêmes de la raison* (Paris: Flammarion, 1979; Italian edition, Milan: Instituto Editoriale Italiano, 1973), esp. pp. 93–103 and 39–48.

23. Crow, op. cit., pp. 256–8.

24. Clarke, op. cit., pp. 33–42.

25. Starobinski, op. cit., esp. pp. 100–2.

26. Michael Fried, *Absorption and Theatricality: Painting and Beholder in the Age of Diderot* (Los Angeles and London: California University Press, 1980), esp. pp. 107–9.

27. See Jennifer Harris, 'The Red Cap of Liberty: A Study of Dress Worn by French Revolutionary Partisans 1789–94', *Eighteenth-century Studies*, vol. 14, no. 3, 1981.

28. Albert Mathiez, *Les Origines des cultes révolutionnaires* (Paris: 1904; Geneva: Slatkine, 1977), p. 34.

29. Détournelle, *Aux Armes et aux arts! Journal de la Société populaire et républicaine des arts* (Paris: 1794), pp. 252–6.
30. Ibid., pp. 258–9, 317.
31. Hunt, op. cit.
32. Maurice Agulhon, *Marianne au combat: l'imagerie et le symbolique de 1789 à 1880* (Paris: Flammarion, 1979); *Marianne into Battle: Republican Imagery and Symbolism in France, 1789–1880* (Cambridge: Cambridge University Press, 1981), ch. 1.
33. See Hannah Mitchell, 'Art and the French Revolution: an Exhibition at the Musée Carnavalet', *History Workshop*, no. 5, 1978, pp. 123–45.
34. Pascal de la Vaissière, writing in the introduction to the exhibition catalogue *L'Art de l'estampe de la Révolution française* (Paris: Musée Carnavalet, 1977), p. 6.
35. Ibid., p. 3.
36. Michel Vovelle, 'Revolutionary Iconography in Town and Country', unpublished paper. This and related themes are pursued extensively in the conference papers published as M. Vovelle (ed.) *Les Images de la Révolution* (Paris: Publications de la Sorbonne, 1988). As Eric Hobsbawm argued in *Bandits* (London: Weidenfeld and Nicolson, 1969; Harmondsworth: Penguin Books, 1972, 1985), a study of the bandit as a figure in peasant society, the hero of the lower classes – reflecting all the ambivalences of their position – is unlikely to appeal to the dominant groups in society.
37. Michel Foucault, *Les Mots et les choses* (Paris: Gallimard, 1966), pp. 230–1. (Translated as *The Order of Things* (London: Tavistock, 1970).)
38. Hugh Silverman, 'Foucault and Derrida: the Origins of History', unpublished paper.
39. Renaud Barral, 'Les Jacobins penseurs de leurs propre révolution' in A. Tosel (ed.), *Philosophies de la Révolution française* (Paris: Vrin, 1984), p. 21: 'Si des hommes comme Condorcet et Saint-Just ont pu s'accorder sur le contenu d'une action politique, les autres Jacobins occupant toutes les positions intermédiaires entre les leurs, c'est que malgré des convictions antithétiques, tous deux réfèrent la politique à la nature, que ce soit pour rechercher son dépassement ou un retour aux origines.'
40. Renaud Barral, 'La Pensée politique des Jacobins, 1789–94', unpublished doctoral thesis, University of Nice, 1982, p. 157.
41. Ibid., p. 18.
42. Sieyès, *What is the Third Estate?*, trans. M. Blondel (London: Pall Mall, 1963) pp. 113, 115 and 117.
43. Murray Forsyth, *Reason and Revolution: The Political Thought of the Abbé Sieyès* (Leicester: Leicester University Press; New York: Holmes and Meier, 1987), pp. 70ff.
44. Ibid., p. 128.
45. Speech of 25 December 1793, quoted in Robespierre, *Textes choisis*, ed. J. Poperen (Paris: Editions Sociales, 1974), vol. 3, p. 99: 'La fonction du gouvernement est de diriger les forces morales et physiques de la nation vers le but de son institution.'

46. See Chapter 1, pp. 30–1.
47. See F. Picavet's exhaustive study, *Les Idéologues: essai sur l'histoire des idées et des théories scientifiques, philosophiques, religieuses, etc en France depuis 1789* (Paris: Alcan, 1891), esp. ch. 1, for an account of the movement's membership and organization. These are discussed more fully in Chapter 6.
48. Volney was acquainted with philosophic circles before the Revolution; but he had made a reputation as a writer on foreign lands and cultures with *Voyage en Egypte et en Syrie* (1789). He was to publish a secular revolutionary 'catechism' in 1792, and become in due course a philologist and geographer of the *idéologues*, as well as a senator.
49. Volney, *Les Ruines: méditations sur les révolutions des empires*, reprint (Geneva and Paris, 1979), chs IV–XI.
50. Ibid., chs XV–XXI.
51. Ibid., p. 94.
52. Ibid., ch. XVII.
53. According to Roland Barthes, 'Le Discours de l'histoire', *Poétique*, 49, p. 15, *Les Ruines* 'complicates historical time by counterposing another time, that of the discourse itself'.
54. '*Les causes de vos dissentiments n'existent pas dans les objets eux-mêmes mais dans vos esprits, dans la manière dont vous percevez* ou *dont vous jugez*. . . . Pour établir *l'unanimité d'opinion*, il faut donc préalablement bien établir la certitude, bien constater que les tableaux *que se peint l'esprit sont exactement ressemblants à leurs modèles*'. Volney, op. cit., p. 243.
55. See John McManners, *Death and the Enlightenment: Changing Attitudes to Death among Christians and Unbelievers in Eighteenth-century France* (Oxford: Clarendon, 1981; Oxford and New York: Oxford University Press, 1985), pp. 340f.
56. As Henry Deneys shows, 'Révolutions sur la scène de l'histoire selon Volney' in Tosel, op. cit., esp. pp. 56–7, Volney has explained the former corruption of human self-love as the product of a psychology misled in the past by despotism into an ignorance of the limits that would satisfy it.
57. Condorcet, *Esquisse d'un tableau historique des progrès de l'esprit humain* (Paris, Editions Sociales, 1971), p. 203: 'la raison humaine se former lentement par les progrès naturels de la civilization'.
58. Ibid., p. 253: 'Le seul fondement de croyance dans les sciences naturelles, est cette idée, que les lois générales . . . sont nécessaires et constantes; et par quelles raisons ce principe serait-il moins vrai pour le développement des facultés intellectuelles et morales de l'homme, que pour les autres opérations de la nature?'
59. Ibid., pp. 225–7; see also Chapter 6, pp. 169–70.
60. *Power, Property and History: Barnave's 'Introduction to the French Revolution' and Other Writings* (trans. and ed.) Emanuel Chill (New York & London: Harper and Row, 1971), pp. 85 and 94.
61. Ibid., pp. 90–91.
62. Barral, 'Les Jacobins penseurs', p. 24.

Part Two

COMMENTARIES

CHAPTER FOUR

Post-revolutionary Histories: Bourgeois Roots for Liberal Culture

This part of the study moves forward into the nineteenth century. This and the following chapter deal with histories written in France. In the decades following the Revolution, histories written directly about it — or related to it — naturally became significant in French culture. As Douglas Johnson put it: 'The Revolution made historians necessary.'[1] The century lived under the shadow of the great revolution which preceded it. Most obviously, in 1830, 1848 and 1871 there were avowed 'revolutions'; and those involved, on whatever side, could hardly avoid taking their inspiration from the great original. At a somewhat slower pace than in the 1790s, France continued to be a nation of changing constitutions. Over the course of the century the state moved from Napoleonic empire; to a restored monarchy (from 1815); to a more limited monarchy in the hands of a different branch of the royal family (from 1830); to a republic (from 1848), back to an empire (under another Napoleon — from 1852); and finally back to a republic (from 1871). So a correct or at least politically agreeable account of the history of the Revolution was naturally much in demand.

That is one reason why the calling of historian advanced in status in the nineteenth century. In addition, history was better organized as an educational activity over the early decades of the century. Historians received public acclaim, official acknowledgement (or, more telling still, discouragement) and, sometimes, state salaries. Of the eight historians I shall look at in this and the next chapter, three (Guizot, Lamartine, Thiers) were also deputies and ministers. Of those, one (Guizot) also became head of government, while one (Thiers) became a minister, head of government *and* head of state. Two others (Quinet and Michelet) drew such crowds to lectures judged unsympathetic to

115

the regime in power that their courses were closed down. Two more (Thierry and Mignet) enjoyed success as writers and journalists. All were able to achieve wide circulation of their opinions in print.

Though the interpretation of the Revolution was a matter of political weight, the immediate political import of the histories that were written is not my subject.[2] On the other hand, the historians do naturally group themselves into approximate political categories, roughly chronological, which shape my exposition. Nineteenth-century historians and social theorists wrestled, as had the revolutionaries themselves, with the peculiar status of the Republic as an ostensibly historical creation of the people. As Claude Nicolet puts it, discussing the difficulty of nineteenth-century republicans:

> The republic contains potentially all that is possible, it is, as it were, the end of history: but, as it is always under attack, it is never fully realized, it is a permanent becoming, and by that very fact it is entirely, and in a most singular way, within history.[3]

The theme on which I wish to concentrate is the insertion of the Revolution into historical time and causality. For these aspects in the historians' thought shape the historical existence accorded to the French people in the Revolution. Chronology and the structure of causality are intimately linked. All the historians offer an explanation of the occurence of the Revolution and its outcome. To do this, they situate it within a *long-term* structure in history, with attendant causally dominant trends and turning points. The nature attributed to the people in the Revolution is a function of those trends. The people may, for example, be inveterately prone to unruly passions. Or they may be able to reassert a long-oppressed appreciation of liberty, or liable to repeat unwittingly the reactions taught them by past oppression.

The structure of time and of causality adopted by the historians entails a view of what is politically possible. This yields the rough political categorization which has a role in grouping them. Some historians considered social change dangerous to attempt. Others ('liberals') implied that it is best to leave the people out of any process of social advancement, or for them to be carefully guided in the process by the rationality of their social superiors. I shall deal with these, who were writing principally during the first four decades of the century, in this chapter.

Finally, some historians were 'republicans'. Their span of activity ran slightly later: from the 1820s to the 1860s. They might take one

116

constituent of the French people (usually the bourgeoisie) to embody the most important element for the Revolution and the progress of the whole. Other 'republicans' thought it in the nature of the French people *as a whole* to be able, under the right conditions, to execute the original intentions of the Revolution. In my view, romanticism made a crucial contribution to the position of these historians. Its empathy with diversity, its emphasis on feeling, and its faith in providence again extended the range of what could be included among the historically effective agents for the Revolution. I shall consider this trend among 'republican' historians in Chapter 5.

By the start of the period dealt with in this chapter, the Revolution, far from being a new beginning, seemed at best a highly compromised attempt to progress. It might even have been a regression in the direction of lower passions – perhaps a culpably foreseeable regression. In other terms, society was not free to re-create itself by an act of will: the movement of historical time was not something to be renewed at will. Reason – or it may even be the faith – which may promote reconstruction, is counterposed to the people who make up society. This looks a far cry from the presumption, predominant during the early years of the Revolution, that the people in some way embodied reason. But, ultimately, it reproduces the same paradoxes.

DE STAËL: PASSION VERSUS RATIONALITY

Though Mme de Staël's *Considérations sur la Révolution française* (1818) is not a history, it did set an agenda for historical writing. It begins with a mémoire of events in which de Staël's father, Necker, had participated. (He had been the most popular of the king's reforming ministers.) It ends with a lengthy discussion of the political system in England, asking, by comparison, whether the French can be regarded as capable of freedom. If de Staël's answer is yes, that is founded upon the hope that the cultural leadership of courageous people of good sense will prevail (as it has at times in the past), rather than upon the expression of particular historical tendencies within society as a whole.

De Staël thus achieves a cautious optimism. But to do so she has had to overcome a suspicion that any rational sense of liberty and justice is beyond the powers of the mass of human beings. De Staël expressed this suspicion in her *De l'Influence des passions sur le bonheur des individus et des nations* of 1796. The work consists of moral reflections, which analyse various passions in an abstract, eighteenth-century fashion.

With a stoic, Rousseauian tone, she condemned almost all the passions as oppressive yokes, which encourage individuals' desires to outstrip necessity.[4] Politically, this underwrites a liberal mistrust of the mass of humankind. Because passions are a 'stimulus which drives man independently of his will', the state cannot completely regiment the people. 'The sole problem of constitutions is, then, to what degree passions can be aroused or repressed without compromising public well-being.'[5]

Though Mme de Staël is more optimistic by 1818, the same structure of thought is in operation. The social order appears as at best an irrational product of rational skills and fortuitous circumstances, assisted by a noble but unstable collective will. An affectionate respect for the stirrings of national consciousness is balanced by caution. Of the storming of the Bastille, she writes:

> 14 July had greatness: the movement was national; a whole people always holds true and natural feelings . . . there was still only good in the souls [of men], and the victors had not had time to be infected with boastful passions.[6]

This mood of compassionate understanding towards destructive passions is sustained even in the account of the fanaticism of 1793.

> In itself the social order is a bizarre construction: . . . the concessions that must be decided upon for it to subsist torment enlightened spirits with pity, satisfy the vanity of some and provoke the irritation of others.[7]

However, de Staël does believe that the fundamental irrationality of passion need not altogether overwhelm political liberty in society. This is partly the fruit of a notion that liberty has long roots in French history. It follows that if liberty is eclipsed, that must be a recent phenomenon — and may be a temporary one. But this liberty has taken the form of independence from the king. It has, she argues, been pursued by various social strata or groups such as the nobility or the church. In that way, liberty can be said to have made real progress before 1789.[8] Hence, de Staël's lengthy discussion of the question: 'Did France have a constitution before the Revolution?'.[9] She argues that the tradition of liberty might have been sustained if abuses of royal power had been stopped before 1789.

There is a clear tactical advantage in adopting this position just after the restoration of the monarchy. It allows one to advocate 'liberty' without suggesting loyalty to the Republic of the Revolution. To the implicit credit of the newly restored nobility of France, de Staël claims that the knights of the past were not supporters of absolutism. [10] In effect, she revives the idea, which had underpinned the hopes of conservative aristocratic reformers in the 1780s, that absolutism obstructed fundamentally benign relations between nobility and peasantry.

Indeed, de Staël's notion of liberty is not the one the revolutionaries themselves had in mind. The freedom from the monarchy sought by various groups in society cannot be a uniform value shared across the nation. Its insertion into history is therefore not the same. It is a feature that exists more or less as the power of the king or the state is limited. It cannot be the motor leading the nation and guiding history.

Since, for de Staël, liberty is of less account in the history of the Revolution, other driving forces take precedence. Priority passes to culture and the sentiment of justice; that is, an awareness that injustice done to others is a loss to oneself. The *ancien régime and* the revolutionary state had overcome the desire for liberty as de Staël has described it. But the sense of justice *can* be cultivated by law and culture. [11] '. . . in Europe . . . it is liberty that is ancient, and despotism that is modern. . . . Were this truth not evident, it would only make more pressing the duty to inaugurate the rule of justice.'[12]

De Staël (like Barnave, whom I considered in the last chapter) relates the historical progress of culture and justice to the growth of commerce, which had placed property in the hands of the middle classes, free from aristocratic ties. [13] According to de Staël, the growing middle classes had been the strongest bastion against the crown's tendency to buy off the nobility's desire for freedom. Whereas the crown can corrupt a narrow elite, a larger class of well-to-do commoners, aware of the value of justice, requires government to follow higher principles.

So long as the privileged classes alone were prominent, the state could be governed like a court, by manipulating the passions and the interests of a few individuals; but once the second class of society, the most numerous and the most active of all, felt its own importance, the knowledge and adoption of a greater system of behaviour was indispensable. [14]

The 'second' classes had been the best hope in pre-1789 France for a living constitution.

What accounts for the outcome of Revolution? In de Staël's terms, the spread of a responsible sense of justice is unavoidably limited. Even the most widespread enlightenment would not equip the people to execute just government − though it could educate them to choose representatives able to do so. Hence, the mistake of the first revolutionary constitution was to ignore this fact and weaken the king's independence as a magistrate.[15] But enlightenment had in fact been confined to a narrow band of French society. Whereas it is the duty of the cultivated to extend enlightenment by mixing with the people,[16] the rich in France had been content to display their wealth to the poor from a distance.[17]

Yet, when all is said and done, even the maximum spread of culture will not remove the grounds for de Staël's pessimism, for rationality is not to be expected in the people. As she says in *Des Circonstances actuelles*, written in 1798, there is 'a mass of the nation, always inert, always immobile, who, in times of trouble, care only to discover the strongest party so as to join it'.[18] De Staël's attitude towards any collective action is sympathetic but muted, because the extent of any rationality is so limited.

Though culture and public opinion provide crucial pegs for optimism, what political stability can be achieved in the modern world rests only upon a faltering balance which the statesman maintains in public opinion: 'The whole movement of attitudes consisted in the wish to exercise political rights, and the whole skill of the statesman was based on the art of managing that opinion.'[19] Because of the limits of enlightenment, then, an equilibrium between state, culture and people has to be sought. This will ensure that each restrains the evils to which the others are prone. But, in this scheme of ideas, no one is free to any great extent to re-form society at will. The room to manoeuvre for both society and the political reformer is narrow. Rather than the essence of the social order's existence, liberty is a chancy achievement with no historical necessity, attained by balancing the things that foster it against those that would prevent it. Society needs slow and lengthy improvement.

De Staël passed on this basic configuration in her view of the Revolution. On the one hand, there is human passion, concentrated especially in the mass of the people, yet containable within political institutions and the play of history. On the other hand, there is the enlightenment of a few.

THE LIBERAL HISTORIANS

Mignet

The texts of the historians of liberal persuasion associated with the journal, the *National*, are more thoroughgoing histories of the Revolution than is de Staël's. Yet we find the same configuration, with a perceptible new inflection in its terms.

Politically, the *National* anticipated, or even encouraged, the Revolution of 1830, with its liberal aspirations. To be politically active in France and hope to see the restored monarchy replaced, one required some accommodation with the past Revolution. The *National* historians, Mignet and Thiers, reached this through a 'fatalism' on several levels. In place of de Staël's self-consciously tragic tone, they adopt a matter-of-fact one. Whatever is recounted seems to be accepted merely as past and beyond reproof. Narration and explanation taken precedence over judgement.

The *National* historians use the same liberal categories as de Staël had done (liberty, justice and culture), and the same deterministic forces (rationality versus passion). They develop that sense in the thinking of de Staël that long-term social developments will, in due course, push forward the realization of liberal freedom. Their conceptual system is able to find positive value in even the negative forces of the Revolution. They situate the acts of individuals, classes and the nation itself on a larger historical plane. On that plane, it is possible for individuals' skilful handling of the social forces to contribute to social improvement.

Mignet's *Histoire de la Révolution française* (1826)[20] places special weight upon the gradual growth of the middle classes. Echoing de Staël, that provides a deterministic grounding in society which underlies the evolution of the culture to support liberal values. The failure of the Revolution is explained by the limited extent of the middle classes' development at the time the Revolution occurred. There are three implicit levels of explanation in Mignet's narrative: long-term insurmountable trends; individual action; and irrational collective passions during interludes of upheaval. Conscious collective action has no place in the scheme. As well as the past failure, this explanatory scheme accommodates possible future success in reform.

Mignet's book is not long. The format is predominantly a narrative, divided into chapters which generally cover periods of only a few months. The tone is rather breezy. Mignet's first concern appears to be a clear, approachable account of events, without rancour or regret. He presents a Revolution played out by individuals who act within a sequence that gives cultural and political dominance to different classes in turn. The centuries leading up to the Revolution had seen aristocratic and monarchical power whittled away by art and then philosophy, which established the pressure for reform.[21] All this owes much to de Staël and, through her, to Voltaire. According to Mignet, a national public opinion, which is essentially the expression of middle-class values, was formed before the Revolution. It was dominant in the legal egalitarianism of the Revolution itself, when privileges were abolished but property defended.[22] But it proved too weak to manage the war and hold off the lower classes. Their 'fears' and 'fanaticism' created conditions for them to dominate in the 'revolution-ary' government of the early 1790s. Power was then taken over by parties more or less divorced from public opinion, whose weakness and dissensions in turn left the way open for Napoleon's dictatorship.[23]

Mignet inserts the hopes and deeds of the individual political agents into the larger-scale forces, which are insurmountable but bear the seeds of cultural progress.

> . . . during their attempts, each class, in power for a time, destroyed of the higher classes all that was intolerant or calculated to oppose the progress of modern civilization.[24]

Culture is supported by economic developments, too. In the midst of the political comings and goings, the growth of private industry and agriculture was laying the material basis for private life to reinvigorate public culture.

> The revolution grew daily more materialised . . . Many illusions were already destroyed. . . . The directorial manners [of the late 1790s] were the product of another society, which had to appear again before the new state of society could regulate its relations, and constitute its own manners. In this transition, luxury would give rise to labour, stock-jobbing to commerce; salons bring parties together who could not draw close except in private life; in a word, civilization would again usher in liberty.[25]

This is hope for progress in the manner of Mme de Staël, supported by the economic categories of Barnave. An overarching, long-term historical progress limits what is possible in the Revolution. But it implies the compensation of optimism for the future. The material, class basis makes 'civilization', which will sustain political liberty, a certain outcome for the long term. And evidently, the material conditions of 'civilization' must have appeared greater by the time the book was published, than they had been in the 1790s. Hence Mignet can safely include reform in his insurmountable, long-term trends. 'When a reform has become necessary . . . nothing can prevent it, everything furthers it.'[26]

In Mignet's account, the preponderant force lies with grand, long-term developments. Yet, by its focus upon specific individuals' courses of action, his narrative manner implies a certain status for the deeds of individuals. The individual's power to act is encompassed by a broad explanation of the balance of forces between individual action and historical determination. At the time of the Revolution, individuals could arrive at no positive achievements, because the basis of civilization was missing. Political agents are therefore excused from complete responsibility for, or power over outcomes because the material, social means for progress were not available. Even Robespierre can be partially excused; he was in charge at a time when 'death became the only means of government'.[27]

But Mignet does extract certain transhistorical prudential rules for leaders, and draws appropriate lessons. These take the form of general factual claims about politics in upheaval. For example, Mignet interpolates a 'truth which for [men's] good ought to be generally known': to the effect that a contested reform creates conditions for the rise of daring, intemperate leaders advocating impractical systems. Likewise, he claims that men in revolutionary situations become obsessed with their own power and ideas.[28] These assertions entail the third implicit level of explanation in Mignet's narrative: irrational collective passions which intervene between long-term progress and the limited scope of individual action.

It is at this point that passion as used in de Staël's scheme of thought makes its appearance in Mignet's. Within the upheaval of the Revolution a distinct causal structure is operating: the irrational force of passion. In spite of the optimistic long-term trend of material and cultural progress over and above them, agents in the Revolution itself are carried along by passion. Passion has been introduced into the explanation so as to provide for what is negative and incomprehensible in the Revolution. The more gradual evolution simply limits the harm agents can do within the Revolution, so that the long-term outcome remains benign, regardless of their passion or prudence. The Revolution has been inserted into a progressive history, then, without being historicized. Except for a small scope for judgement in political actions, it remains a distinct period of history dominated by the inchoate: passion.

Thiers

The major popular history of the 1820s and 1830s was that by Thiers, which began to appear in 1823. Thiers' style of historical thought and writing matches the shrewd, pragmatic politician he in due course became. As Interior Minister, briefly Prime Minister and in due course President of the Third Republic, he protected limited liberal, constitutional government, and pursued a nationalistic foreign policy.[29]

This statement at the close of his enormous history nicely reflects Thiers' political values as regards the Revolution:

> The Revolution, which was to give us liberty, and which prepared everything for us to have it one day . . . was to be a great struggle against the old order of things . . . the new society would be consolidated in the shelter of its sword, and liberty could come one day. It has not come, it will come.[30]

As in the views of de Staël and Mignet, the Revolution is located in an inevitable long-term progress. In that chronology, it has yet to realize its purpose. Thiers' different explanatory levels show how that can be so. Thus, Thiers can afford to be tolerant. He has spoken, he writes, 'without hatred, pitying error, respecting virtue, admiring greatness, endeavouring to grasp the grand designs'.[31]

The structure and tone of the work mirror the agnosticism. It consists mostly of detailed accounts of events in the political and military centres, put together with some care from records and recollections. Of itself, this tends to confine the motive force to the conscious, political centres — as against the relatively inarticulate mass of the people. Thiers emphasizes the importance of the plane of relations with other states, too, with their comparable centres of power. Overlaying this narrative approach, his book is divided into periods for each different constitutional regime.

The long-term and the international planes are especially important to Thiers' causal explanation because (like a Trotsky of the bourgeois revolution) he believes that liberty will not be possible until the Europe-wide struggle against the past is complete. The international plane is also a figure in a realm of long-term historical necessity, such as we met in Mignet. Obstacles to liberal rationality in politics are destroyed on the long-term plane, though not by rational action. Like Mignet, only more explicitly, Thiers claims (in his conclusion) that by the time the Revolution and the revolutionary wars were over, the destruction of the old order both in France and in Europe had at last created the conditions for liberty.

In this long-term realm, the significance of negative, destructive aspects of the Revolution is reversed. History has used non-rational, unintentional action, outside the control of the agents caught up in it, to open the way for liberty by destructive processes. A 'chance combination of various circumstances brought the catastrophe, whose day could be postponed, but whose arrival sooner or later was inevitable'.[32] Against such long-term forces what can the participants do? According to Thiers, Louis XVI was prevented from running with the tide by the court's fear of the people.[33] On the other hand, Mirabeau, moved by his 'great passions', indignation at despotism and abuses of power, launched himself into the tide, destroying institutions out of a spirit of vengeance, directed at 'an unknown future'.[34] The need to destroy so that liberty can be established is paramount, then; individuals seem able only to fall in with that need unconsciously. On Thiers' account, the fury which destroyed the abuses of power is beyond comprehension and control. Nevertheless, it is a positive, progressive historical force, because the vested interests defending abuses could only be moved by an enormous, irrational anger. Reason, on the other hand, has to wait for the power of irrational forces to have done. In considering the Revolution itself, liberty consciously sustained by the people is implicitly postponed.

Thiers' attitude towards the Terror illustrates the place he accords to the irrational forces destroying for the benefit of liberty, and to the responsibility of individuals in relation to them. Thiers presents the moods of the people in a moment of social upheaval and danger as more or less unavoidable currents which have to be accommodated. 'A revolution whose unforeseen but inevitable outcome had been to raise the lower classes of society against the upper classes was bound to awaken envy . . . and release brutal passions'.[35] Again, in a struggle between 'moderate' and 'pitiless systems' of government, the latter, says Thiers, will win control.[36] Under certain conditions, there seems no alternative to passion and violence. On the other hand, the politician can handle these passions with more or less propriety and skill, according to the situation that he finds himself in. The Jacobins as a whole seem justified in their extreme line by the need to hold some sway over the people in extreme times. Thus the club, 'by its long-standing and its sustained violence, always won out over those who wanted to be more moderate or even more violent'.[37]

The human passions that were the impediment to a just society in the liberal conception of Mme de Staël, appear in Thiers' history in a different light according to their location in society and in time. In the people, they are inevitable, yet unwittingly beneficial functions in revolutionary upheaval and its consequences in war. In the sphere of individual political leadership, however, passions can only be excused as a necessary device to maintain power[38] — and justified to the extent that power itself is necessary or well used.

For Thiers, the long-term movement of history is towards liberty. Within the Revolution the people's secular passions have a threatening, irrational character; but, as with Mignet, there is a role for the irrational in history and in the people. Rationality and intention are not to be found in the people, however, and a gap opens between any will they have and its realization in the real world. But the Assembly or the leaders within the Revolution can make the nation's will a reality.

This is characteristically liberal thinking: a special assembly whose *raison d'être* is to represent the rational will of the nation. The legislature was an 'enlightened assembly', 'convinced of its rights', whose 'mere expression of will' constituted the core of the Revolution. 'That is the Revolution in its entirety; so much for the first and noblest act; it is just, it is heroic, for never has a nation acted with more right or more danger'.[39] Yet, in practice the legislature slipped into pursuing its own private interest once selflessness and drama of abolishing privileges faded, and the details had to be worked out.[40] The Assembly's acts on behalf of the nation then acquire a somewhat ironic standing, divorced from action in the real political world. It was, says Thiers, 'swollen with pride in its ancient power'.

In sum, the dynamics of explanation underlying Thiers' account give the people a blind power to destroy and an abstract power to form and express a national will. But the latter exists only at one remove, through the work of the representative assembly. The political leader possesses the freedom to juggle political forces within loose moral limits in order to make the national will a reality. People and leader are all embraced by a realm of long-term forces that are themselves blind, illiberal and cruel. They require an inflexible uniformity[41] and, though they will tend to produce liberty, are not themselves components of liberty.

In the last analysis, we return once again to the tension between abstract principle and real, historically evolving humanity. We have once again abstract justice and rational will above history. This is rather unsatisfactory. For history can be written about the *groundwork* for liberty and the nation, but not about those things in themselves. They belong to an abstract place in the future, after the manoeuvrings of politics and timeless popular anger have cleared the way. Liberal rationality occupies a space outside history, and political compromises mediate between it and the realities of social life.

CONCLUSION

Looking back over the work of de Staël, Mignet and Thiers, it is possible to see a definite movement governed by the opposition, identified first in de Staël, between passion and rationality. Implicit in de Staël's view, there is a causal plane which is made explicit by Mignet and Thiers, beyond the Revolution and its chaos of passion. The important movement of history is therefore displaced to this plane outside the Revolution. Counterposing the people to reason removes the Revolution and liberty from history in a full sense. The public cannot be, as it was in the Revolution's own self-image, the conscious bearer of a universal value. The public is inchoate nature opposed to rational progress in history. So freedom does not evolve within the history lived by those promoting liberty in the Revolution.

Though it started out from a position apparently reversing that of the Revolution, the configuration of rationality and passion derived from de Staël ends with the same paradox of an abstract ideal. It represents liberty as an abstraction, by counterposing it to nature and to the public. The people are a more or less menacing breeding ground of natural passion, and hence the enemy of conscious, rational social order. Rationality is a virtue found in individuals, though sometimes it can be seen translated in a limited fashion into the public arena. Liberty, on the other hand, is a long-term product of history. It cannot be observed coming about in the actions of individuals or the history of the Revolution itself. Liberty is excluded from the empirical content of the Revolution and saved for the future.

NOTES

1. Douglas Johnson, *Guizot: Aspects of French History, 1787–1874* (London:

Routledge and Kegan Paul; Toronto: University of Toronto Press, 1963), p. 326.

2. This has been acutely dealt with by François Furet, *La Gauche et la Révolution française au milieu du XIX siècle: Edgar Quinet et la question du Jacobinism, 1865–1870* (Paris: Hachette, 1986).

3. 'La République contient en puissance tout le possible, elle est, si l'on veut, la fin de l'histoire: mais, comme elle est toujours attaquée, elle n'est jamais pleinement réalisée, elle est un devenir permanent, et par là même elle est entièrement et singulièrement dans l'histoire' (Claude Nicolet, *L'Idée républicaine en France (1789–1924)* (Paris: Gallimard, 1982), pp. 133–4). Nicolet's essay also provides a broad study of how different political ideologies of the republic intertwined in the nineteenth century in relation to the sense of history.

4. Mme de Staël, *Oeuvres complètes* (Paris: Firmin Didot, 1822), vol. 1, pp. 170–1.

5. 'Le seul problème des constitutions est donc de connaître jusqu'à quel degré on peut exciter ou comprimer les passions, sans compromettre le bonheur publique' (ibid., p. 108).

6. 'la journée de 14 juillet avait de la grandeur: le mouvement était national; . . . l'émotion de tout un peuple tient toujours à des sentiments vrais et naturels . . . il n'y avait encore que de bon dans les âmes, et les vainqueurs n'avaient pas eu le temps de contracter les passions orgueilleuses' (Mme de Staël, *Considérations sur la Revolution française*, vol. 1, pt 1, ch. 22, p. 241).

7. 'L'ordre social est en lui-même un bizarre édifice: . . . les concessions auxquelles il faut se résoudre pour qu'il subsiste, tourmentent par la pitié les âmes élevées, satisfaient la vanité de quelques-uns, et provoquent l'irritation et les désirs du grand nombre.' (ibid., vol. 2, pt 3, ch. 15, p. 113).

8. Mme de Staël, *Considérations sur la Revolution française*, 2nd edn (Paris, 1818), vol. 1, pt. 1, ch. 2.

9. The title of ibid., pt. 1, ch. 11.

10. Ibid., vol. 3, pt. 6, pp. 377f.

11. Ibid., vol. 1, pt. 2, ch. 23.

12. ' . . . en Europe, comme en France, ce qui est ancien, c'est la liberté; ce qui est moderne, c'est le despotisme . . . Quand cette vérité ne serait pas évidente, il n'en résulterait qu'un devoir plus pressant d'inaugurer le règne de la justice . . .' (ibid., vol. 3, pt. 5, ch. 1, pp. 9–10).

13. Mme de Staël's *De la littérature* (1800; considered in Chapter 5) examined more closely the impact of cultures on society and societies on cultures, from ancient Greece through to modern Europe, especially France under Louis XIV and in the eighteenth century.

14. 'Tant que les classes privilégiées avaient seules une grande existence, on pouvait gouverner l'état comme une cour, en maniant habilement les passions ou les intérêts de quelques individus; mais lorsqu'une fois la seconde classe de la société, la plus nombreuse et la plus agissante de toutes, avait senti son importance, la connaissance et l'adoption d'un plus

grand système de conduite devenait indispensable' (Mme de Staël, *Considérations*, vol. 1, pt 1, ch. 3, p. 53).

15. Mme de Staël, ibid., vol. 1, pt 2, ch. 15.
16. Ibid., vol. 3, pt 6, p. 378.
17. Ibid., vol. 2, pt 3, ch. 15.
18. 'une masse dans la nation, toujours inerte, toujours immobile, qui, dans le temps de trouble, n'a d'autre soin que de connaître le parti le plus fort, afin de s'y rallier' (Mme de Staël, *Des Circonstances actuelles qui peuvent terminer la Révolution et des principes qui doivent fonder la république en France* (ed. L. Omacini (Paris: Droz, 1979), pt. 1, ch. 3, p. 106).
19. 'Tout le mouvement des esprits [in 1789–91] consistait dans le désir de s'exercer des droits politiques, et toute l'habileté d'un homme d'état se fondait sur l'art de ménager cette opinion' (Mme de Staël, *Considérations*, vol. 1, pt 1, ch. 19, p. 210).
20. F.A. Mignet, *History of the French Revolution* (London: Bell, 1889).
21. Ibid., esp. pp. 7–8.
22. Ibid., esp. pp. 52–4 and 110.
23. Ibid., esp. pp. 333 and 337–40.
24. Ibid., p. 314.
25. Ibid., p. 315.
26. Ibid., p. 2.
27. Ibid., esp. p. 247.
28. Ibid., pp. 248–9 and 251.
29. J.P.T. Bury and R.P. Tombs, *Thiers: 1797–1877: a Political Life* (London: Allen and Unwin, 1986).
30. 'La Révolution, qui devait nous donner la liberté, et qui a tout préparé pour que nous l'ayons un jour . . . devait être une grande lutte contre l'ancien ordre des choses . . . la nouvelle société allait se consolider à l'abri de son épée, et la liberté devait venir un jour. Elle n'est pas venue, elle viendra' (A. Thiers, *Histoire de la Révolution française* (22nd edn, Brussels, 1844), vol. 2, pp. 585–6).
31. 'sans haine, plaignant l'erreur, révérant la vertu, admirant la grandeur, tâchant de saisir les grands desseins' (ibid.).
32. 'un concours fortuit de diverses circonstances amenait la catastrophe, dont l'époque pouvait être différée, mais dont l'accomplissement était tôt ou tard infaillible' (ibid., vol. 1, p. 14).
33. Ibid., chs 2 and 4.
34. Ibid., pp. 17–18.
35. 'Une révolution dont l'effet imprévu, mais inévitable, avait été de soulever les basses classes de la société contre les classes élevées, devait réveiller l'envie . . . et déchainer les passions brutales' (ibid., vol. 2, p. 143).
36. Ibid., vol. 1, p. 338.
37. 'par son ancienneté et par une violence soutenue, l'avait constamment emporter sur tous ceux qui avaient voulu se montrer plus modérés ou même plus violents' (ibid., p. 94).
38. Leaders ought not to substitute their *private* interests for that of the

nation, as the court had done, or add their *personal* passions to the unavoidable passions of the crowd: 'De cruelles personnalités ajoutent les haines individuelles aux haines d'opinion; le discorde est excité au plus haut point' (ibid.). Danton seems to show up in a particularly unfavourable light in these terms. He is 'l'homme passioné, violent, mobile, et tour à tour cruel et généreux' (ibid., p. 143), who deploys his own passions to exacerbate those of the people in order to maintain power. In his revolutionary ardour he wanted to conserve his power base, and 'penchait sur toutes les idées de vengeance que repoussaient les Girondins' (ibid., p. 173). Robespierre's particular penchant, on the other hand, is envy; but he is paradoxically excused by his own meanness of spirit: 'pas assez grand pour être ambitieux' (ibid., vol. 2, p. 62).

39. 'C'est toute le Révolution; c'en est le premier acte et le plus noble; il est juste, il est héroïque, car jamais une nation n'a agi avec plus de droit et de danger' (ibid., vol. 1, p. 91).

40. Ibid., p. 40.

41. While sympathizing with the feelings of the peasants cruelly put down in the Vendée, Thiers holds that their suppression was necessary because there must be 'une règle uniforme et absolue dans les grandes réformes sociales' (ibid., vol. 1, p. 310).

CHAPTER FIVE

Idealist and Romantic Histories: The Return of the Oppressed

HISTORY AND ROMANTIC SENSIBILITY

The liberal historians took their French Revolution carefully strained. They liked the liberal values, but found the rest dangerous and difficult to comprehend. So the actual social content of the Revolution appeared to them like a storm in history. The leaders caught up in it had weathered it as best they could. The historians could grasp it only as passion, the wild side of humanity irrupting into history. The most they could say for the Revolution itself was that it made it possible to look forward: to a new dawn when the quiet ripening of political good sense from before 1789 could begin again, in soil freshly watered by the destructive force of the Revolution.

The *aesthetic* values of romanticism were able to transform this restrained posture. Yet, they came initially from *opponents* of revolutionary values. The opponents questioned the revolutionaries' view that history was a domain for rational self-determination. They emphasized what lay outside the rational in human life: religious sentiment, private emotion and traditional mores. In the minds of the opponents these were so many obstacles to the rationalist revolutionary project. But those who were more sympathetic to the Revolution could develop that interest as well. They, too, could extend their gaze further back and deeper into opaque social phenomena. They, too, began to look for ancient and medieval roots of the Revolution, but found its *progressive* direction. They, too, embraced those levels of social life rejected by the liberal historians. Their romantic understanding – allied, in due course, with idealism – reintegrated the '*ir*rational', on a new footing, into the historical ontology in accounts of the Revolution. Their romantic empathy with buried currents in humankind gave a new

131

expression to the sense that the people could actively engage in a revolution.

Before we look more closely at the historians who adopted this path, it is helpful to clarify the romantic impulse in history by looking briefly at some of its originators, French and otherwise: Chateaubriand, Hugo, Burke, Herder and Scott. Their romanticism represents a departure from the classical idealization of truth and reason, as identified in Chapter 3. But it proceeds to this from starting points in the Enlightenment.

Chateaubriand's first historical work was a thoroughly Enlightenment undertaking: a survey of the great revolutions in history. The *Essai historique, politique et morale sur les Révolutions anciennes et modernes considérées dans leurs rapports avec la révolution française* (1799) compared purported revolutions in three historical ages: Greek, Roman and Christian. From this *scientific* inquiry, Chateaubriand drew a profoundly *anti*-rationalist conclusion: the importance of an unquestioned religion to the social order. Each age had suffered a 'revolution' through the decline first of religious and then of political authority. 'As soon as men begin to doubt in religious matters, they doubt in political ones. Whoever dares to seek the foundations of his religious faith enquires before long into the principles of his government.'[1] Chateaubriand's analysis encouraged the historian to look further back than the Enlightenment (or even the late-medieval towns) in order to explain the French Revolution. The Revolution was rooted in the long-standing decline of the Christian Church: the corrupting influence of the Crusades; the Reformation; and only then the Enlightenment and 1789.

But Chateaubriand's attitude towards the general movement of history was more influential than his anti-Enlightenment explanatory framework. It reasserted an historical agenda with Christianity at the centre of the chronology. It developed other Enlightenment currents: nostalgia for lost natural simplicity, and stoicism at the futility of history. The *Essai* ends with a whimsical evocation of natural liberty in the 'Night of the Savages of America', and a postulate of cyclical necessity governing men's history.[2] Chateaubriand's hugely successful *Génie du christianisme* (1802) followed his conversion to Christianity. It left all of the previous rationalist findings in place, but introduced a new romantic posture that emphasized the sentimental appeal of religion — rather than evidence and argument. It was time, according to Chateaubriand, to show that Christianity 'accords wonderfully with the movements of the soul, and can enchant the spirit . . .'[3] Religion cannot change history, but now it can reveal how God is miraculously transforming its meaning. Viewed mystically like this, history *is* moving forward.[4]

Chateaubriand applied to history a new, romantic aesthetic and tone. These are especially evident in his posthumous *Mémoires from beyond the grave*. He recollects an active career in public life under Napoleon from a position of wistful, self-deprecating proximity to the great. His writing conveys a new disposition: the sensitive individual can embrace inwardly the shadowy forms stirring behind history. The irreducible force of history, on the other hand, can bear individuals along on its fringes.

The strands of romanticism in France formed briefly in the 1820s into an explicit movement. One of its 'manifestos',[5] Hugo's preface to the historical drama *Cromwell*, spelt out more explicitly the new aesthetic and emotional posture towards history. Each of the different societies that evolve in history (primitive, antique and modern — that is, Christian) has had, in Hugo's view, a specific literature and a specific imagination related to its political order. (Madame de Staël had used the same idea, in her *De la littérature* (1800), to demonstrate perfectibility running through human history — indeed, it was she who gave the term 'romantic' to one modern form of literature.) Hugo draws several consequences from the link between each particular imagination and its society. He undercuts the abstract ideals of classicism with the notion of an evolving aesthetic diversity. He subsumes the private imagination — the artist's included — under a historically determinate character, which suits its time and place. He conveys the confidence of belonging to a mysterious, providential order that can reconcile the romantic to the vicissitudes of history. He encourages an acceptance, indeed an attachment, to historical diversity. According to Hugo, indeed, the modern imagination has in particular to embrace the diverse, the *non*-uniform, the sinister, and those principles that *contend* within a particular historical reality. For Christianity has incorporated melancholy tensions into the modern consciousness: tensions between the material and the spiritual; between the soul and the body; and between the beautiful and the grotesque. The modern universe, according to Hugo, is that of historical drama. In sum, Hugo's romanticism directs the writer to respond to what is diverse and exotic in historical reality.

Burke, Herder and Scott were three non-French sources for the ideas underpinning this romantic disposition. Burke had introduced the contrast between the orderly aesthetic value of 'beauty' and the mysteriously awesome pull of 'the sublime'. Furthermore, he had emphasized the importance in the social world of what is long-standing or historically particular — as against the eighteenth century's liking for abstract, transhistorical principle. He attacked the contemporary dominance of 'sophisters, economists and calculators'.[6] Burke advocated wise husbandry of the historical legacy of a society. Yet, as more than one commentator has pointed out, Burke's line of thought is derived from a rationalist eighteenth-century principle: that of utility.[7]

Herder's view of history (published in the 1780s) portrayed historical forces dwarfing the intentions of individual actors. Each nation, according to him, is led through historical time by its *Volksgeist*: the spirit of the people which determines its character and destiny. Herder, too, was stoutly opposed to the Revolution, arguing that French revolutionary ideas must be excluded from Germany. Yet, through Quinet (who translated his *Thoughts on the Philosophy of History* in 1827), his views on history linked the Enlightenment (in the form of Montesquieu's geographical determinism) to the ideas of nineteenth-century historians (Quinet and Michelet) who included the collective spirit in their histories.

Walter Scott's historical novels, notably *Quentin Durward*, also contributed to historical perception in France. They encouraged a reassessment of the feudal period, which is a feature common to many of the histories I will look at in this chapter.[8] And they conveyed the diversity of human beings in history in a way that drew affection for them from readers.[9] Yet this, too, was no rejection of rationalism.[10] It was a by-product of the analysis of different societies' evolution which had been undertaken by Scottish Enlightenment historians such as Ferguson and Millar (who had themselves extrapolated from Montesquieu). Again, the romantic taste for diversity in history was licensed by rationalist concepts for historical analysis.

We can now extrapolate how the romantic influence might be felt with regard to history. On the basis of ideas found in Enlightenment rationalism itself, romanticism reverses the classical view of history. Romanticism is unafraid of contradiction, the irrational and what is beyond immediate comprehension. It embraces what is peculiar to the historical moment as of value in itself, or as part of a mysterious but providential evolution. Far from seeking abstract ideals in the classical past — or anywhere else — romanticism focuses attention on what is diverse, peculiar, or eccentric. It is drawn to what (in classical thinking) was uninteresting, distasteful or even disastrous. The rationalist sense that history has a direction is recovered, therefore, though the direction may have gone behind the cloud of a shifting, socially evolving imagination. Indeed, direction and worth may now be found even in the confusion and human suffering that fills so much of history. Finally, because the private imagination shadows the movement of history, writers may now identify themselves, in a mysterious way, with historical movement itself. By the 1810s, one sees, in the social thinking of Saint-Simon, the first of a tradition of visionary utopian writers. They put themselves forward as prophets able to realize a version of the Revolution enhanced by a romantic sense of dramatic possibilities in history.[11] But social theorists belong in Chapter 7. My concern in this chapter is with the written histories.

THIERRY: THE ROMANCE OF THE FRENCH RACE

Thierry and Guizot developed versions of French history in which the long-term sources of the Revolution were traced further back even than in de Staël's thinking: right to the fall of Rome. In their accounts, the centuries since that time witness gradual suppression of earlier forms of liberty. The Revolution itself emerged, somewhat more positively, as a *revival*, on new terms, carried out by the provincial bourgeoisie.

In the context of the restored monarchy, this extended chronology and new causal account of the Revolution were clearly useful to bourgeois-liberal politics. However, Thierry and Guizot also made subtle innovations in the way the reader could both understand history and feel about it. Thierry organized the history of the French with a strongly romantic appreciation of diversity, which made France's past an exciting current in which his readers could swim. For his part, Guizot, more theoretically sophisticated, introduced an idealist conceptual apparatus that explained the strands of French history as complex manifestations of European 'civilization', which contemporary society could advance still further. In different ways, the two friends were both reconstituting the people as they had appeared in the Revolution, out of historical elements from the distant past. As these historians represented them, the French belonged to an active, creative movement for political liberty which had culminated in the Revolution. They and their readers were therefore encouraged to believe themselves capable of participation in the future realization of the purposes of the Revolution.

Thierry started to publish the articles that were to become his *Lettres sur l'histoire de France* in 1817.[12] Calling for a new perspective in French history, he himself adopted visionary evocation as the purpose of his writing. He aimed, he said, to 'penetrate to the hearts of men across the distance of the centuries . . . represent them living and acting . . . They have been dead for . . . hundreds of years . . . but what does that matter to the imagination?'[13] According to Thierry, the task of the historian is to look for diversity rather than uniformity in his subjects.[14] For over forty years, as a historian and journalist, he continued to pursue the evocation of the lives and activities of France's long-dead forebears.

The *Lettres* advance the idea of a native tradition of liberty that was reasserted in 1789. That original liberty, which had been gradually suppressed by the central power over the centuries, was attributable to racial diversity. Thus, Gaul is a charming picture of doomed, but vigorous diversity:

> all the races of men that mixed to produce one nation, ours . . . the primitive diversity of their manners and ideas . . . the gradual decline of the old civilization, the growing ignorance of legal tradition, the loss of enlightenment, the oppression of the weak and the poor . . .[15]

According to Thierry, the Frankish invaders, by suppressing the established ways of the Gauls, began a long tradition of oppression from Paris.[16] The vigour and diversity they put down were, however, reborn by the steady growth of free communes during the Middle Ages, with the unwilling sanction of royal authority.[17] The word 'bourgeois' at that time 'expressed at once the ideas of personal freedom and of active participation in municipal sovereignty'.[18] Yet, by 1789, this manifestation of liberty had declined to such an extent that merely a bastardized version remained.[19] The Revolution's suppression of the remaining local autonomy was a blessing. A national constitution, to put French liberty on a more formal footing, had become necessary.[20] The Revolution emerges from the story as an act undertaken by 'opinion and the public will' to revive liberty 'when the mass of the nation felt the hollowness . . . of restoring ancient rights'.[21]

In this account, diversity is both the aesthetic preference of the historian and the essence of freedom. Thierry adapts the long-term trend culminating in the Revolution to romantic taste. His thesis also places the historian at the fulcrum of the struggle for the nation's liberty. It is a rhetorical posture comparable to that of the revolutionary journalists. Thierry begins his first Letter on a personal note. He identifies himself with the forebears. Alluding to his earlier political activity as secretary to Saint-Simon, he claims that the enthusiasms of his youth have now been replaced by an involvement in the French people's own long struggle for justice and liberty.[22] The heroes of this struggle, as Thierry then describes them, are humble people full of 'patriotism and energy'.[23] These people, who are the true bearers of the tradition of liberty, have been oppressed by their masters and passed over by historians. If the historian's task is to evoke their diversity, then in fulfilling it he is also the channel for their values: the French tradition of freedom.

Thierry wanted to lead his readers to identify themselves with the French people of history, as he himself had done. Furthermore, by the manner in which he achieves that, the readers are clearly encouraged to take up the age-old fight for liberty. The romantic colour Thierry uses in evoking the French can give the reader a sense of participation. The strands that motivate the history are presented as elements in the racial identity of the French. Thierry is a 'racist' in an innocent sense that is no longer available: he simply believed that a people's racial heritage formed whatever identity it had. So, the slow fusion of racially peculiar culture and mores, which he lovingly describes, have made up the nation. Like inherited family resemblances, this racial inheritance can appear as the free property of its bearers. It can, therefore, be counterposed to ineluctable climatic conditions à la Montesquieu.[24] Thierry can then portray 1789 as a *free* act which brings to fruition something belonging to the nation, to Thierry himself and to his intended readers. The Revolution is the action of the people as Thierry has constituted them, expressing their unsuppressible inherited identity. This accounts for the tone of his closing remarks:

> and thus there came about that immense gathering of men, possessing civil liberty but lacking political rights, which undertook in 1789, for the sake of France as a whole, what their ancestors had done in simple towns in the Middle Ages. We who still look upon it, that society for modern times, struggling with the debris of the past, of conquest, of feudal obligations and absolute royalty, let us not worry ourselves for it . . . it has conquered all the powers that have been vainly recalled.[25]

Thierry's imaginative, romantic way of identifying the people at the heart of the Revolution gives reassurance about the future and generates a sense of involvement in an inevitable long-term historical process.

GUIZOT: REPUBLICANISM AND FEUDAL SOCIETY

Guizot performed a similar reorientation of overarching causal structure and of attitude. He, too, regarded 1789 as the revival, in a new form, of the earlier spirit of civic freedom and nascent political liberty among the bourgeoisie of medieval France. His originality lay in the theoretical basis of his work.

Guizot's overarching theme is the growth and evolution of 'civilization'.[26] The concept has a romantic tinge. Like Thierry, Guizot held that diversity was the source of progress in civilization.[27] His first critical work (*Vie des poètes français du siècle de Louis XIV* (1813)) had pursued the romantic issue (from de Staël) of the links between artists' imaginations and their historical epoch. However, via French intermediaries, Guizot acquired a German idealist conceptual framework. He held that there were different mores constituting civilization in different places and times (what he calls its different 'moral states'). All were versions of the underlying forms of the social character of human beings (similar to Kantian categories). The given 'moral state' constitutes the individuals and groups that are active in history. By highlighting these levels of social existence, Guizot advances, in effect, a distinct historical ontology and distinct analytical method.

In Guizot's account, a rich diversity formed feudal society after the fall of Rome, generating first the feudal system, and then the political liberties of the towns, which the monarchy superseded. 1789 revived them. This is the same story as Thierry's, though Guizot regards the centralizing royal power in a more favourable light. However, the role of racial heritage in Thierry is taken over by elements of the 'moral state': the development of the law, culture, social relations and private attitudes. By analysis and comparison of legal records and other documents, Guizot attempts to gauge speculatively how the given principles and practices of civilization were articulated in the reality of social life.

So the writing traces the growth of 'civilization' through history. The essential elements of modern civilization can be found in the Roman, the Christian and the German legacies brought together through the barbarian invasions.[28] Guizot thus embeds the Revolution in a chronology going back a very long way. These are the elements of social life articulated already at the very foundation of European history: central power, professional administration, municipal organization, monarchical authority, aristocratic rank, democratic debate, doctrine regulating social life, free association and self-governing

assemblies. Yet this combination was unstable. The rule of Charle-
magne and the feudal system swept it aside. Again, elements essential
to civilization continue: individual consent (via oaths), clear conditions
of association, consent to taxation, public participation in justice, and
so on. 'All the rights of individuality' were established.[29] And
alongside feudalism, there arose the government of the free communes:
a unique asset in European civilization, preserving the principles of
election and participation handed down from the post-Roman
period.[30] But feudal society lacked a focus for the good of society *as a
whole*. In Guizot's view, it was therefore 'insupportable and odious'.[31]
Its justifiable suppression over the centuries culminated in the
rationalization of 1789. Commune society, for its part, was already
decadent by the fourteenth century.[32]

In Guizot's view the moral state in 1789 could not sustain the social
order. This explains the difficulties of the Revolution. Along with
what was objectionable in feudalism, the eighteenth century had
destroyed that 'poetic character, that truth' which had helped people to
adopt willingly the manners of their society. The society created by
the Revolution therefore lacked internal loyalty to social mores. ' . . .
the revolution of the last century unleashed a social revolution; it
concerned much more people's reciprocal relations than their internal
and personal dispositions; it wanted to reform society rather than the
individual'.[33] In other words, the Enlightenment had neglected the
private conscience and feelings of the citizen. A barren division
prevented people from relating facts to general principles and vice
versa.[34] Guizot's intellectualism arrives at the romantic view of the
social role of sentiment.

> Civilization consists in essence of two things: the development of the
> social and the intellectual condition; the development of the exterior
> and general, and of the internal and personal nature of man; in a word,
> the perfection of society and of humanity.[35]

Like Thierry, Guizot not only expounds an interpretation of the past,
but also prompts a feeling of participation in the direction of its long-
term chronology. History, as Guizot wrote it, has a particular role in
the understanding necessary for civilization to get back on the rails. It
brought fact and principle together, showing how the elements of the
moral state of a society are articulated. And its renewed interest in the
Middle Ages allows the public to 'understand the role that the
imagination plays in the life of man and of society'.[36] Hence, Guizot

displays an idealist, even an Hegelian idea of a world where history is made by the interaction of human agency and human thought with the objective given.

> We are thrown into a world that we have neither created nor invented; we find it, we look upon it; we study it: we have no choice but to take it as a fact . . . As agents, we do otherwise: when we have observed external facts, knowing them generates in us ideas of something better; we feel duty-bound to reform, to perfect, to regulate what there is; we feel able to act upon the world, to extend the glorious empire of reason. That is the mission of humankind . . . [37]

Guizot constructed history by interlocking conscious change within the imaginations and thought of both individuals and societies. The Revolution, like other history, was the interaction of human beings articulating their projects in the terms of the given state of society. Yet history has a direction; and the Revolution is the latest manifestation of that direction. So, by his manner of composing history, Guizot encouraged his readers to complete it consciously. The change that is in process would, he says, contribute to the 'permanent, regular, peaceful character of the social condition that is being established and appearing on all sides', a condition founded on 'convictions common to all'.[38] Guizot not only describes deep-rooted reasons for the course of the Revolution, he also advances its aims for conscious realization.

QUINET: REPUBLICANISM AND
THE SPIRIT OF CHRISTIANITY

Edgar Quinet's thinking extended yet further the chronology that embraced the Revolution. According to his *Le Christianisme et la Révolution* (1845), the Revolution was the revival of the deep spirit of Christianity, that sense of human growth first revealed in the life of Christ.

> Christianity remains locked away in tombs up to the time of the French Revolution, when we can say that it revives, takes shape, is touched and felt for the first time in the hands of non-believers, in institutions and in the living law.[39]

The book is a romantically personal, even a mystical assessment, interspersed with expressions of the writer's own intuitions. Christ's life was the historic moment which revealed to him the infinity of the soul in human beings. The Revolution was the first social realization of the core of Christianity, which the complex of doctrine and Church institutional development had covered over. When feudalism is brought to an end by the Revolution, Quinet feels that, 'at last, in the Constituent Assembly, modern times have added the declaration of the rights of man to the ancient Credo'.[40]

Quinet's approach reversed the priority given to institutional forms in Guizot's idealism. For Quinet, the development of rites, institutions and doctrines added nothing to the spiritual meaning of Christianity. It simply extended the power and institutional base of the Church: 'the whole of the Middle Ages worked on the declaration of the rights of the Church'.[41] New Testament ideals of equality and fraternity, for example, were held back by the Augustinian doctrine of authority. Quinet's view of history is itself a more mystical idealism. According to Quinet, the long-term direction of history is to realize in social life the double nature of human beings as both flesh and spirit. Christ was the incarnation of this nature.

> . . . one who knows in detail the way that dogma was shaped knows in his heart how civil and political history is shaped. Modern humanity is made, as in antiquity, in the image of God; there is nothing in that supreme ideal that we ought not to aim to realize one day in institutions and laws.[42]

In Quinet's account, the Nicean Council fused religion and classical philosophy in a creed stating that double nature. Medieval movements, such as the rise of the communes, receive scant attention. The Reformation is recognized solely as the validation of individual conscience — though for a humanity no longer equipped to live by it. The Revolution alone comes near to realizing the union of flesh and spirit in social life.

Evidently, religion is going to be crucial in the Revolution itself. Quinet's account focuses on how institutionalized Christianity rejected the separation of the French Church from Roman Catholicism (the so-called 'civil constitution of the clergy') and set out to defeat the Revolution in the Vendée uprising. Because the culture of human growth had been driven out of religion and the religiosity of the French nation suppressed by counter-reformation, the revolutionaries' own response was ineffective. The cult of the Supreme Being was unable to supply the need for a national religion. Instead, by persecuting private consciences in the Terror, the Revolution ended by matching the papal authoritarianism it was opposed to. In short, the revolutionary movement acted blindly. It tried to constitute itself in a religious observance which recognized the modern, individual conscience; but it failed because it could not cast off the legacy from the past.

Compared with Thierry's or Guizot's accounts, Quinet's long-term history reverses the relationship between the Revolution and its historical roots. In Quinet's historical ontology, the need to recover roots is outweighed by the need to transcend them. It is necessary to *undo* much of the ancient past in the name of its hidden principle – to redo the work of 1789–94. As Furet neatly puts it, the '1789-ism' of Guizot's generation was 'the acceptance of a society and the search for the government it needed', whereas the '1793-ism' of Quinet's generation was 'the inventory of promise aborted and of a society that needed to be remade'.[43]

Quinet's romantic idealism is accordingly more marked than that of the earlier historians. It defies the surface events and the temporal sequence of history. The aims of the Revolution are taken as a sacred message in history. Human romantic heroes act in concert with the Revolution, on a plane where time is not a merely linear process. Time has intense moments where cosmic conflict appears from beneath the surface of events. One such moment is the debate in the Assembly on the civil constitution of the clergy. In Quinet's terms, the revolutionaries were deciding to turn from Catholic authoritarianism and combine civil with religious renewal.

> Audacious in the face of royalty, the Constituent Assembly hesitates in the face of Catholicism; at the bottom of its heart it is free; but it does not admit it . . . The clergy demand a more explicit submission. At that moment Mirabeau rises and goes to the window looking out on the . . . terrace, and points with his finger at the *palace whence the signal went out for the Saint Bartholomew's day massacre*. Everyone fell silent; all sensed that France, at that moment, had taken a great step.[44]

The spiritual strand in history, repeatedly frustrated, makes of historical acts the *repetition* of a drama that is always on the point of resolution. The early Christians and the French can be placed on the same side.

> We too, we are in a time when we are told that new barbarians close in on the old society. There they are, people say, on the threshold; they demand admittance . . . What shall we do? Who will march before the

new barbarians, like another Saint Leon? Shall we say that the world is going to end? We shall say that a new epoch will begin . . . What remains to be done then? This. Establish a truce between the city of God and the city of man; reunite the one and the other under the same principle, enlarge the second by hoisting the standard of law and of right from the first . . . we can build a mansion of justice, liberty and truth big enough to house us all.[45]

In Quinet's timeless drama, the human spirit approaches that ideal where social order and religious values will in the end be united. The drama takes place on a plane of reality that is concurrently historical, spiritual, emotional and ideal. Quinet adopts the dispositions of nineteenth-century romanticism and idealism, so as to combine causal explanation and the freedom to transform the social world. So his ontology expresses something of the excitement of change felt by the revolutionaries. It also encourages the human spirit to go back to earlier points in time and advance further towards the ideal. But to account for the Revolution, Quinet translates its reality into the ideal.

In due course, Quinet himself felt its weakness. In exile after the fall of another republican revolution (to Napoleon III), he addressed more sanguinely the question of the Terror. In both the 1790s and the 1850s, it seemed, revolutionaries could collude with France's past to resurrect the oppression which they were seeking to destroy.[46] Quinet now recast his earlier idealism, where a religious *message* lay within the empirical course of history. He developed, instead, a more static sociology of religion. This change made the failure of the Revolution an outcome of objective factors, and swamped the implicit, heroic freedom of historical agents.

La Révolution (1865) sets out this more sociological approach. The key sociological principle appears in connection with the Vendée revolt:[47] one religion can only be defeated by another. Religion, Quinet argues, grasps the life-experience of people in society more deeply than the revolutionaries understood.[48] Hence, the Republic's victory over the religious rebels was illusory. The Jacobins ignored the need for tolerance of the individual; they reimposed the old world's discipline upon the modern, individualist world.[49]

In Quinet's later historical ontology, heroic action is easily impeded by wrong objective conditions.

If the nation is not mature, the man who rises above her perishes an unknown martyr, leaving no trace. If the time has not arrived, if the ground is not prepared, the plant that has grown at the pinnacle of the species perishes stifled, without issue.[50]

In the last words of his book Quinet adopts a rhetorical posture reminiscent of that I described for Saint-Just in Chapter 1. He places himself in the tragic role of one who embraced his own ruin at the hands of necessities he had himself identified.[51] But he refuses to let go altogether of the idealist element of his thinking: 'others are born in better conditions; if just one [plant] found appropriate conditions, it would produce a vegetable revolution and a new world'.[52] And he closes the book insisting defiantly on the possibility of hope.

> even when souls seem extinguished, dead, must we despair? Not at all. All of nature protests and teaches us hope in spite of ourselves . . . What are we persons of a day, tangled up with the colossal, immortal persons called nations . . . They laugh at us and our gloom, trusting in a future they can delay but not diminish.[53]

Quinet's history marks the full expression of idealism and romanticism in defining the character of the Revolution. It is idealist because it views history as the realization of the ideal. Even when Quinet interpreted the course of the Revolution more in terms of scientific sociology, this idealism persists. It is romantic by virtue of the historian's romantic empathy with the past. Quinet believed he could refer to the ideal in past history, in the Revolution, and in the future, and so make it available as an objective of conscious human action in the present.

LAMARTINE: THE ROMANTIC EPIC OF THE REPUBLIC

My two remaining historians are the most republican in the sense that they portray the French nation as a whole entity capable of acting as a historical agent in the Revolution. This perspective represents a return to that of the revolutionaries themselves.

The interest of Lamartine's popular *Histoire des Girondins* lies not so much in its explanation of the Revolution as in its rhetorical posture. Lamartine was not a historian, but a poet and an independent politician. He was briefly figurehead of the provisional government set up by the Revolution of 1848, the year after his history was published. He talked of himself as the founder of a *'Parti sociale'*, which could resolve the problem of how to integrate the proletariat. Looking back over his career, he wrote that he had 'popularized healthy revolutionary principles . . . The way to be read in the highest and the lowest circles [of society] is to touch and engage the human heart.'[54] He had sought a style to communicate the possibility of collective political action – in particular to the new proletarian class, which was waiting for action from the political elite.[55] Like Quinet, Lamartine wanted to present objective historical realities as feasible objects of human action. His solution was the romantic epic. The heroes of the epic can blend together and give expression to the historical cross-currents residing in the people. Forming and reforming society appears a hazardous but achievable goal.

Lamartine's style unites a romantic taste for the particular and the picturesque with epic narrative. Some of the classic features of epic are present. Much time is spent introducing individual figures and tracing them back to their particular historical roots. This resembles the folk epic, where the lineage of the sword may be traced at length while it is held aloft waiting to strike. The first four books are largely dedicated to introducing the various political figures in play: Mirabeau, the king, and then (the ostensible heroes) the deputies from the Gironde. This may appear an obtuse distraction from the action. But in fact, its effect is to convey the action at another level. The individuals are both crucial and peripheral. The reader learns about the Revolution *through* this procession of *dramatis personae*. In recounting Mirabeau's death, for example, Lamartine tells us how the Revolution had gone beyond the rational, constitutional phase, which this one man could now no longer sustain. This manner of presentation fuses the actions of individual agents with epic forces on an enormous historical stage.

The role of individuals is to bear with difficulty and skill the buffeting of forces greater than themselves. Lamartine's book is 'the history of a small number of men who, thrown by providence into the greatest drama of modern times, contained in themselves the ideas, the passions, the faults, the virtues of an epoch'.[56] The course of historical events is accounted for by how these individuals master the historical forces. Mirabeau himself is 'the image of certain men whose, as it were, collective genius forms itself in the model of their epoch and epitomizes in them alone the individuality of a nation'.[57] Carnot, who overhauled the way that troops were assembled and directed at the enemy, invents the 'modern' form of warfare: that of the sovereign people.[58]

The epic forces in Lamartine's history are often identified in terms of the cultural and racial lineage of a figure. Mirabeau's family origins in the culture of the Italian republics and Machiavelli are fully described (along with the detail of his amorous past!). Lamartine is linking the individual with various great principles of organization running through the modern world. The principles are fighting it out *through* the individuals: reason; republicanism; patriotism; religious liberty; the democratic principle of the sovereignty of the people; humanistic 'faith in humanity'; and so on. But these forces are not merely abstract. They come into existence in conjunction with historically particular groupings, influences, heritages and forms of social or economic organization. Take, for example, Mme Roland. By virtue of her artisanal origins, she possessed, for Lamartine, both the simplicity of the people and the enlightenment of the aristocracy. These are qualities, he tells us, which might have regenerated the nation.[59] Likewise, the city of Lyons is a 'republic of interests', or a 'sociable democracy' — safe, wealth-conscious, intellectually dull. To the Jacobinism of the North[60] Lyons opposed the heritage of the old southern European republics (better preserved away from the absolutist state in Paris [61]).

As for the Girondins, the heroes of the action, they were adaptable 'démocrates de circonstances', trying to maintain political power after the departure of the great actors from the stage. They epitomize a realistic, tolerant republicanism, which is sympathetic to property. But they face Robespierre and Danton, the 'démocrates de principe', whose political posture 'fascinates the people'.[62] They are unable to survive in the political climate of the day, with a suspicious, uncomprehending people. They are the epic heroes of the drama of modern republicanism (in which Lamartine saw himself): a republican constitution can be clearly set out, but its underlying principles have not as yet been communicated to the people.

What historical ontology does this epic convey? As Lamartine portrays them, the deeds of the individual actors manifest contending principles and forms of organization. These in turn may arise because of historical social conditions, such as the impact of absolute government or the distribution of property. Groups, individuals and organizations struggle to master the flow of historical forces — sometimes succeeding. There is a 'mysterious correlation which exists between acts and their consequences'.[63] Yet actions are often turned in directions other than those intended by the agents. The same principles may have different outcomes in different conjunctures. The individual is granted a limited freedom by the complex of mysterious historical forces.

Within this movement, the hardest of all groups to bring into

146

existence, the people itself, is also the most important. In the Revolution, the people, 'for whom all of politics was sentiment', were filled with anger, and 'understood nothing of the thinking of the Assembly', with its respect for abstractly defined institutions.[64] The 'abdication' of the constitutional Convention, once the constitution was written, was therefore the turning point of the Revolution. For it happened at a time when 'the nation did not wish to reign', and needed leadership that would convey the meaning of the constitution to the people. Instead of that 'factions ruled . . . a people that does not know how to take and hold all that belongs to it tempts tyranny and anarchy at the same time'.[65]

In sum, Lamartine employed the romantic taste for the particular to identify historic currents as the living undertow of human action and evoked sentiment alongside his exposition of abstract principles. In this way, he sought to revive the Revolution's idea of the nation as an agent in history and to convey to the people a sentiment of its potential for action.

MICHELET: THE PEOPLE AS THE IDEAL

Michelet is the last historian I want to consider because he took the developments I have been following to their furthest point. His writing brings the epic manner of Lamartine to the expression of a still more purified idealism than Quinet's. He extended his gaze to comprehend the people as an undifferentiated unity. They became the unique force at the centre of the historical ontology. Michelet gave an account in which the Revolution appeared, once again, to be the product of the people as such: 'the essential basis of history is in the thinking of the people. Without doubt the republic was floating in this thinking'.[66]

Like Lamartine, Michelet wrote with a romantic sensibility to convey the ideal at work in the French people. For him, writing history would both account for the past and help to leave the people capable of grasping their own identity and exercising their freedom for the future. Like Quinet, who was his close friend in the 1840s and 1850s, Michelet interpreted the collective action of the Revolution as the embodiment of humanity's own ideal principle. But, unlike Quinet, he did not ground his ideal in religious revelation, but in the very essence of collective action. In the Revolution, the people constituted the dominant force in history, by virtue of coming together as an active unity. Or rather, since they manifested no principle from outside of themselves, the people constituted themselves and discovered their ideal at the same time. For Michelet, the ideal embodied in the people did not have to come from outside, because it was the principle inherent in social unity, namely, the principle of justice.

Before Michelet begins his *History of the French Revolution* in earnest, he expounds the ideal principles in play in the sequence of events. For, as he says, 'I cannot without this inquiry advance one step'.[67] This exposition 'defines' the Revolution. In contrast to past domination by the Church and the principle of grace, the Revolution is: 'The advent of Law, the resurrection of Right, and the reaction of Justice'.[68] Key moments in the history then follow, introduced as instances of conflicting principles subsidiary to the battle of Grace and Justice. The book proceeds through a series of such moments: the Bastille, the king's flight to Varennes, the popular invasions of the legislature (notably, 10 August 1792, which brought the monarchy to an end), and so on. An epic build-up to each moment emphasizes the ideals that are going to be in conflict when the climax is reached. The overall principle, gradually emerging throughout, is that of the people itself, pursuing *its own* principle of action.

Take, for example, the king's flight to Varennes. Building up to the key event, Michelet sets out the advice offered by various politicians, courtiers and foreign powers, each following their particular principles.[69] As for the king himself, he manifested the loyalty of all Christian kings. He was

> still a stranger by virtue of a sentiment external in his eyes to all nationality: a stranger in his religion. For the Christian the nation is a secondary thing . . . All kings have a special religion; they are dedicated to royalty.[70]

Following the king's flight, the proper focus of sovereignty is in doubt. The next two books portray the growing awareness in thinking circles of the need for a republic. The principles in play within the participants' actions are again fully evinced. The debate on the inviolability of the Assembly, for example, is among 'the first republican acts'[71] because it belongs to an attempt to relocate the sovereign power.

The build-up to the Terror receives a similar treatment: a thorough exposition of how ideal principles are manifest in the events. Though the story begins with the personality of Marat, he only has an impact because the principle at the base of the nation's existence was obstructed.[72] Patriotic men found themselves isolated where the nation's greatest enemy (the king) was at its head. The nation therefore lacked all internal coherence, and Marat's peculiar delirium could spread to others. Unable to contain their own passions, journalists and militants called up 'an artificial force of exaggeration in violence'.[73] In the final analysis, then, Michelet finds that it is the Assembly's weakness as a focus of sovereignty that encouraged the militant journalists' in their disreputable course. In trying to speak for the interests of conflicting groups (the privileged, the aristocrats, the monarchists) as well as common people, the Assembly was 'profoundly heterogeneous and confused, like the chaos of the *ancien régime*, whence it sprang'.[74]

The fundamental battle going on beneath the surface of the Revolution is between the principle of Justice and that of Monarchical Grace. Michelet traces the notion of Grace to the religion of the Middle Ages. Grace asserts the dependence of humans, for salvation or for whatever else is good, upon an arbitrary, higher power. According to Grace, humanity is the author of evil. The principle expressed in the Revolution, on the other hand, is the Justice created by man for man. This is fundamentally opposed to the position entailed in the principle of Grace. It is founded on mutual love and collective unity. The Revolution 'founds fraternity on the love of man for man, on mutual duty — on Right and Justice. This base is fundamental, and no other is necessary'.[75] The evils of the old monarchy derive from the faults involved in the principle of Grace. Arbitrary abuses of law, docility over famine, the haughty, grasping self-interest of the Church: all these are made possible because France 'comprehended politics only as devotion and love' towards the god-like monarchy.[76] Men were divided from each other instead of united by justice and mutual love.[77]

The people holds a peculiar position in relation to the emerging ideal of Justice. Justice is the principle by which a nation creates *itself*. It is the principle that makes possible independent self-regulation, that is sovereignty. If it only acts autonomously, therefore, the people follows its own inherent principle. Because justice belongs to its nature, according to Michelet, the people can *sense* what is right and what it should do. As an example, he cites the story of one poor woman's fight on behalf of the unjustly imprisoned Latude.[78] It demonstrates that, in spite of centuries of monarchical callousness, the ordinary people have retained an implicit feel for what is right. Or again, on the day the Bastille was stormed, the people sensed the direction that the conflict between the principles of past and future had to take, and intuitively acted on their own logic.

> The future and past both gave the same reply; both cried Advance! And what is beyond all time – beyond the future and the past – immutable right said the same. The immortal sentiment of the just imparted a temper of adamant to the fluttering heart of man . . .[79]

Furthermore, once they have *sensed* it, the people are able to *create* what is right. Their acts transcend the limitations felt by other actors: 'The attack on the Bastille was by no means reasonable. It was an act of faith'.[80] When the Assembly is paralysed, incapable of acting for the nation, the people steps in to resolve the crisis of legitimacy.

> The moderate who ought, one would think, to have been more keen-sighted and less dazzled, saw nothing of this. Strangely enough, passion took a better view; it perceived that everything was danger . . . and strove to get clear of it.[81]

The people marched to Versailles and brought the king back to Paris, to be subject to the sovereign assembly. So, Michelet has taken us a long way from the view of the people that we found in de Staël. For the liberals, the people represented the natural disorder of passion. For Michelet, the people's passion is not natural disorder, threatening to reason: it *unites* passion and the highest rationality.

In Michelet's historical ontology, the people, acting as a nation, therefore have the solidest existence of all. This is partly because they are close to natural material needs, such as hunger, which bring them together in the common bonds of ordinary people.[82] But it derives, as well, from Michelet's general ontology of human emergence. Taking up Vico's phrase, 'Humanity is its own Prometheus',[83] Michelet saw history as a realm in which humans *develop themselves* out of nature. He examined the natural evolution itself in a later series of whimsical books about material nature.[84] For him, the pinnacle of human evolution is reached when humanity self-consciously pursues principles that it has itself invented and validated. Where that point is reached, rational freedom is realized in history: nature is in accord with history. Hence, where the people achieve that autonomy, the opposition of reason and nature is overturned.

Accordingly, in describing the people in the Revolution, Michelet always stresses its autonomy. The crowd at the storming of the Bastille was not promoted by orators: the action was carried out by those 'who had also the devotion and the strength to accomplish their faith. Who? Why, the people – everybody'.[85] The invasion of the Assembly on 10 August 1792 was the action of the people, 'I mean . . . the mass of people of all classes'.[86] 'We must not seek the action of parties' in the march to Versailles; it was 'unanimous', and even those who did not participate 'rejoiced' in the outcome.[87] Other levels of social existence are subsidiary to the ideal principle embodied in the people, with their unique capacity for sovereign unity.

In 1846, Michelet broke off from his history to make a personal testament of his aims in writing. *Le Peuple* openly expressed how his historical writing was a quest for romantic self-identification[88] with the nation. Indeed, his writing was intended to be a contribution to the process of constituting the nation. The task calls for personal sentiment as well as scholarly technique. To advance beyond the conventional historians, Michelet writes, one must consult the heart: in history 'Thierry saw a *narration* and Monsieur Guizot *an analysis*. I have called it *resurrection.*'[89] So Michelet openly supplemented Thierry and Guizot with a different emotion. He included emotions in his construction of the ordinary people. The people have 'a richness of sentiment and a goodness of heart' combined with 'a vital warmth', he writes; the nation is 'the great friendship'.[90] Michelet's autobiographical 1868 Preface to the *History of France* spoke of what he felt to be a life-long intimacy with the French nation: 'cherished France with whom I have lived, whom I leave with such deep regret!'[91] Passages in the history also imply that the nation needed, and could offer a unique union in love; for example, this apostrophe to the underlying principle of the nation, Justice:

> For thou art truly love, and identical with Grace.
> And as thou art Justice, thou wilt support me in this book . . . Thou wilt be just towards me, and I will be so towards all. For whom have I written this, but for thee, Eternal Justice?[92]

Empathy is justified as a historical method because oppression and patronage have covered over natural sentiments. We have, therefore, in Michelet's view, to set aside such social forms ('an artificial thing and born of circumstances'), and return to 'the invariable and natural relations between human beings'.[93] It is this which produces in Michelet's writing what one commentator has called a 'multiple revelation' of the people.[94]

151

CRITICAL REVIEW

Michelet's is an elevated portrayal of the revolution of and by the people. He interpreted the most obscure strata of society as embodiments of the most high-flown ideal principles. Yet, it is striking, as Linda Orr points out, that the people do not speak for themselves.[95] The revolutionary orator may speak for them; but, more often, the historian himself is left to do it. Indeed, much modern commentary upon his work refers to the frustration of Michelet's literary enterprise, especially to his inability to find a voice for the united humanity whose historian, then prophet, he wished to be.[96] With a historical ontology of Michelet's kind, how well does the weight of interpretation sit upon individuals and individual acts? As he is the extreme point of idealist and romantic development, it would be revealing if Michelet has any difficulty interpreting his historical subjects in terms of his ideals.

In theory, individuals become either the spokespersons or the bearers of the evolving, conflicting ideals. Almost without exception, however, individuals in Michelet's account of the Revolution do not embody ideal principles successfully. Lafayette, for example, is an unconscious republican who becomes the tool of reaction at the Champs de Mars.[97] Poor Paine, though solidly loyal to the republic, slips into contradiction when he declares against trying the king.[98] Mirabeau was 'destined to complete the sum of contradictions'.[99] More than any one else, he embodies, for Michelet, the impossibility of acting for the two principles at war within the motivations of the Revolution. 'The monster of the time, I mean the discord of the two principles, their impotency for creating anything vital, must, to be well perceived, be seen in one man'.[100]

The more revolutionary politicians hardly fare better. Robespierre is overtaken by the logic of a political situation which he cannot control, and by his own naturally tyrannical character. He destroys the strongest advocates of the Republic. Danton manages to escape partially an infecundity which seems to be human destiny in Michelet's account. He has a somewhat lurching intuition of the people's need for justice.[101] Then he falls prey to the jealousies within the Jacobins and the conspiracy of the Right.[102] The ideal principles embodied in the Revolution seem very difficult to attach firmly to individuals.

On the other hand, it seems easy for those who are *against* the Revolution. There always seems to be a terrible coherence in their action. Michelet finds no difficulty in attributing clear and even, for a long period of time, successful cynicism to the Church. It has jealously guarded its wealth over centuries and can easily hoodwink the Assembly. 'This was clear, simple and vigorous; the clerical party knew very well what they wanted. The Assembly knew it not.'[103] Likewise, the court party usually seems to exhibit striking coherence in their plans. For example:

> a show of strength was needed to make it strong in the belief in its own strength. That could only happen with a riot, with a victory over a riot. The royalists in the Tuileries, and the constitutionals in the Assembly, certainly wanted that.[104]

For Michelet, history is fundamentally motivated by the spiritual growth of principles for the unity of the people. But the people's principles have to be intuited, whereas the deeds of self-serving individuals are easily understandable. It appears to be so much easier to identify narrow, self-interested agents precisely because they are narrow and self-interested. They follow a clearly identifiable focus: the specific individual and his advantage. The deeds that transcend that level and serve the higher order of the sovereign people have no such specifiable focus. Once principles are embodied in specific individuals, I would suggest, they become limited by the specific social structure where those individuals move. Hence the ideal principles are circumscribed by those individuals' interests, and become something less than those of the self-creating unity of the people as a totality. The union of rationality and freedom, of nature and history, can only be maintained so long as the will that miraculously combines these contradictions is not specified too closely.

In their writings, the 'republican' historians I have been considering returned to a portrayal of the Revolution in which the public or the people held a central role in the action, as it had done in principle for the revolutionaries themselves. This reverses the way of thinking about the Revolution which had opposed the passion of the people to the rationality of the leadership or the cultural heritage of the few. Idealism in the 'republicans'' view of social reality and a romantic taste in their interests enabled them to pay attention to the people in new ways. They extended the range of their chronology, and broadened the subject matter of their histories, to embrace a larger range of social actors. They accordingly reduced that abstraction in the notion of the public which had appeared in the contemporary portrayals of the Revolution. They identified anonymous masses as historical actors *through* ideal principles which they were said to embody: race; legal and institutional form; social organization and mores peculiar to their culture; religious belief; shared emotions; higher principles motivating their deeds. Michelet, in particular, made the people the unique embodiment of the principle of social harmony.

In brief, the republican historians did not always succeed in portraying the Revolution in their chosen terms. Their stories are often inspiring, but fall short in coherence, with historical entities that remain vague. At one extreme, Michelet places upon the nation the greatest power to act; but he has the greatest difficulty in identifying the underlying principles in historical individuals' actions. It might be said that the later histories recognize the need to give the people an identity in history, but have difficulty specifying the mechanism behind the historical action of a society as a whole. The dynamics of the revolutionaries' own perception of what they were doing is recovered in the republican historians, then; but so, too, is some of the tension between abstract, rational unity and empirical reality.

NOTES

1. Chateaubriand, *Essai sur les révolutions* Et *Génie du christianisme*, ed. M. Regard (Paris: Gallimard, 1978), pt. 2, ch. 40, p. 392.
2. Ibid., ch. 57, pp. 441–8, p. 432n.
3. '. . . se prête merveilleusement aux élans de l'âme, et peut enchanter l'esprit . . .' (Chateaubriand, *Génie*, pt. I, bk 1, ch. 1, p. 470).
4. In a footnote to the remark under note 2, which he added in a later edition of the *Essai*, Chateaubriand adds a crucial inflection to the image of a circular history. Man, he says, prescribes 'des cercles concentriques qui vont en s'élargir . . . dans un espace infini'.
5. See René Debray, *Chronologie de Romantisme* (Paris: Nizet, 1963), ch. 10.
6. Edmund Burke, *Reflections on the Revolution in France*, ed. Conor Cruise O'Brien (Harmondsworth: Penguin, 1968), p. 170.
7. See J.R. Dinwiddy, 'Utility and Natural Law in Burke's Thought: a reconsideration', *Studies in Burke and his Time*, XVI, no. 2 (1974–5); and C.B. MacPherson, *Burke* (Oxford: Oxford University Press, 1980).
8. Scott himself wrote, in language that could as well be found in many of the later historians, that 'the Feudal system of France, like that of the rest of Europe, had, in its original composition, all the germs of national freedom' (Sir Walter Scott, *Life of Napoleon Buonaparte, with a Preliminary View of the French Revolution* (Edinburgh: 1827), vol. 1, p. 63).
9. See Harry E. Shaw *The Forms of Historical Fiction: Sir Walter Scott and his Successors* (Ithaca, NY and London: Cornell University Press, 1983) esp.

ch. 3: Scott, says Shaw, concentrates 'on the forces that bind individuals together in historically distinctive societies' (p. 128).

10. See Duncan Forbes, 'The Rationalism of Sir Walter Scott', *Cambridge Journal*, VII (1953).

11. See D.O. Evans, *Social Romanticism in France* (Oxford: Clarendon, 1951).

12. They were published in book form in 1820–7.

13. 'pénétrer jusqu'aux hommes à travers la distance des siècles; il faut se les représenter vivants et agissants . . . Il y a sept cents ans que ces hommes sont morts . . . mais qu'importe à l'imagination?' (Thierry, *Histoire de la conquête de l'Angleterre par les Normands* (Paris: 1825), quoted in Pierre Moreau, *Le Romantisme* (Paris: Gigard, 1932), p. 137).

14. Thierry, *Lettres sur l'histoire de France* (Paris: Garnier, 1935), pp. 32–3.

15. 'toutes les races d'hommes qui s'y sont mêlées pour produire un la nôtre . . . la diversité primitive de leurs moeurs et leurs idées . . . la décadence graduelle de l'ancienne civilisation, l'oubli croissant de traditions légales, la perte des lumières, l'oppression des pauvres et des faibles . . .' (ibid., pp. 46–7).

16. Ibid., Letters II, VI and VIII.

17. Ibid., Letters XXIII–XXV.

18. 'à la fois les idées de franchises personnelles et de la participation active à la souveraineté municipale' (ibid., p. 431).

19. Ibid., p. 206.

20. Ibid., p. 413.

21. 'ce travail nouveau de l'opinion et de la volonté publique . . . la masse nationale eut senti à fond le néant pour elle d'une restauration de droits historiques' (Thierry, *Essais sur l'histoire du Tiers Etat* (1850; Paris: Furne Jouvet, 1866), p. 259.

22. Thierry, *Lettres*, p. 14.

23. Ibid., p. 18.

24. 'La constitution physique et morale des peuples dépend bien plus de leur descendance et de la race primitive à laquelle ils appartiennent que de l'influence du climat sous lequel le hasard les a placés.' (1824, quoted in P. Moreau, *Le Romantisme*, Paris: de Gigord, 1932, p. 146.)

25. Thierry, *Lettres*, p. 431: 'et ainsi se trouva formé cette immense réunion entreprit, pour la France entière, ce qu'avaient exécuté, dans de simples villes, ses ancêtres du moyen âge. Nous qui la voyons encore, cette société de temps modernes, en lutte avec les débris du passé, débris de conquête, de seigneurie féodale et de royauté absolue, soyons sans inquiétude sur elle . . . elle a vaincu toutes les puissances dont on évoque en vain les ombres.'

26. Lectures delivered in 1828–30 and published as *Histoire de la civilisation en Europe* (Paris: 1828) and *Histoire de la civilisation en France* (Paris: 1829–32); references in my text are to Paris: Didier, 1853, *Histoire de la Civilisation en France depuis la chute de l'empire romain.*

27. See Douglas Johnson, *Guizot: Aspects of French History* (London: Routledge and Kegan Paul; Toronto: University of Toronto Press, 1963), pp. 337–40.

28. Guizot, op. cit., vol. II, Lesson 30.
29. Ibid., p. 81.
30. Ibid., vol. IV, Lessons 16–19.
31. Ibid., vol. III, p. 228.
32. Ibid., vol. IV, Lesson 19.
33. 'la révolution que le siècle dernier a fait éclater est une révolution sociale; il s'est bien occupé de changer la situation réciproque des hommes plus que leurs dispositions intérieures et personnelles; il a voulu réformer la société plutôt que l'individu' (ibid., vol. I, p. 110).
34. Ibid., pp. 22–6.
35. 'civilisation consiste essentiellement dans deux faits: le développement de l'état social, et celui de l'état intellectuel; le développement de la condition extérieure et générale; et celui de la nature intérieure et personnelle de l'homme; en un mot, le perfectionnement de la société et de l'humanité' (ibid., p. 6).
36. Ibid., vol. III, p. 235.
37. 'Nous sommes jetés dans un monde que nous n'avons point créé ni inventée; nous le trouvons, nous le regardons; nous l'étudions: il faut bien que nous le prenions comme un fait . . . Comme acteurs, nous faisons autre chose: quand nous avons observé les faits extérieurs, leur connaissance développe en nous des idées qui leur sont supérieures; nous nous sentons appelés à réformer, à perfectionner, à régler ce qui est: nous nous sentons capables d'agir sur le monde, d'y étendre le glorieux empire de la raison. C'est là le mission de l'homme' (ibid., vol. I, pp. 25–7).
38. 'le caractère permanent, régulier, paisible, de l'état social qui se fonde et s'annonce de toutes parts' (ibid., p. 23).
39. Edgar Quinet, *Le Christianisme et la Revolution* (Brussels: Wonters, 1845), p. 87: 'Le christianisme reste ainsi enfermé dans les tombeaux jusqu'à l'heure de la révolution française, où l'on peut dire qu'il ressuscite, qu'il prend un corps, qu'il se fait, pour la première fois, toucher, palper par les mains des incrédules, dans les institutions et dans le droit vivant.'
40. Ibid., p. 72: 'enfin, les temps modernes ont ajouté, dans l'assemblée constituante, à l'antique *Credo*, la déclaration des droits du genre humain'.
41. Ibid.
42. Ibid., p. 79: 'celui qui connaîtrait, dans ses détails, la formation du dogme, connaîtrait dans son esprit la formation de l'histoire civile et politique. L'humanité moderne est faite comme l'antiquité, à l'image de son Dieu; il n'est rien dans cet idéal suprême que nous ne devions prétendre réaliser un jour dans les institutions et les lois.'
43. François Furet, *La Gauche et la Révolution française au milieu du XIX siècle: Edgar Quinet et la question du Jacobinisme, 1865–70* (Paris: Hachette, 1986), p. 17.
44. Quinet, op. cit., p. 243: 'Audacieuse devant la royauté, l'assemblée constituante hésite devant le catholicisme; elle s'est affranchie au fond

du coeur; elle n'en fait pas l'aveu . . . Le clergé demande une soumission plus explicite. Alors Mirabeau se lève; il s'approche de la fenêtre de la terrasse . . . et il montre de doigt le *palais d'où est parti le signal de la Saint-Barthélemi*. Tout le monde se tait; chacun sent que la France, en ce moment, vient de faire un grand pas.'

45. Ibid., pp. 91–2: 'Nous aussi, nous sommes en des temps où l'on assure que de nouveaux barbares s'approchent de la vieille société. Les voilà, dit-on, déjà au seuil; ils demandent à entrer . . . Que ferions-nous? qui marchera au-devant des nouveaux barbares, comme un nouveau saint Léon? Dirons-nous que le monde va finir? nous dirons qu'il va recommencer une époque nouvelle . . . Que reste-t-il donc à faire? le voici. Etablir la trêve entre la cité de Dieu et la cité de l'homme; réunir l'un et l'autre dans le même principe, agrandir la seconde en y arborant la loi et le droit de la première . . . nous pouvons bâtir une maison de justice, de liberté, assez grande pour nous tous abriter.'

46. See Furet, op. cit., ch. 2. Furet argues that, in the 1860s, Quinet employed the categories of idealist thought to generate a view that was disagreeable to those still attached to a faith in republicanism. His analysis tends, however, to overstate the conceptual differences between the earlier and the later Quinet.

47. Edgar Quinet, *La Révolution*, 6th edn (Paris: 1869), vol. 2, pp. 37–41.

48. Ibid., bk. 21, chs 9, 11, 12 and 14.

49. Ibid., pp. 125–6.

50. Ibid., pp. 127–8: 'Si la nation n'est pas mûre, l'homme qui s'élève au-dessus d'elle périt martyr inconnu, sans laisser de trace. Si le temps n'est pas venu, si le sol n'est pas préparé, la plante qui s'est développée au faîte de son espèce périt étouffée sans postérité.'

51. Ibid., pp. 440.

52. Ibid., pp. 127–8: 'd'autres sont nées dans des conditions meilleures; si une seule a trouvé un milieu convenable, elle a pu produire une révolution végétale et un monde nouveau.'

53. Ibid., p. 439: 'Mais lors même que les âmes sembleraient éteintes ou mortes, faudrait-il désespérer? Nullement. La nature entière proteste et nous enseigne l'espérance en dépit de nous . . . Que sont nos personnes d'un jour, aux prises avec ces personnes colossales, immortelles que l'on appele nations? . . . elles se rient de nous et de nos tristesses, se confiant dans un avenir qu'elles peuvent ajourner sans l'amoindrir.'

54. 'a popularisé les principes de la saine révolution ; . . . Les moyens de se faire lire en bas, en haut . . . C'est de toucher le coeur humain en l'intéressant' (quoted by H. Guillemin, *Lamartine et la question sociale* (Paris: Plon, 1946), ch. 3; see Lamartine, *Histoire des Girondins*, ed. Jacques (Paris: Plon, 1984), p. 25).

55. See Lamartine, op. cit., p. 23.

56. Ibid., p. 29: 'l'histoire d'un petit nombre d'hommes qui, jeté par la Providence au centre du plus grand drame des temps modernes, résument en eux les idées, les passions, les fautes, les vertus d'une époque'.

57. Ibid., p. 31: 'l'image de certains hommes dont le génie pour ainsi dire collectif se modèle sur leur époque et incarne en eux seules toute l'individualité d'une nation'.
58. Ibid., pp. 549–51.
59. Ibid., p. 165.
60. Ibid., pp. 282–3.
61. Ibid., pp. 566–9.
62. Ibid., pp. 857–9.
63. Ibid., p. 29.
64. Ibid., p. 139.
65. Ibid., p. 280: 'les factions règnent . . . un peuple qui ne sait pas prendre et garder tout ce qui lui appartient, tente à la fois la tyrannie et l'anarchie'.
66. Michelet, *Histoire de la Révolution française* (first published 1847–53), vol. 3, bk. 5, ch. 4, the Flammarion edition (Paris: no date), p. 69.
67. Michelet, *History of the French Revolution*, trans. C. Cocks, ed. G. Wright (Chicago: University of Chicago, 1967) p. 120.
68. Ibid., p. 17.
69. Ibid., vol. 2, bk. 4, ch. 12, Flammarion edn.
70. Ibid., trans. C. Cocks, ed. G. Wright, pp. 178–9: 'encore étranger par un sentiment extérieur (à ses yeux) à toute nationalité: étranger de la religion. Pour le Chrétien la patrie est une chose secondaire . . . Les rois ont tous une religion spéciale; ils sont dévoués à la royauté.'
71. Ibid., vol. 3, bk. 5, ch. 6, Flammarion edn.
72. Ibid., vol. 2, bk. 4, ch. 8.
73. Ibid., trans. C. Cocks, ed. G. Wright, p. 399.
74. Ibid., bk. 2, ch. 6, pp. 265–6.
75. Ibid., introd., pt. 1, p. 22.
76. Ibid., introd., pt. 2, p. 42.
77. Ibid., introd., pt. 2.
78. Ibid., introd., pp. 74–8.
79. Ibid., bk. 1, ch. 7, p. 163.
80. Ibid., bk. 1, ch. 7, p. 162.
81. Ibid., bk. 2, ch. 6, p. 266.
82. Ibid., bk. 1, ch. 5, p. 136.
83. Michelet's autobiographical, 1868 preface to the *History of France*, trans. Edward K. Kaplan in his *Michelet's Poetic Vision: a Romantic Philosophy of Nature, Man and Woman* (Amherst: Univ. of Massachusetts, 1977), p. 150. See also Anne R. Pugh, *Michelet and his Ideas on Social Reform* (New York: Columbia University Press, 1923), pp. 69–72.
84. See Linda Orr, *Jules Michelet: Nature, History, Language* (Ithaca, NY: Cornell University Press, 1976); and Kaplan, op. cit.
85. Michelet, op. cit., bk. 1, ch. 7.
86. Ibid., bk. 6, ch. 1, Flammarion edn, p. 3.
87. Ibid., bk. 2, ch. 8, trans. C. Cocks, ed. G. Wright, p. 281.
88. Michelet also criticizes the romantics in *Le Peuple* (ed. P. Viallaneix (Paris: Flammarion, 1974)). But what he finds wrong in them is not

romantic empathy as such. It is their lack of life experience among the people. In Michelet's view, the romantics were consequently prone to see the masses merely as ugly and degraded. 'Les romantiques avaient cru que l'art était surtout dans le laid . . . S'ils étaient descendus eux-mêmes, par leurs souffrances personnelles, dans les profondes réalités de la vie de cette époque, ils auraient vu que la famille, le travail, la plus humble vie du peuple, ont eux-mêmes une poésie sainte' (p. 63). See also the 1868 Preface pp. 159 and 164.

89. Michelet, *Le Peuple*, p. 73.
90. Ibid., pp. 64, 72 and 147.
91. Appendix to Kaplan, op. cit., p. 168.
92. Michelet, op. cit., trans. C. Cocks, ed. G. Wright, p. 80.
93. Michelet, *Le Peuple*, p. 201.
94. Pugh, op. cit., p. 93.
95. Orr, op. cit., pp. 6–7.
96. This particular formulation is given by Paul Vialleneix, 'Les Silences de l'histoire' in P. Vialleneix (ed.), *Michelet cent ans après* (Grenoble: Presses Universitaires de Grenoble, 1975). Linda Orr, op. cit., argues that Michelet's reflections on the 'metamorphosis' of nature into self-creating humanity express his desire to speak for humanity as a whole. He moves to these reflections when his hope of speaking for and arousing the people of France is frustrated. In the end, though, the overall enterprise is lost in the ambivalence of speaking for others *per se*. Roland Barthes, *Michelet* (Paris: Seuil, 1974) refers instead to how Michelet tries to make 'the other' speak in history. The attempt expresses Michelet's hopeless aspiration for the social classes of his day to dissolve into one voice.
97. Michelet, op. cit., bk. 2, ch. 7 and bk. 5, ch. 8.
98. Ibid., bk. 5, ch. 4.
99. Ibid., bk. 2, ch. 7, trans. C. Cocks, ed. G. Wright, p. 270.
100. Ibid., bk. 2, ch. 6. p. 266.
101. Ibid., bk. 6, ch. 5.
102. Ibid., bk. 17, ch. 2.
103. Ibid., bk. 3, ch. 9, trans. C. Cocks, ed. G. Wright, p. 415.
104. Ibid., bk. 5, ch. 8, Flammarion edn, p. 141: 'il fallait un coup de vigueur qui lui rendît force en la faisant croire forte encore. Cela ne pouvait se faire sans une émeute, sans la victoire sur une émeute. Les royalistes aux Tuileries, les constitutionels à l'Assemblée, la désireraient certainement.'

CHAPTER SIX

Perspectives on Social Stability and Transformation

This chapter moves from histories of the Revolution to nineteenth-century theoretical accounts of it. The historians took a longitudinal view, in which the Revolution was the fruition − or frustration − of some long-term movement in French society. Those thinkers I call 'theorists', on the other hand, are of interest for their ideas on how, in general, a society remains stable or undergoes transformation. Any such 'theorists' in the nineteenth century were acutely aware of the historical fact of the Revolution. Their discussions of change referred to it and attempted to grasp its character. Taken all in all, their discussions give us a sense of the range of positions that are available in order to understand social transformation as epitomized by the Revolution. In this chapter, I will be considering those discussions.

Of course, though they are not historians, these thinkers pursued their ideas in the same historical context. They can be divided into five groups, or schools of thought, falling into a very approximate time sequence. They follow a trajectory comparable to that of the historians. They began from a position that is profoundly at odds with the Revolution's optimism about deliberate, conscious change by the nation or the people. The principal aim of Burke and the counter-revolutionary polemicists was to show how such social change was simply beyond the scope of human agency. The later schools, however, usually acknowledged some long-term evolution which made change possible, or even inevitable. Their differences arise because they situate the dynamic of evolution at different levels. They postulate an ideal moral growth; or they trace a cultural development; or they identify socio-economic processes in tension with political ones.

Having critically examined the thinkers in each of these groups, I return to the issue that embraces both them and those involved in the

Revolution itself: the extent to which a body of self-determining social agents can promote deliberate social transformation. The culture of the Revolution (and its difficulties) centred on this issue. To consider the 'theorists'' response to it charts the distance they travelled from the thinking – and the conceptual difficulties – of the revolutionaries. It also permits an assessment of whether there are answers available to give a coherent account of the role of human agents in the Revolution.

COUNTER-REVOLUTIONARY POLEMICISTS: CONSTRAINTS BEYOND THE SCOPE OF POLITICS

At the very moment that groups involved in the Revolution were fighting, each according to their own model, to establish a new political order, there were those who opposed it root and branch. From the sidelines, the 'counter-revolutionaries' set about showing that the entire enterprise could not possibly succeed. The revolutionaries' projects were essentially political: through a political reconstruction, they aimed to put into effect universal principles for a rational society. In addition, some held that, due to the evolution of contemporary French society, this was the best historical moment to realize those principles. By contrast, the counter-revolutionaries drew on ideas of overwhelming forces and constraints from outside the political realm, arguing that these were at odds with the direction proclaimed by the politics of the Revolution.

The argument of Burke's *Reflections on the Revolution in France* was precisely along those lines. He enlarged the range of factors in the life of a society that could in principle contribute to the character of the political order, and to its continuance. Burke claimed that, whereas the English of 1688 had undertaken a modest improvement, the French of 1789 were attempting an impossible reconstruction. The power of Burke's argument lies in the possibility that unnoticed factors in the character of a society will undermine the projects of political reconstruction.

Burke eulogized England's political inertia,[1] which is, according to him, the source of her political and social vigour. He points up the importance of numerous unthought-out customs and habits of mind. Quite at odds with the spirit of the Enlightenment, he even grants a useful role to prejudice.[2] These various elements originating in society constrain politics from outside. Who, following the logic of Burke's argument, can know before attempting to transform the social order,

161

which elements in social life are constitutive of it? Any of those elements may be vital to the survival of the entire society. The consequent risk involved in any political reform is stated most explicitly in a passage from the *Appeal from the New to the Old Whigs*, where Burke defines the essence of a people as a corporation. A people, he states, is an artificial entity, created by a common accord with quite particular form and character.

> A number of men in themselves have no collective capacity. The idea of a people is the idea of a corporation. It is wholly artificial; and made like all other legal fictions by common agreement. What the particular nature of the agreement was is collected from the form into which the particular society is cast. Any other is not *their* convention. When men, therefore, break up the original compact or agreement, which gives its corporate form and capacity to a state, they are no longer a people . . . Alas! they little know how many a weary step is to be taken before they can form themselves into a mass, which has a true politick personality.[3]

In short, Burke portrays a social world in which many mysterious powers beyond the grasp of politics preserve stability and cohesion.

To broaden the range of elements essential to the nature of society, as Burke does, makes revolutionary politics impossible. It is absurd to reconstitute the state on the basis of general, abstract principles which are foreign to the particular character of the state in question. Likewise, it is impossible to reformulate a social contract from scratch. If Burke is right, any founding principles – a contract, for example – must embrace past, present and future generations – not to mention uniting our lower and higher natures.[4] The task of founding a new order cannot be entrusted to the new political class in the Assembly, as the Revolution did in 1789. Jurisprudence gathers its wisdom slowly, says Burke, mixing 'the original principles of justice' with numerous 'human preoccupations'. So the maintenance of the law requires 'the most delicate and complicated skill', which 'is not taught *a priori*'.[5] Skilful action on the political level can guide human society to a limited extent, but cannot reconstitute it. In general, human beings must accept inherited social practices and surrender to the mysterious forces and obligations which maintain social life.[6] Any political programme aiming to go beyond these limits is absurd. Democracy above all is 'shameful', because it accords to the people a freedom of action and an authority which ought only to be exercised in 'trust to the one great master, author and founder of society'.[7]

Although they are hard to alter, the factors that Burke refers to outside the political sphere are substantial social institutions, such as legal conventions or the given practice and functioning of the Church. It appears that French counter-revolutionaries, by contrast, did not have the option of falling back on the power of pre-existing social reality. They were faced with the sudden and complete disappearance of all established social institutions. Hence the emphasis in their thinking on a cosmic Providence, directed by God.

Abbé Barruel, indeed, explains the collapse of all the institutions of the *ancien régime* — social, religious and political — as the punitive will of the Almighty.[8] In Barruel's view, God wanted the ruling classes of the *ancien régime*, who had been subverted by philosophical and materialist ideas, to be faithful to their own principles. Hence, he claims — ingeniously — that the revolutionary crisis, far from demonstrating the bankruptcy of the *ancien régime*, shows how God himself sanctions its existence in the long term. The revolutionaries' victory is temporary: merely God's scheme to purify the regime that He loves. By reference to a force outside all the existing political and social reality, Barruel preserves a sacred right and inevitability for the defeated *ancien régime*.

Writing shortly after the Terror, de Maître makes the providential will of God still more cosmic — not to say sinister.[9] According to him, though the history of the human race has been marked by violence and destruction, these are nothing less than God's own devices to realize his ultimate order. Periods of social revolution are a sort of miracle, when God, in order to reach his long-term goal, sets aside the accepted rules of the social order. By their sufferings, God is punishing the French and training them in preparation for the future reimposition of the monarchy by the use of 'invincible Nature'.[10] The religious tone of de Maître, like that of Barruel, expresses a mystical, God-fearing response to the upheaval of the Revolution. It is a spirit that, with the terms changed, reappeared in Chateaubriand.

Jacques Mallet du Pan also appealed to forces outside politics.[11] But, by contrast, his thinking was relatively realist. Certainly, du Pan likens the Revolution, dramatically, to the historic cataclysm that took place with the destruction of Roman civilization by the barbarians. And, once again, the outcome is beyond the will of the political agents involved. On the other hand, his analysis accounts for events in terms of real political and social mechanisms. He describes how Europe-wide impoverishment, poisoning social relations, has produced a general militarization and then a war. In due course, he argues (prophetically), the war will destroy the very revolutionary regime that has had recourse to it. Du Pan was the counter-revolutionary writer with the highest hopes for benign intervention from a quite terrestrial source. He advocated an alliance of European powers to restore France to order and return her to the family of European monarchies.

Overall, these counter-revolutionary writers, by referring to factors or forces outside the political realm, threw into relief how limited are the powers of human beings to direct revolutionary change. In each case, a force beyond conscious human will is turning the course of the Revolution towards an outcome quite different from that envisaged by those nominally in control. In a profound sense, politically-directed change appears impossible.

PROGRESSIVE GERMAN IDEALISM: KANT, FICHTE AND HEGEL

In Germany, where Burke's organicist thinking was particularly well received,[12] the authorities held political change firmly at bay during the period of the Revolution. The appeal to forces beyond the political realm appeared there, not in opposition to revolutionary aspirations, but in support of them. They refer to an ontological level not only beyond politics, but beyond the real world altogether – to the transcendental world of the rational spirit seeking its own ideal nature. This transcendental world guarantees the direction of change in the empirical world.

Kant's remarks on the Revolution in 1798 indicate, albeit briefly, the progressive idealists' strategy.[13] Kant grounds his case on the sentiments felt by those outside France at the sight of the Revolution. In his view, it is part of an effort to perfect humanity. Whether the present Revolution succeeds or not, he argues, responses abroad indicate a profound enthusiasm for the ideal. One day, this enthusiasm will transform human history. It demonstrates that reason can recognize and follow pure morality. In Kant's view, pointers like this underpin a distinctive, *philosophical* knowledge of law and liberty. This licenses the *philosophical* prediction that Kant makes: that the task undertaken by the French Revolution will some day be taken over by the broader evolution of humanity as a world-wide union.

This strategy absorbs given historical realities into another history. This latter history is surer than the one known from observations of humans in the past, to which we give the name 'history'. Called 'anthropology' in Kant's terminology, it is founded on the notion that the human race perfects itself. Come what may at the empirical level, the struggle for perfection remains a firm, even a predictable fact on the transcendental level. Viewed on that level, the Revolution in France is merely an imperfect case of a greater evolution towards perfection. The French Revolution as it actually occurred is taken over and turned into a moment in another history, operating on the transcendental level. By raising our sights towards the ideal, Kantian idealism diminishes the weight of all the shortcomings in the empirical world, where political change is actually pursued.

Whereas Kant's tone in support of the Revolution was measured, his disciple, Fichte, went to far greater lengths. His *Considerations on the French Revolution* (1793) uses Kant's philosophical strategy in an explicit defence of the Revolution against the attacks of German critics. But while the political position is explicit, the text makes barely any precise reference to the revolutionary events that were taking place as Fichte was writing. Fichte declares that it is Kant's philosophical 'revolution', rather than 1789, which has been the greatest creative act accomplished by the human spirit.[14] He then sets about a painstaking exposition, in the Kantian manner, of the means by which it is possible to attain pure principles for judging political change in general. The Revolution itself is pushed into second place: it is merely a 'striking picture for those with the weakest insight'.[15] As with Kant, the work of the empirical historian is set aside because it deals only with the past, the 'childhood' of the human race. To judge an event like a revolution properly we need instead the work of the philosopher, together with the 'laws of experience' which are written in the human heart, and which constitute 'an empirical psychology'.[16] Once he has set out the rules to judge historical events, Fichte seeks to demonstrate the right, indeed the obligation, of a people to change its constitution as the French have done. The crucial defence of such an act is that the change advances the unique human privilege of 'infinitely perfecting itself' by realizing the 'culture of liberty'.[17]

In this argument, the actual political struggles have once again been displaced from centre-stage by forces beyond the level where political action takes place. In idealism, political acts are related to a transcendental level. Idealism meets the force of the counter-revolutionaries' strategy quite effectively. For it, too, moves on to a level opposed to and outside the control of present politics. But, unlike those extra-political forces summoned up by the counter-revolutionary writers, these forces are human. They are transcendent potentialities of the conscious human spirit. Hence, they are even present, in some sense, in the actions of those involved in the Revolution. And they make progressive historical change inevitable, so that the purposes of the Revolution are bound to be realized in due course. So, the philosopher, referring to an alternative transcendent level of reality, speaks for a human race that contains within itself the transcendent spirit of perfectibility which inspired the Revolution. The idealists reformulated, on their transcendent level, the confidence in historical change which the actual outcome of the Revolution had undermined.

Though, all told, as much critic as supporter of the Revolution, Hegel pursues the same kind of defence. Overall, his philosophy inserts the ideal certainty about historical destiny into the empirical social world. His support for the Revolution waxed and waned in the course of his career as he struggled to integrate a rational direction into history. But he did maintain an optimism that the Revolution was a historic point of departure for a new sort of political progress.[18]

Hegel was critical of one central notion of the Revolution; namely, of the rationality of constituting the state on an abstract idea of the nature of mankind (or, in the Kant–Fichte version, an abstract idea of its future destiny). According to Hegel, this sort of politics is founded on the sovereignty of individuals, in the manner of Rousseau. Because the will of the individual is ranked as a 'general' will in Rousseau's sense – equivalent in worth to the will of the state – it can be transposed directly on to the will of the state. In the Revolution, therefore, abstraction had overturned the state in the name of pure thought:

> when these abstract conclusions came into power, they afforded for the first time in human history the prodigious spectacle of the overthrow of the constitution of a great actual state and its complete reconstruction *ab initio* on the basis of pure thought alone, after the destruction of all existing and given material. The will of its re-founders was to give it what they alleged was a purely rational basis, but it was only abstractions that were being used; the Ideal was lacking; and the experiment ended in the maximum of frightfulness and terror.[19]

Hegel, for his part, advocated a rationality which would integrate transcendent abstraction in the development of social practices and legal institutions in the historical world. In Judith Shklar's words, what he thought was needed was a 'scheme of juristic society as the integrative political order of independent men'.[20] The forces outside politics, which opponents and idealist defenders of the Revolution drew upon, would be reintegrated into the political realm. Hegel sustained an optimistic view of historical progress with a *history* of consciousness, or 'Spirit', in which the Revolution had a central place. The history of Spirit demonstrated how the transcendent ideal was being realized in social institutions. It relocated the Revolution in a larger chronology, like that of some later French theorists and idealist historians, with the Reformation as its crucial moment. This also removed the focal point of history from France to Germany[21] – as Kant and Fichte had implicitly done.

Positive accounts of future political prospects and judgements on particular regimes appear later in Hegel's writing.[22] The sixth chapter of *Phenomenology of Spirit* (1807) gives the essential problematic for the history of Spirit as it concerns the Revolution. According to the *Phenomenology*,[23] the culture of modern society is that of a world that is conscious of itself. The inner tensions of that culture appear in three historical moments. Arbitrary absolute monarchy conflicts with the individualistic (i.e. the market) economy. Meanwhile, consciousness of self is alienated by the idea of it that the Enlightenment advocates. Only then – the third historical moment – is anarchy unleashed by the 'revolutionary self' of the French Revolution. So the Revolution embodies a contradiction born long before, in the Enlightenment and in the atomization of society into individuals. Human consciousness has been conceived in isolation from all social institutions and lacked rationality in the sense that Hegel advocated. Hence, an idea of liberty arose which was adapted to individuals abstracted from society: 'universal' but empty. In Hegel's view, this 'freedom' underwrote the Terror. Having no links to the real world, it could only promote acts of destruction. First, it destroyed given social organization, and then it turned on individual human individuals – that is, it turned on rivals for power.

Where does Hegel's view leave social change and stability? In spite of being critical, it broadened and deepened the idealist defence of the Revolution and of social change. Jacob Ritter advances two key elements in his exegesis of Hegel's view.[24] Firstly, Hegel believed that humankind's relationship with its own history had been fundamentally transformed by the Revolution. Secondly, because of this, philosophy can, according to Hegel, advance a fresh account of political and social liberty for the future. In spite of the setback, humankind can now participate in making its own history. In Hegel's view, the argument runs, the Revolution definitively overturned the sanction of tradition and custom.[25] For it derived the social order from first, 'natural' principles. That is a historic transformation in humankind's manner of comprehending and organizing their world. In Hegel's words, 'the entire mass of former representations and concepts, the bond of the world', collapsed.[26] From then on, the guiding concepts and representations of the social world must come through the activity of thought. But what made the Revolution, in Hegel's terms, 'world-historical' was that it brought self-consciousness into historical reality.[27] Philosophy therefore has a new and crucial relationship to the modern, post-revolutionary world. It is now needed in order to apprehend the truths that are fundamental to its own time.[28] According to Hegel, the Revolution bequeathed the contemporary age no political order. Philosophy must therefore provide the age with a response to the chronic, destructive negativity in the will of individual agents.[29] But it can do so: with a defence of the Revolution which reveals how its pursuit of self-emancipation derives from the transcendental Ideal.[30]

Social change is also implicit more broadly in Hegel's philosophy. This is a source of both strength and weakness. On the one hand, change appears to be inevitable, because all empirical determinations of Spirit are limited in scope. By treating social institutions and forms of thought dialectically, Hegel perpetually shows how their defining boundaries make them unstable and unsatisfactory. He then analyses change on three social levels of empirical society: the economic, the intellectual and the institutional. Furthermore, the direction of change, inherent in the transcendental Ideal, guarantees that a new and more comprehensive integration of consciousness will come about. In short, the Ideal underwrites the process of social change. That is the significance of Hegel's dictum that everything which is real is also rational. Whatever is truly substantial and likely to survive in the empirical world must, Hegel maintains, be coherent in terms of the dynamics of consciousness which he has analysed on the ideal level. So Hegel establishes that social transformation is both necessary and safe. On the other hand, he then takes it to be so many manifestations of the Ideal. At bottom, both the transformation and the stability of the human world are motivated by a dynamic from beyond not only the political world, but the empirical world in its entirety.

CONDORCET TO COMTE:
THE REVOLUTION AND INTELLECTUAL PROGRESS

A group of French thinkers grounded a measured optimism in long-term cultural evolution. Like the later French historians and the

German idealists, they took the Revolution as an event which, though it had turned out badly, none the less belonged to a benign progress in the long term. Long-term evolution could dissolve society, but it could also establish a post-revolutionary regime that would be sound and suitable for the modern world. These thinkers situate the dynamic of change in the growth of knowledge, or of culture more generally. For them, the Revolution was a product of the historical movement springing from these levels of society. Condorcet (whom I considered in Chapter 3) and the *idéologues* saw intellectual life as the source of the collapse, but also of possible progress. Later, Saint-Simon and Comte identified a historical dynamic operating *between* intellectual life and broader social organization − that is, since the fifteenth century, the commercial economy. For collapse to be followed by benign change, intellectual life had to be better adapted to social organization. By proposing a wider-ranging dynamic for social change, these thinkers approached the breadth of the idealist account.

At the very moment when the regime of the Revolution he had fostered was pursuing him, Condorcet invented the theoretical strategy that could reassure progressively-minded intellectuals. He deduced benign evolution from a scientific law which had been, to his mind, evident in history since the advent of Cartesianism. It is that a human is 'an intelligent being, able to develop chains of reasoning and acquire moral ideas'.[31] Since the seventeenth century, then, 'human reason' can be seen 'forming slowly through the natural progress of civilization'.[32] The greatest source of hope for the future of humankind is therefore the influence of learning and science 'on the rightness of people's minds'. Above all else, the increasing and increasingly widespread grasp of knowledge serves human progress: it 'is of truly universal usefulness'.[33] As Condorcet describes things, a slow historical transformation originates in the intellectual life of society, and embraces the present revolution in a hidden progress.

Under the Directory, the *idéologues*[34] recovered Condorcet's work and revived his line of thought. They were an extensive body of teachers and thinkers who gathered around the educational and scientific institutions of the Directorial regime of 1796–9. They aimed to promote intellectual progress of the type postulated by Condorcet. To their minds, a political and pedagogic programme could ensure that the progressive achievements of the Revolution would survive. They were therefore concerned with the analysis of the growth of knowledge and the training of citizens' minds. For them, the change Condorcet saw originating in intellectual life became not merely a historical framework, but an active force. If properly managed, it was capable of intervening in the Revolution. They put forward a more detailed account than Condorcet's of the relations between pure ideas, intellectual life, and institutions of public education which circulate ideas. For intellectual advance can be managed, and revolutionary change can be cultivated.

Destutt de Tracy, author of the movement's seminal *Eléments d'idéologie*, set out the revoutionary inspiration of their programme. In 1795, under threat of execution, de Tracy imagined analysis as a programme to save the direction of the Revolution.

> In the future, I will always begin from this point . . . The product of the faculty of thought or perceiving = knowledge = truth. In a second work on which I am working, I show that one should add three other terms to this equation: = virtue = happiness = sentiment of loving; and in a third I will prove that one should add these: = liberty = equality = philanthropy.[35]

A properly developed intellectual evolution, then, would promote the emotional and moral unity which the nation lacked. De Tracy and the *idéologues* took up what the Revolution aspired to — a united, active public — through a more analytical programme. The transformative aims of the Revolution could come about in a different time-scale, on the basis of underlying intellectual progress.

From the start of a bizarre career as writer and self-styled prophet, Saint-Simon was concerned with the role of intellectual life in the Revolution. For him, however, intellectual life in modern France could bring about *either* a collapse *or* a recovery. Which it would be depended on the relationship with the demands of production. In *Les Considérations sur les mesures à prendre pour terminer la Révolution* (1820), for example, he attacked the educated professional classes for not matching up to the responsibilities they had acquired in the Revolution. *Le Catéchisme des industriels* (1823) explained how their failure came about. In 1789, power was seized on behalf of a professional class rising with social development. But that class was not close enough to the most fundamental basis of legitimacy in modern society — the production of material goods — so the Revolution was blown off course. To establish a sound post-revolutionary regime, power had to be in the hands of those involved in industrial production — the 'industrials'.

Behind these proposals about the political position of one class or another, there is a new conception of the dynamic of social change which gave rise to the Revolution. The dominance of a given body of intellectuals or a given way of thinking is not necessarily, as the *idéologues* had contended, an adequate means to foster social change. Intellectual development, though it is a *force* for change, is legitimate only if it is in accord with the true foundation of social progress in more fundamental activities. There is a dynamic of change from within society; but it operates on two levels: the intellectual and the economic. It is possible for these two levels of society's existence to go amiss, or to be in conflict with each other. That was what happened in 1789.

In *Le Nouveau christianisme*, (1825) Saint-Simon describes the ideology needed for modern, industrial society; that is to say, the course of development intellectual life ought to adopt. Since the fifteenth century, he maintains, the growth of Europe has biased culture. The preoccupation with individual interests and particular facts has impeded social cohesion. Though this preoccupation is essential for material progress, it is not adequate for fusing humans into a society:

> the human spirit has detached itself from the most general viewpoint; it has given itself over to specialities; it has concerned itself with the analysis of particulars, of the private interests of the different classes of society; it has worked to lay down the secondary principles to serve as the basis for the different branches of knowledge. During this second period [of history], the opinion gained ground that general concerns, on general principles or the general interests of the human race, were just vague metaphysical matters and could not contribute effectively to the progress of enlightenment or the perfection of civilization.[36]

The dynamic of social transformation arises in economic organization. This is also the basis for legitimacy. Yet, it may in itself distort cultural life, which is also necessary for a successful transformation of society. Saint-Simon concludes that, for social harmony to be achieved following the Revolution, there needs to be a new religion. The cultural level of society has to step in to compensate for a distortion produced by economic organization.

Saint-Simon shares with Hegel and many later thinkers an idea of why society dissolved in the Revolution. Society, according to them, was atomized into individuals lacking the necessary sense of common values. The new faith (which Saint-Simon's disciples, 'Saint-Simonians', were to evangelize after his death) would spread general ideas of the social good, that were in harmony with the dominance of industrial production.

Comte's work, two decades later, amounts to a more systematic version of Saint-Simon's perspective. For Comte, the Revolution represented the inevitable crisis or 'critical' period that brings any era of history to an end. In the case of the Revolution, it was the crisis in the second of the three great eras of world history: the 'metaphysical' era. But the Revolution was a fruitful crisis, because it belonged to a benign overall progress. As Saint-Simon had also held, the evolution of thought had undone the social order. But this would certainly give way to a renewed order in the future, and to a new kind of thought.

Immediately prior to the Revolution, according to Comte, individuals had been deprived of the authority of religion and common values.[37] They were vainly searching in metaphysics for the coherence they needed in their social world. Three forms of metaphysical deism (each sketched out by one of the three great geniuses of the Enlightenment: Voltaire, Diderot and Rousseau) were leading towards social breakdown.[38] The three great political orientations in conflict in the Revolution (Girondin, Dantonist and Montagnard, respectively) followed these deisms. But they were quite incapable of producing the sort of synthesis needed for social unity.[39]

In Comte's thinking, the tendency towards social change derives from a dynamic on the same social levels as for Saint-Simon: socio-economic organization and culture, plus the relationship between them. But, there are differences. Comte is more systematic. And, whereas Saint-Simon describes a political conjuncture in which the participants simply adopted a mistaken political course, Comte turns the Revolution into a moment in the emergence of inevitable contradictions. He emphasizes a destructive dynamic operating on the socio-economic and cultural levels. Disorder arises because cultural life is not up to the demands of social organization:

> Organic evolution being unable to satisfy the needs made evident in the critical movement, social upheaval became inevitable, and became all the more indispensable in order to procure a decisive extension and a wider diffusion for regenerative conceptions.[40]

For Comte, a revival of social order would, however, follow from the seriousness of the upheaval. An ideology would grow up that was better able to supply 'regenerative conceptions'. This is Comte's term for that antidote to the failure of the Revolution which is advocated by all the thinkers in this school. In Comte's case, regeneration would come from his own system, for which he coined the name 'Sociologie'.

POLITICS VERSUS SOCIETY: DE TOCQUEVILLE

De Tocqueville's *The Ancien Régime and the Revolution* (1856) looks rather like a history. But it is really a work of political sociology. Its very shape indicates where de Tocqueville sees the dominant force in the Revolution. Rather than the course of events, de Tocqueville describes at length the strategy pursued by the *ancien régime* to centralize power and suppress all centres of resistance. De Tocqueville is expounding a theoretical account of the Revolution, in which the dynamic for change exists in a dialectic between political and social structures. Saint-Simon anticipated one version of this dynamic: that in which the forces for change arise in economic development and impose revolution upon the political system. I will return to that version in the socialist or Marxian development of Saint-Simonian ideas. De Tocqueville's uniquely original version identifies a form of society fostered by the state itself, which distorts the aspirations towards change in society at large.

The state proceeds ingeniously. It gives individual members of society the *impression* that they are independent. In due course, they lose the capacity to combine in mutual defence against the central power or to be involved in public affairs.[41] This is de Tocqueville's perspective on social atomization. But in his case, the trend originates in the centralization of the state, rather than in society at large.

The Revolution itself is also largely the outcome of misguided action by the state. From the middle of the eighteenth century, the absolutist state adopted public-spirited aims: to reform the administration and better the condition of the less privileged. This coincided with the growth of a reforming impulse in society at large. The authorities disseminated a new esteem for the interests of the whole; that is, the belief that the 'nation as a whole has sovereign rights, while the individual citizen was kept in the strictest tutelage'.[42] But the state's new posture was actually promoting dissent. By 'championing the cause of the underprivileged', they also 'made them acutely conscious of their wrongs'.[43] Paradoxically, then, the state generated its own downfall — giving rise to de Tocqueville's oft-cited dictum that

it is not always when things are going from bad to worse that revolutions break out. On the contrary, it more often happens that when a people which has put up with an oppressive rule over a long period without protest suddenly finds the government relaxing its pressure, it takes up arms against it.[44]

The state itself was at the root of the 'rankling discontent' and hostility to the past[45] that was to inspire the Revolution.

The net effect of all the changes which absolutism has encouraged in society is this. French society had a strong impulse to change in the direction of equality — which, according to de Tocqueville, is characteristic of the modern world. But it was incapable of exercising over itself the necessary free government. The old nobility, who had possessed the capacity to resist central authority, had been largely undermined. The peasantry, on the other hand, had been encouraged. The impulse in the direction of change came, therefore, from both embittered illiterates and men of letters, giving 'free rein to their imagination'.[46] The surviving capacity for joining in a free government briefly asserted itself; but it was shallow. Soon, society reverted to that expectation which administrative centralization had taught: that the state will ride roughshod over individual members of society in pursuit of the public good. The people seized the central power to pursue its inhuman urges to revenge. Then, in due course, Napoleon took up where the old centralized government had left off.

In de Tocqueville's political sociology, modern society does have an independent tendency to demand self-government and equality. These do not always produce the consequences they did in France. *Democracy in America* (1835) describes a more benign outcome. But the impact of public institutions on society is again the key factor. In America, de Tocqueville makes clear, they have fostered political participation.[47] What is more, state institutions have so little power that errors by the people can have little real impact.[48]

In the European context, on the other hand, 'the legislators conceived the imprudent project of destroying . . . rather than instructing and correcting, and, without wishing to teach [the people] to govern, they thought of nothing but distancing [power] from the government'.[49]

In effect, then, the governments of the centuries before the Revolution were able to pass down an acceptance of centralized power, which could, as by inertia, determine the overall direction of the Revolution. Hence, in his notes, de Tocqueville comments on 'the powerlessness of any man or men in particular at the start of the Revolution and so long as its own drive lasted'.[50] In sum, according to de Tocqueville's account, the Revolution arises from a dynamic between society and the state. But it was the state, in the final analysis that had determined the kind of political demands society would make.

SOCIETY VERSUS POLITICS: FRENCH SOCIALISTS AND MARX

Whereas de Tocqueville's work in the 1850s indicated an inertia directing the Revolution, socialist writers preferred to see 1789 as an *incomplete* revolution. It stood in need of a second, complementary struggle for social transformation. To support this position, in due course, they developed the economic explanations of the Revolution found in such earlier accounts as those of Barnave and Saint-Simon. This economic view, which gave pre-eminence to the dynamic between society and the state, gradually extended from the conceptual range of utopian socialist writers of the 1830s, such as Philippe Buonarroti or Etienne Cabet.

Certainly, Buonarroti's influential and highly discursive account (published in 1828) of Babeuf's egalitarian conspiracy of 1796, hardly reflected economic terms of analysis. He identified economic forces with industrialization, as commended (to his mind) by English political economy. In opposition to that, he favoured Rousseau and Mably's 'French' perspective, which centred on the love of virtue rather than money.[51] In the Revolution, this perspective was represented by Robespierre, Marat and Saint-Just, who attempted to promote the moral growth of the nation.[52] Yet virtue naturally belongs to the poor and uncorrupted people. Buonarroti relates their victories against the 'egoist' party (in invading the legislature), and their final defeat by the 'conspiracy', funded by foreign money, which unseated Robespierre. Through such explicit voluntarism, Buonarroti bequeathed a romantic moralism and a demonology of the Revolution.

Cabet's *Histoire populaire de la Révolution française* (1839) employed political categories – or even possibly Kantian moral ones – rather than economic ones. For him, the united French people are a model of 'the upward march of the nations towards happiness and liberty'.[53] In his history, the course of events in the Revolution was determined by the conflict between the political demands of the people and the resistance of the aristocracy and the monarchy. Even the aristocracy's opposition to reform is not so profoundly rooted in society as not to be susceptible to reform. The unhealthy education of the *ancien régime*, Cabet believed, had formed them as they were. These views remain essentially within the perspective of Jacobinism, which maintained that the transformation of society could be achieved by moral reconstitution.

There is, however, an economic category at the centre of Proudhon's analysis – though it is simply the degree of hardship experienced by the people. His *Idée générale de la révolution dans le 19me siècle* (1851), written during a period of republican government (and hence political ascendancy for the Left), presented 'revolution', in 1789 and since, as an irresistible force, arising from the cry of the people against poverty. The state had to tame this force lest it were overturned by it. According to Proudhon, it was the conflict between the people and the monarchy that provoked 1789. So the actions of the Revolution itself are understood in terms quite similar to Cabet's. Yet they did originate from an economic source. Thus, to avoid a repetition of 1789, Proudhon advocated a programme of economic change (à la Saint-Simon) which would bring the state under the interests of the industrial economy.

We can expect that Marx would offer an account of the Revolution where a dynamic relationship between society and the state would be articulated through social classes in conflict. A fairly simple interpretation of the Revolution in such terms is contained in some other bald statements from the classics of the 1840s. According to *The Communist Manifesto*, the Revolution 'abolished feudal property in favour of bourgeois property'.[54] In *The German Ideology*, he writes that the French bourgeoisie, in 'the most colossal revolution that history has ever known, was achieving domination'.[55]

The interplay between classes and forms of property is explained more fully in an article of 1848:

> In 1789 the bourgeoisie was allied with the people against the monarchy, the nobility and the established church . . .
>   . . . the bourgeoisie was the class that *really* formed the van of movement. The *proletariat* and *the strata of the burghers which did not belong to the bourgeoisie* either had as yet no interests separate from those of the bourgeoisie or they did not yet constitute independently developed classes . . .
>   . . . The bourgeoisie was victorious in these revolutions [in England and in France]; but the *victory of the bourgeoisie* was at that time the *victory of a new order of society*, the victory of bourgeois property over feudal property, of nationality over provincialism, of competition over the guild, of partition over primogeniture, of the owner of the land over the domination of the owner by the land, of enlightenment over superstition, of the family over the family name, of industry over heroic laziness, of civil law over mediaeval privilege.[56]

It appears that the bourgeoisie promoted first the Revolution (with some help from rival classes), and then the political structure which the Revolution created for society. In the political struggle, the new dominant social class obtained power over the state, and used that power to advance a transformation of society along lines agreeable to it.

The Revolution is, therefore, the product of tension between society and the political set-up. Social and political transformation originates in society, whence a newly dominant class has emerged to force change upon both state and society itself. They are a conscious medium through which society imposes the change it needs in the political and social regime. The idea that a dynamic between the bourgeoisie and the state underlay the Revolution, has organized much modern Marxist historical writing.[57]

Yet, even from Marx's earliest thoughts on the Revolution, the position is more complicated. The tension between society and politics has a dynamic independent of classes. For one thing, though the bourgeoisie is the agent promoting the social transformation, it is itself the product of a prior social transformation. Secondly, from the tone of Marx's remarks above, it is clear that the transformation wrought by the Revolution achieves historical progress over and above the mere interests of the bourgeoisie. The bourgeoisie are the servants of a greater movement. (Indeed, Marx believed it would push them aside in due course.) Thirdly, Marx argues that the political and legal order which the bourgeoisie created in the Revolution is riven with contradiction. As he puts it in *The German Ideology*:

> liberal private property-owners, at the beginning of the French Revolution gave private property a liberal appearance by declaring it one of the rights of man. They were forced to do so if only because of their position as a revolutionising party; they were even compelled not only to give the mass of the French (rural) population the right to property, but also to let them *seize actual* property, and they could do all this because thereby their own 'how much', which was what chiefly interested them, remained intact and was even made safe.[58]

For all these reasons it seems, therefore, that from as early as the 1840s, Marx believed that fundamentally the bourgeoisie were *not* the masters of the historical situation in the Revolution — even if they appeared free and dominant agents.[59]

As political realities around Marx changed in the middle of the century, he seems to have felt even more that the opposed classes in the Revolution could be embroiled in forces beyond them — even where they themselves have generated the forces in question. The resurgence of revolutionary bourgeois republicanism in the late 1840s, followed by its demise in the face of Napoleon III's dictatorship, suggested precisely this. The defeat undermined any earlier impression of the bourgeoisie's unchallengeable political dominance. Accordingly, in *The Eighteenth Brumaire of Louis Bonaparte*, written in 1851–2, Marx turned a more jaundiced eye on the independent power of the bourgeoisie. Now he stressed the inexorable growth of the state following the 1789 Revolution. 'The task of the first French Revolution', he says, had been 'to destroy all separate, local, territorial, urban and provincial powers in order to create the civil unity of the nation . . . to carry further the centralization that the absolute monarchy had begun'.[60] This trend (the same, of course, as de Tocqueville had placed at the centre of his thesis) had swallowed up independent bourgeois political power in 1799 – as in 1852.

For Marx, the bourgeoisie does not have a free hand in making the Revolution. The outcomes are not altogether in its grasp: the dynamic between society and politics produces something independent of its will. At bottom this is because of the contradictory nature of social unity which the bourgeois revolution has to seek, so as to counter the atomization of society into class-bound individuals. Though his explanation of the nature and origin of atomization is distinct, throughout his career, Marx understood this dialectically. To that extent, he remained within the terms set by Hegel. The Revolution meant the political arrival of individualist or bourgeois society, trying to escape its inherent limitations through a political structure which claimed to constitute social unity. On this account, Marx does not explain the Revolution so much as a transformation imposed by one class of society on the political structure. Rather, it is the process by which complex tensions within a changing social structure were transposed into a paradoxical political structure.

According to Marx's later political commentaries, these paradoxes make themselves felt in the culture and in the politics of the Revolution. The symbolism employed by 1789 shows how,

> unheroic as the bourgeois society is, it still required heroism, self-sacrifice, terror, civil war, and battles in which whole nations were engaged, to bring it into the world. And its gladiators found in the stern classical traditions of the Roman republic the ideals, art forms and self-deceptions they needed in order to hide from themselves the limited bourgeois content of their struggles and to maintain their enthusiasm at the high level appropriate to great historical tragedy.[61]

Marx holds that the contradictions in the political order give rise to the demise of both the 1789 and the 1848 revolutions. The post-1789 political order, run by the bourgeoisie, gives way to Napoleonic dictatorship.

> It is no longer the monarchy that appears to have been overthrown but the liberal concession extracted from it by a century of struggle. Instead of *society* conquering a new content for itself, it only seems that the *state* has returned to its most ancient form, the unashamedly simple rule of the military sabre and the clerical cowl.[62]

The enlarged state apparatus that took over from both 1789 and 1848 was still a political palliative to society's endemic problem of atomization.

> The first French Revolution with its task to found national unity (to create a nation) had to break down all local, territorial, townish and provincial independence . . . Every minor solitary interest engendered by the relations of social groups was separated from society itself, fixed and made independent of it and opposed to it in the form of the state interest, administered by state priests with exactly determined hierarchical functions.[63]

The autonomous, centralized state, fully grown under the two Napoleons, countered the divisive effects of competing social interests. It ejected interests firmly into the private sphere, and imposed the unity of the nation, located within itself.

Though Marx's analysis is more political later in his career, the source of these tendencies is expressed in a Hegelian manner in the early texts. It is the interplay between atomization (which renders social identity private) and the need for a public unity. Marx described this as early as 1843. The Revolution, he argued, attempted to counteract the class identity of members of society, previously represented in different estates. It made distinctions between individuals a private matter, and concentrated a countervailing public identity in political life:

> . . . the French Revolution completed the transformation of the political classes into social classes, in other words, made the class distinctions of civil society into merely social distinctions, pertaining to the private life but meaningless in political life. With that, the separation of political life and civil society was completed.[64]

On the other hand, Marx argued, this strategy over atomization was radically incoherent. The very notion of a merely private identity (and, hence, the complementary public unity which the Revolution had tried to promote) was self-contradictory. It was an effect of modern, capitalist-market society. Members of civil society could not in reality be atoms, he argued.[65] Their essential human properties, their material need of each other, dominates their supposedly private existence. In consequence, the Revolution was pursuing a 'political superstition': that 'civil life must be held together by the state'. It is due to the 'terrible illusion' in modern bourgeois society of 'self-estranged natural and spiritual individuality'. With due adjustment made for the new historical material and the greater apparatus of political analysis, Marx's account of the character of the Revolution in his last writings still employs this structure of thought.

CRITICAL ASSESSMENT: THE AGENTS OF CHANGE

We can now return to the question of agency in the Revolution. To what extent are a body of self-determining social agents promoting deliberate social transformation? The sequence of theorists of change that I have set out began from a position that social transformation was outside the control of those involved. But this position was largely qualified by the later theorists, as various levels of causation were incorporated into their theoretical explanation. This amounts to renewed opening for some version of agency among those involved in the Revolution — although it will be very limited when compared to the extreme of historical romanticism in Michelet's discovery of collective agents in the people-nation. On the other hand, the theories do furnish some coherent positions to accommodate the human agent along the lines the Revolutionaries had in mind. I should like to reconsider a thinker from each of the last four groups. How can they conceptualize that central idea of the Revolution's culture: human agents directing historical transformation?

We have seen that Hegel was critical of the idea of rationality by which the Revolution understood individual action.[66] None the less, his underlying ontology redeemed something to human agency. It guaranteed that social change was necessary, benign and rational — since, like all reality, it is governed by the transcendental Ideal. A besetting difficulty is reiterated by a number of commentaries on Hegel's view of the Revolution. How can the transcendental Ideal be at one and the same time *beyond* the real world and the basis of the rationality that arises *within* it? In terms of human agents trying to direct the Revolution, are they embodiments of rational progress or merely ciphers of something beyond their understanding and their world? This issue, variously addressed by commentators, indicates the scope and the limitations of human agency in Hegel's approach.

Herbert Marcuse derives his critical position in *Reason and Revolution* from the Marxian use of alienation and reification. According to Marcuse, Hegel's view of the Revolution amounts to an unwitting critique of alienation under capitalism. In reality, the individual will, as critically analysed by Hegel, has been misdirected by the private market economy. It is this which accounts for the historical content of the Revolution.

Certainly, Hegel saw the private market economy as an essential historical precondition of the Revolution. The individualist economy created the tension between the 'public' will of the monarch and the 'private' will of individuals in their economic existence. In Marcuse's view, Hegel correctly pointed out how the Revolution abstracted the will of such 'private' individuals into a rational, 'general' will, which is fundamentally inadequate for social and political order. Human agency is, therefore, stillborn in the revolutionary era's misconception of it: it is determined by a private sphere which it cannot rise above.

But Marcuse rejects Hegel's own route to a solution in the ontology of the transcendental Ideal.[67] According to Marcuse, the human will has been narrowed *not* by any fundamental ontological facts of its nature, but by the dominant contemporary experience of free will, which reflects its exercise in the private market. Hegel was wrong to accept that particular version of human will as universal. This falsely generalized what is historically particular; the 'law of competitive society' became a 'law of nature'. 'The "nature" of free will is conceived in such a way that it refers to a particular historical form of the will, that of the individual as private owner'.[68] To counteract that kind of individual will, Hegel relocated rationality in the Ideal as expressed in established social and political institutions. In terms of the problem of agency in the Revolution, Marcuse contends that Hegel correctly identified the symptoms of individual powerlessness among agents in the Revolution. But then he wrongly diagnosed the symptoms as part of a universal, natural condition, and so opted to make *any* human will into a mere reflection of the transcendental Ideal.

Jacob Ritter, on the other hand, argues that Hegel is perfectly well aware that the problem of the human agent has been posed by *historical* conditions. It may also be solved within them. His interpretation both comes nearer to what Hegel actually wrote and brings Hegel's perception of history closer to that of the revolutionaries. Philosophy can show how the historical future may transcend the dichotomy opposing abstract individuality to established institutions. This is the aim of the *Philosophy of Right*.[69] When the Enlightenment set aside tradition and the claims of tradition, it confined the scope of objective necessity to the thing-like objectivity of the material world. Hegel's philosophy is intended to show an alternative objective necessity: the *interplay* of individual and received social institutions, working out the transcendental Ideal in contemporary history. So, the transcendental Ideal is no diversion from the real world and the problem of agency in it. Reason can only progress in the world where that subjective will and objective institutions are united in the individual agent. The *Philosophy of Right* expounds the necessary resolution of the two — in Shklar's words, a 'scheme of juristic society as the integrative political order of independent men'.[70] For Hegel therefore, says Ritter, 'History is itself the realm in which the Idea is actual and at work; the reason of the age is present in that which is, and theory has to bring it forth from the age as its concept'.[71] On Ritter's account, the Ideal is a reality both in and of history. Hegel's juristic scheme is a historically determinate solution offered the human agent for the historically determined negativity of the human agent. It is a basis for achieving the self-emancipation of the individual as the Revolution envisaged it.

Ritter can then defend Hegel against Marcuse's line of attack; that is, that Hegel unwittingly abstracted the individual agent from the private market on to a universal ontological plane. Ritter argues that Hegel wanted to see the private market extended for the sake of its short-term historical benefits. He had understood English political economy very well. He realized perfectly well that 'the revolutionary idea of the freedom of all is founded in the emergence of modern labour society'.[72] But he also held that the market society has a civilizing, historical role. It diffuses a world-wide system of needs, which generates self-interested individuals, who can, in due course, free society from its past.[73] But, on the other hand, market society has to be historically transcended. That is the point of the *re*integration of objective, legal-political tradition, as advocated in the *Philosophy of Right*. In short, Hegel holds the private market to be the historical *precondition* of a future free individual agency, reintegrated into the rationality of an objective framework.

But can this interpretation of Hegel on the evolution of human agents succeed in representing them as agents of change in the Revolution? Habermas has argued that, of itself, Hegel's reference to the Ideal divorces the revolutionaries from their objective circumstances.[74] Human purposes, confronting circumstances that are objective to them, are ravelled up with those circumstances in the same transcendental bundle.

> . . . an objectively revolutionary event is comprehended in categories that are borrowed from subjective revolutionary consciousness, but are now only to be valid for the subject of history as a whole . . . in order to guarantee the realization of the revolutionary demand in history, a subject must be substituted for this history, which invents the ultimate aim of a theoretically pre-designed plan . . .[75]

That is to say, subjectivity and objectivity are together lost in the Ideal. Hegel split the actions of those involved in the Revolution away from any rational, progressive purposes they might have, because, Habermas argues, he 'desired the revolutionizing of reality, without any revolutionaries'. Indeed, as Hegel aged, he progressively drove a thicker wedge between rational freedom and the deeds of the actual revolutionaries.[76]

In sum, we can say two things regarding the agents of social change in Hegel's philosophy of revolution. In its underlying reference to the Revolution, it is an attempt to show the philosophical and historical conditions of free, self-emancipating human agency — such as the revolutionaries felt they were exercising. But, it marginalizes actual human agents from the ontological level of rationally executed change. Hegel is unable a priori to conceive social transformation and free, rational human agency together in the same people.

We may say much the same of Comte's thinking. He, too, fails to identify any basis for free, rational action by those involved in processes of change. We have already seen that, in Comte's interpretation of the Revolution, cultural life at the time was 'critical' and, hence, inadequate to prevent the breakdown of the social order. This was why those involved lost control in the Revolution. Under what conditions might human agents regain control? Describing the Revolution itself, Comte indicated the conditions of satisfactory progress: 'a positive reconstruction of universal morality, worthily applied to all classes by a unanimously respected priesthood'.[77] We have a chance to see what Comte meant because he pursued active involvement in the Revolution of 1848. So much, indeed, did Comte (like others) regard this period as a rerun of 1789, that he dated the volumes of the *Système de politique positive* by the years since 1789: 1852 appearing as the 'Sixty-third year of the great Revolution', and so on.

Comte reacted to the 1848 revolution by announcing the formation of a 'Positivist Society'. This was intended to fulfil a role analogous to that of the Jacobins in 1789: it would 'facilitate the coming of a new spiritual power'. But now, according to Comte, the way was clear for the Revolution to pass on from 1789, which had been a negative, 'critical' phase. 1848 was a positive phase, when social change can be advanced by rational human agency. It would be the function of the Positivist Society to direct this.

It emerges from the general 'Plan' of the new society[78] that its task was one of 'sentiment rather than reason' and would be managed from above by its leadership. The problem was to reconcile the instinct for order with that for progress. This could be achieved by a 'reorganization of opinion and social mores', which would rebuild a more effective version of the spiritual organization of medieval Europe. Comte believed that this new structure would readily obtain acceptance from 'spirits tired of mental anarchy and unable to resist at base the force of philosophical demonstrations'.[79] Clearly, in the Revolution's second, more propitious phase, initiative lay with organized intellectuals. Writing in 1854, Comte provides the rationale for his top-down view of rational human agency in the Revolution. The Revolution had recognized public opinion as supreme. The difficulty in political organization is to distinguish opinion from desire. Ordinary citizens express desires which are, in their terms, irreducible: but they do not understand what means are necessary in order to realize those desires. Questions of means must therefore be the province of 'those who are learned in politics', who devote exclusive attention to them.[80] In other terms, for Comte, interests had to be radically separated from power. 'A primary condition for a publicist who wants to take a wider view, is to abstain from all employment or public office: who can be at one and the same time actor and spectator?'[81] For Comte, that is to say, directing historic change *had* to be kept apart from living in it. He could not conceive of rational agency involved in social transformation.

We have seen that de Tocqueville thought the process of the French Revolution was beyond the power of those involved. On the other hand, the situation he described in America gives some scope for democratic action − though it is significantly limited in its effects. Over there, at least social agents promote deliberate change. De Tocqueville appeared to offer two different sociologies: one for the *ancien régime* and one for the new democracy.[82] But he did not achieve a historical sociology that could embrace the Revolution itself. Further analysis allows us to follow the dynamics of de Tocqueville's thinking.

184

De Tocqueville had only one concept available to cover the social agents in the Revolution: that of democracy. For him, this was fundamentally a socio-economic concept (the levelling of status hierarchies), rather than a political one. In moving from the analysis of America to that of France, the concept got swamped by a purely political one: that of centralized power. Hence, we find a paradoxical hybrid for a political sociology: 'democratic despotism'.[83] This is a physiocratic term in which the people are a notional source of sovereignty and an 'undiscriminated mass'. The sociological category embraces humans in society only as legal symbols and passive objects of government.

The category of democracy hardly figures, then, in the *Ancien Régime*.[84] De Tocqueville loses the only sociological concept he has available to comprehend political action in society. It may be this theoretical lacuna which draws de Tocqueville to what Hayden White calls the 'tragic irony' mode of employment: that is, one where human action is encouraged by the lure of clear, achievable goals, only to find that human nature turns out different from what it appears.[85] More important for my present discussion, the lacuna prevents de Tocqueville from paying attention to political action within the society of the Revolution itself. Indeed, he describes the Revolution as 'a rather uninteresting period of transition that separates the administration of the Ancien Régime from the administrative system created by the Consulate'.[86] As Furet comments, this is 'a truly astounding remark for a man who wanted to write a history of the Revolution'. It shows to what extent de Tocqueville's theoretical thinking fails where it ought to embrace social agency.

It is evident that Marx's view of the Revolution leaves the ostensible agents of change in a quite paradoxical position. Even though they appeared dominant, the bourgeoisie were never really the masters of the Revolution. Bourgeois society required an illusory unity epitomized in the state to counteract its endemic divisions. Consequently, the attempt to construct or direct political transformation was bound to slip away from them in the state's autonomous projection of unity.

We cannot define Marx's theoretical account of human agency in history without reference to his general theory of history, disputed as that is. The most influential current view is that Marx was a 'technological determinist'.[87] Yet, though this can be well supported by exegesis of Marx's theoretical texts, it offers little with which to understand the attitude he expressed in discussing particular moments of history, such as the Revolution. Technological determinism deals in historical entities that are too long-term, and too deterministic to embrace the ambivalence of historical agents tangling with an organized illusion.[88] Gregor McLennan, however, has loosened the hold of large historical entities in Marxist historical interpretation.[89] He distinguishes old-style 'speculative' history from realist 'theorizing', with its more modest aim of informing interpretations of particular historical moments.

On the other hand, my view is that Marx derives his position on the Revolution from the idea of alienation. Melvin Rader offers an interpretation of Marx's general theory of history underpinned by the concept of alienation.[90] According to Rader, historical change in Marx can be accounted for by the breakdown of equilibrium in social systems. There is a dialectic of breakdown that is both objective and subjective, in which alienation grows up between human beings and their society, and is then resolved in the breakdown. We can, therefore, attribute to Marx two explanatory mechanisms operating in parallel: the changing socio-economic conditions and the alienation of collective identity in the state. If this view is sound, agents in the Revolution would be involved in both economic and ideological processes, and both would have a genuine impact on historical outcomes.

Incorporating this view, we could interpret Marx's version of the history of the Revolution thus. Human agents may well be consciously trying to manage the reality in which they exist. But the illusory pursuit of unity in political life is a genuine part of that historical reality. So, under the weight of that misconception (which is strongly encouraged by their conditions of existence), historical agents attempt to direct events *and to define* their own identity as historical agents. Many of the events of the Revolution are therefore the product of human agency: but the agents are labouring under a more or less explicable *misconstruction* of their reality and of themselves in it.

The exegesis of Marx's work being as complex as it is, this interpretation of his views on history cannot but remain tentative. It sounds like an amalgam of Marx's own problematic and manner of thought plus a very modern use of the concept of alienation.[91] None the less, it yields a powerful interpretation of the role of human agency in the Revolution. The participants figure as free agents in a perfectly understandable sense; and − understandably, too − their agency is limited by the effectiveness of their grasp of reality, their own position, and their shared identity. Marx, interpreted in this fashion, offers an account of human agency in the Revolution, capable of doing four things at the same time. First, his view is consistent with the unintended out-turn. Yet, secondly, it reflects the revolutionaries' sense of their own power to generate change. Thirdly, it embraces and relates both the objective circumstances of action and the subjects' intentions. Finally, it leaves deliberate, rational action possible, under certain circumstances.

NOTES

1. Burke, *Reflections on the Revolution in France*, ed. C.C. O'Brien (Harmondsworth: Penguin, 1968), pp. 181–5.
2. None the less, see Chapter 5, note 7 for references to the argument that Burke built upon Enlightenment principles.
3. Burke, *Works* (London: Holdsworth and Bull, 1834), vol. 1, p. 524. See also Isaac Kramnick, *The Rage of Edmund Burke* (New York: Basic Books, 1977); and *idem*, 'The Left and Edmund Burke', *Political Theory*, vol. 11, no. 2 (1983).
4. Burke, *Reflections*, pp. 193–5.
5. Ibid. p. 152.
6. This respect for tradition is not at all incompatible with a utilitarian defence of modern economic liberalism. As is argued by C.B. MacPherson, *Burke* (Oxford: Oxford University Press, 1980), this is a version of the Hobbesian argument that the social order is established and maintained by the power of a limited and sovereign state.
7. Burke, *Reflections*, pp. 190–2.
8. Abbé Barruel, *Le Patriot véridique, ou discours sur les vraies causes de la Révolution actuelle* (1789); *idem, Histoire du clergé pendant la Révolution française* (1792).
9. Joseph de Maître, *Considerations on France* (1799: Montreal and London: McGill-Queens University Press, 1974).
10. Ibid., p. 130.
11. Jacques Mallet du Pan, *Considérations sur la nature de la Révolution de France et sur les causes qui en prolongent la durée* (London 1793). De Pan's analysis is quite remarkably like that put forward in the 1970s by François Furet.
12. See Jacques Godechot, *La Contre-Révolution: Doctrine et action, 1789–1804* (Paris: Presses Universitaires de France, 1961), ch. 7.
13. Immanuel Kant, *Der Streit der Fakultäten (The Contest of the Faculties)* (Köningsberg, 1798), §§6–7.
14. Fichte, *Considérations sur la Révolution française,* trans. Jules Barni (1858), ed. M. Richir (Paris: Payot, 1974), p. 103.
15. Ibid., p. 80.
16. Ibid., pp. 96–100.
17. Ibid., pp. 126 and 115.
18. See Z.A. Pelczynski, 'Introduction' in Hegel, *Political Writings*, trans. T.M. Knox (Oxford: Clarendon, 1964).

19. Hegel, *Philosophy of Right*, trans. T.M. Knox (Oxford: Oxford University Press, 1952; 1967), p. 157.

20. Judith Shklar, *Freedom and Independence: a study of the Political Ideas of Hegel's 'Philosophy of Mind'* (Cambridge: Cambridge University Press, 1976), p. 208. See also Hegel, *Philosophy of Right*, op. cit., p. 156.

21. Thus, according the Hegel, *Philosophy of Right*, §§358–60, the 'German' state-type will fulfil the essential task, that of uniting the modern 'objective' state with a free and 'subjective' association.

22. By which time Hegel is more optimistic about contemporary German states. See the commentary by Merrold Westphal, *History and Truth in Hegel's 'Phenomenology'* (Atlantic Highlands, NJ: Humanities Press, 1978), pp. 173–81.

23. Esp. Ch. 6, § BIII Hegel, *The Phenomenology of Spirit*, trans. A.V. Miller, ed. J.N. Findlay (Oxford: Oxford University Press, 1977) ch. 6, pp. 357–60.

24. Jacob Ritter, *Hegel and the French Revolution: Essays on the 'Philosophy of Right'* (London and Cambridge, MA: MIT Press, 1982), a partial translation, by Richard Dien Winfield, of *Metaphysik und Politik: Studien zu Aristoteles und Hegel* (Frankfurt: Suhrkamp Verlag, 1969). References are to the MIT edition.

25. Ibid., pp. 53–8.

26. Quoted in ibid., pp. 53–4.

27. Ibid., p. 51.

28. Ibid., p. 40.

29. Ibid., p. 45.

30. Ibid., p. 50.

31. Condorcet, *Esquisse d'un tableau historique des progrès de l'esprit humain* (1794) ed. Hincker (Paris: Editions Sociales, 1971), p. 207. Condorcet is also discussed in Chapter 3, p. 107.

32. Ibid., p. 203.

33. Ibid., p. 244.

34. See F. Picavet, *Les Idéologues: essai sur l'histoire des idées et des théories scientifique, philosophiques, religieuses, etc en France depuis 1789* (Paris: Alcan, 1891), esp. ch. 1.

35. Quoted in Emmet Kennedy, *A Philosopher in the Age of Revolution: Destutt de Tracy and the Origins of 'Ideology'* (Philadelphia: American Philosophical Society ('Memoirs' series), 1978), pp. 36–7.

36. H. de Saint-Simon, *Le Nouveau christianisme* (Paris: Rhombus, 1921), p. 63: 'l'esprit humain s'est détaché des vues les plus générales; il s'est livré aux spécialités; il s'est occupé de l'analyse des faits particuliers, des intérêts privés des différentes classes de la société; il a travaillé à poser les principes secondaires qui pouvaient servir de bases aux différentes branches de ses connaissances; et, pendant cette seconde période, l'opinion s'est établie que les considérations généraux, sur les principes généraux et sur les intérêts généraux de l'espèce humaine, n'étaient que des considérations vagues et métaphysiques, ne pouvant contribuer

efficacement aux progrès des lumières et au perfectionnement de la civilisation.'

37. Comte, *Système de politique positive* (Paris: 1851–4), vol. 3, pp. 566–76.
38. Ibid., pp. 580–97.
39. Ibid., pp. 595–600.
40. Ibid., p. 596: 'L'évolution organique ne pouvant donc satisfaire les besoins manifestés par le mouvement critique, une commotion sociale devenait alors inevitable et se trouvait autant indispensable afin de procurer aux conceptions régénératrices une extension décisive avec une libre propagation.'
41. A. de Tocqueville, *L'Ancien Régime et la Révolution* in *Oeuvres complètes*, ed. J.P. Mayer (Paris: Gallimard, 1953), pt. 2, ch. 8 and pt. 3, ch. 8. De Tocqueville regards mutual defence as a particular feature of the old nobility.
42. Ibid., p. 187.
43. Ibid., p. 199.
44. Ibid., p. 196.
45. Ibid., p. 191.
46. Ibid., p. 223.
47. A. de Tocqueville, *Democracy in America*, ed. J.P. Mayer and M. Lerner (London: Collins, 1968), bk. 1, pt. 1, ch. 5.
48. Ibid., bk. 1, pt. 2.
49. Ibid., introduction: 'les législateurs conçurent le projet imprudent de la détruire au lieu de l'instruire et à la corriger, et sans vouloir apprendre'.
50. A. de Tocqueville, *L'Ancien Régime*, p. 176: 'Impuissance d'un homme ou même des hommes en particulier au début de la Révolution et tant que son impulsion propre a duré'.
51. Michel Buonarroti, *Conspiration pour l'Egalité, dite de Babeuf*, ed. Robert Brécy and Albert Soboul (Paris: Editions Sociales, 1957), vol. 1, pp. 26–8.
52. Ibid., p. 38.
53. Cabet, *Histoire populaire de la Révolution française* (Paris: Pagnerre, 1839), p. 145.
54. Karl Marx and Frederick Engels, *Selected Works in Two Volumes* (Moscow: Foreign Languages Publishing House; London: Lawrence and Wishart, 1958), vol. 1, p. 47.
55. Karl Marx and Frederick Engels, *The German Ideology* (London: Lawrence and Wishart, 1965), p. 210.
56. 'The Bourgeoisie and the Counter-Revolution' in *Selected Works in Two Volumes*, vol. 1, pp. 67–8.
57. See Chapter 7, pp. 202–4.
58. Marx and Engels, *German Ideology*, p. 227.
59. Cf. François Furet, *Marx et la Révolution française* (Paris: Flammarion, 1986), emphasizes Marx's view of the illusory character of that social unity which the bourgeoisie seeks to place in the state. This, in Furet's view, explains why it was the state (rather than the bourgeoisie) which

was the final beneficiary of the Revolution. As against my description of a gradual inflection after 1850, Furet also argues that Marx's view of the Revolution evolved through three phases.

60. Karl Marx, 'Eighteenth Brumaire of Louis Bonaparte' in Karl Marx, *Political Writings*, ed. David Fernbach, vol. 2, *Surveys from Exile* (Harmondsworth: Penguin, 1973), p. 237.

61. Ibid., p. 148. This is Marx's view of the use of the classical past, which I discussed in Chapter 3.

62. Ibid., p. 149.

63. Karl Marx, *The Civil War in France* (1871) in Karl Marx, *Political Writings*, ed. David Fernbach, vol. 3, *The First International and After* (Harmondsworth: Penguin, 1974), pp. 246–7.

64. Marx, *Critique of Hegel's 'Philosophy of Right'*, ed. J. O'Malley (Cambridge: Cambridge University Press, 1970) p. 80.

65. Karl Marx and Frederick Engels, *The Holy Family* (1844), in *Marx and Engels Collected Works* vol. 4 (London: Lawrence and Wishart, 1975), pp. 120–2.

66. See above, p. 166.

67. Herbert Marcuse, *Reason and Revolution: Hegel and the Rise of Social Theory* (Oxford: Oxford University Press, 1941; London: Routledge and Kegan Paul, 1967), esp. pp. 186–7.

68. Ibid., p. 187.

69. Ritter, op. cit., pp. 59–68.

70. Shklar, op. cit.

71. Ritter, op. cit., p. 67.

72. Ibid., p. 73.

73. Ibid., pp. 68–78.

74. Jurgen Habermas, 'Hegel's Critique of the French Revolution' (1963) in *idem, Theory and Practice* (London: Heinemann Education, 1974), esp. pp. 138–9.

75. Ibid., p. 138.

76. See Chris Arthur, 'Hegel and the French Revolution', *Radical Philosophy*, no. 52 (1989).

77. Comte, op. cit., vol. 3, p. 610.

78. Quoted in P. Arnaud (ed.), *La Politique d'Auguste Comte* (Paris: Armand Colin, 1965), pp. 62–5.

79. Ibid., p. 65.

80. For a critical analysis of the philosophical underpinnings of Comte's view of knowledge and its unwitting conservative consequences in politics, see Ted Benton, *Philosophical Foundations of the Three Sociologies* (London: Routledge and Kegan Paul, 1977), esp. ch. 2 and pp. 32–45.

81. Appendix to vol. 4 of Comte, *Système de politique positive*, quoted in Arnaud, op. cit., pp. 58–61.

82. It is arguable that this is not the appropriate term. See Sasha R. Weitman, 'The Sociological Thesis of Tocqueville's *The Old Régime and the Revolution*', *Social Research*, vol. 33, no. 3 (1966).

83. Tocqueville, *Ancien Régime*, pt. 3, ch. 3, p. 183.
84. For a fuller discussion, see Seymour Drescher, *Dilemmas of Democracy: Tocqueville and Modernization* (Pittsburg: Pittsburg University Press, 1968).
85. Hayden White, *Metahistory: the Historical Imagination to Nineteenth-century Europe* (Baltimore, MD and London: Johns Hopkins University Press, 1973).
86. Quoted by François Furet, *Interpreting the French Revolution* (Cambridge: Cambridge University Press, 1981), p. 160.
87. See G.A. Cohen, *Karl Marx's Theory of History: a Defence* (Oxford: Clarendon, 1978); and William H. Shaw, *Marx's Theory of History* (London: Hutchinson, 1978).
88. Notwithstanding the inherent difficulties, structuralist historians (such as Régine Robin in *La Société française en 1789: Sémur-en-Auxerre* (Paris: 1970)) have tried to expound a Marxist version of the Revolution exclusively in terms of the power of the coming mode of production. The attempt is roundly criticized from a Marxist point of view by George C. Comninel, *Re-thinking the French Revolution: Marxism and the Revisionist Challenge* (London and New York: Verso, 1987), discussed further in note 74, p. 222.
89. Gregor McLennan, *Marxism and the Methodologies of History* (London: Verso, 1981). McLennan demonstrates the effect of his theoretical position with, *inter alia*, a critique of how the modern Marxist historian Albert Soboul feeds objective processes back into the agents' motivation (pp. 183–6). I analyse Soboul at greater length in Chapter 7 below.
90. Melvin Rader, *Marx's Interpretation of History* (New York: Oxford University Press, 1979), esp. ch. 3, §§ 5 and 6 and ch. 5, § 6.
91. Especially in the work of New York-based philosophers, such as Bertell Ollman (see his *Alienation: Marx's Conception of Man in Capitalist Society* (Cambridge: Cambridge University Press, 1971)) and Norman Fischer.

CHAPTER SEVEN

Postscript: the Coherence of the Revolution in Modern Theories and Histories

The Revolution and the revolutionary wars were the background of nineteenth-century writing on social change. Theory and history in the twentieth century have, if anything, had a still more unnerving experience of upheavals to inform their portrayals of revolution. The Stalinist outcome of the socialist revolution in Russia, together with the murderous growth of fascism, have conditioned much thinking about social transformation since the Second World War. We can find many traces of this in portrayals both of revolution in general and of the French Revolution in particular. By the late 1980s, however, with the thaw in the Cold War and the weight of those historical events gradually easing, there are signs that the notion of a social transformation has gained a new currency. (One of the most surprising has been the overt claim by stoutly anti-socialist governments in Britain and the USA to have brought about a 'Thatcherite' or 'Reagan' 'revolution'.) If the twentieth-century experience of upheaval has been too painful to provide material for an understanding portrayal of revolution, then perhaps the French Revolution may make up for this. After all, since the nineteenth century, the Revolution has, as it were, made good in a modern European democracy.

My final chapter examines some theories of social transformation (philosophical, sociological and historical) since the Second World War. Naturally, these range much further from the French Revolution than their nineteenth-century equivalents did. I then move on to describe how historical studies have portrayed the French Revolution

Material in this chapter originally appeared in 'Who made the French Revolution?', *Radical Philosophy*, 53, Spring 1989.

over the same period, and consider their development. As I am now discussing current theories and histories, it seems appropriate to add more critical assessment to my exegesis of trends.

Once again, the question of human agency in the Revolution is a crucial yardstick. How is the role of agents in the processes of change understood? A coherent answer to this question enables the theoretical and historical writings to embrace upheavals such as the French Revolution. If we consider general theoretical accounts of revolution alongside histories of the Revolution in France, it appears that the historians have gone further than the theorists in comprehending some kind of rational agency within their chosen case. Theoretically interpreted, the historians lead the way, I would contend, where they show how the actions of those involved in the Revolution are structured through the culture that portrayed those agents to themselves. The rationality and the effectiveness of the agents can be understood in terms of the culture — as can their limitations.

THE RATIONALITY OF SOCIAL UPHEAVAL: PHILOSOPHICAL CURRENTS

Post-war philosophy of social change naturally referred to upheavals more modern than the French Revolution. Karl Popper's was the most influential. It aimed to counter late nineteenth- and early twentieth-century theories of historical progress (especially Marxist ones), by arguing that deliberate, large-scale social change cannot be rationally understood, or, therefore, rational in itself. Popper's thinking has contributed a crucial element of the contemporary conception of revolution, and we will find traces of it in the work of historians on the French Revolution.

Popper's attack, classically stated in his *Poverty of Historicism* (1944), makes explicit its reference to those upheavals of the first half of the twentieth century with a dedication to 'men and women . . . who fell victims to the fascist and communist belief in Inexorable Laws of Historical Destiny'.[1] The argument is not aimed at the rationality of change as such. Its target is a certain 'holistic' conception of history which, according to Popper, underpinned revolutionary attempts to produce change. This 'historicism' 'assumes that *historical prediction* is . . . attainable by discovering the "rhythms" or the "patterns", the "laws" or the "trends" that underlie the evolution of history'.[2]

Against historicism, Popper deploys his earlier philosophy of science, grounded in truth-functional logic and intended to demarcate rational from irrational inquiry. The burden of the philosophy of science was that, since scientific generalizations could not be functions of the instances they embrace, any science produces only provisional hypotheses, tentatively predicting outcomes under narrowly specified conditions. Assertions about large trends, with loose prior conditions, are therefore inherently unscientific and irrational. And so it is for social science and history. Rational claims about the course of society or of history as a whole are impossible. 'History', writes Popper, 'like any other kind of inquiry, can only deal with selected aspects of the object.'[3] Popper insists, on the contrary, upon 'methodological individualism': the view that statements about society in general are at bottom reducible to statements about individual members of society.[4] Driving society in history's direction is as irrational as making claims to know that direction. What Popper calls 'utopian' attempts to transform society do not lead to improvement; they unleash totalitarian coercion to force people into the predetermined outcome.[5] Only cautious 'piecemeal' social engineering, a far cry from revolution of any kind, can therefore be rational or scientific.

Isaiah Berlin also contributed something to this post-war current of anti-revolutionary thinking. On the one hand, he extended Popper's critique of historicism. In his essay *Historical Inevitability* (1954), he argued that the idea of necessary historical progress had mistaken myth for history, so as to evade moral responsibility for the outcomes of action. His affinity with Popper is evident from his inclination towards methodological individualism, from his insistence on the primacy of facts over theories, and from his belief in the essential triviality of such general laws as do figure in historical investigation.[6] In addition, Berlin's influential distinction between negative and positive liberty[7] cast a sinister light over attempts to organize rational political harmony. Berlin traced to the late eighteenth century the doctrine that 'positive' freedom could be achieved by subjecting human beings to the higher side of their nature. The coercion that, in his view, this doctrine licensed was plainly meant to resemble the Jacobin as well as the totalitarian programme. In sum, Berlin contended that deliberate large-scale historical change was misdirected, morally suspect and of doubtful benefit. Revolutionary politics were clearly placed under a heavy cloud by such views.

Ernst Gellner tried to admit one global conception of historical progress under the Popperian dispensation.[8] According to Gellner, the last two centuries' global 'totalizing' concepts of social progress have failed, because they do not offer scientific explanations, reasonable moral choice or an account that squares with twentieth-century history. Gellner argues that there is, however, one major social change that dominates the modern world, though it is neither total nor all good: world-wide industrialization.[9] He calls for a 'neo-episodic' account of progress to accommodate this. Unlike earlier ideas of progress, it would be based upon evident fact. And, its basically utilitarian presumptions would make it 'possible to base moral thought on the notion of progress without indulging in some kind of mystical and dangerous pantheism'.[10] Finally, Gellner's 'neo-episodic' view of progress would be, logically speaking, unpresumptuous, and so would encourage a 'type of sceptical, hesitant perception which characterises transitions, which in turn is defined in terms of genuine doubt, and lack of fixed identity'.[11] Gellner's position loosened Popper's demarcation of science and rationality. It admitted substantial content in a positive account of the direction of history, but tried to keep both feet on the ground and to face uncertainty without flinching.

More recent work by Raymond Boudon in France has pushed the limits of the Popperian framework back further.[12] By redefining the character and role of theories of change, Boudon shows that minor amendments to the logic of Popper's programme make a space for rational claims about historical change. These amendments admit the intellectual genre of theories of social change, or philosophies of history. Boudon respects Popper and uses the same logic, though to different effect. He defends a notion of 'conjectural' or 'formal theories' (rather than scientific theories in the acknowledged, Popperian sense) which saves the various types of theory of change from the charge of being unscientific. Boudon thus undercuts the earlier critique of social change from the standpoint of a supposedly scientific logic. In Boudon's view, if we shift theories of social change into the purely formal role, there is room for a 'well-tempered determinism', which avoids the mechanistic predictability that Popper and others had found so unpalatable. Boudon also argues that there is nothing inherently unscientific in theorizing *un*predictability in change,[13] if that is the situation one has to deal with. A theory of change may perfectly well include the possibility that the closed situation it theorizes will prove to be (or become) a matter of 'chance' in the real world.

Boudon's strategy loosens the strict limits which had disfranchised ideas of change and progress by testing them against the truth-functional logic. That test assessed ideas of historical progress against the truth-functional model, in which knowledge is supposed to reflect the real world passively. On Boudon's account, theories of history and of change can be permitted to fit more loosely with reality. The real world can be a partly open domain, embraced by a 'scientific' idea of chance, in which agents may grasp a certain freedom of action. On the other hand, this liberalization does no more than square the fact that change and freedom occur in history with the requirements of a certain notion of logic and scientificity. It does not enlighten us about the experience of activity in history. Gaps for human agency are formally admitted without agency being understood. A view which is less committed than Boudon's to the belief that objectivity is founded on reflection, might place the human agent back in the flow of historical movement. In the end, I would argue, a relationship between active human beings and historical change must be understood as something more creative than ideas more or less adequately reflecting the world. A different idea of human experience and knowledge is necessary to account for the place of agency in social and historical processes. Philosophical currents along these lines have made their appearance in France in the last two decades.

In 1960, Sartre attempted to bring his phenomenological approach to bear on the dominant French version of Marxism, which he, too, saw as totalitarian. His *Critique of Dialectical Reason* tried to provide a Marxist account of revolutionary historical action by social groups, while preserving the ontological status of individual experience. The twentieth-century background is much the same as for Popper and his allies: totalitarian movements ostensibly pursuing progress. But Sartre argued that, from time to time, the 'seriality' of society made up of discrete (indeed, opposed) individuals was reversed. Individuals then come together in 'fused groups', which are ontologically the equal of individuals, except that they are also able to change the course of history. The paradigm of such fusions, Sartre believes, is the formation of groups within class struggle, as described by Marxism. 'What matters, in a history conditioned by class struggle, is to show the passage of oppressed classes from the collective state to the revolutionary praxis of the group.'[14] Sartre's prime example of a fused group engaging in successful praxis is the crowd that stormed the Bastille,[15] for which he shows an esteem that compares with Michelet's.

Sartre's philosophy is openly 'holistic' in the sense that Popper rejected: it takes the whole to be more than the sum of its parts. The praxis of groups in struggle, by temporarily forming a totality which seizes and changes given social practices, makes history intelligible. Sartre extended his earlier phenomenological philosophy of meaning to cover the group in history. When such a group forms a shared intention, that intention is inserted into the reality of the world. Yet Sartre insisted on the tentative but autonomous character of active groups in struggle, so as to prevent their being made the objects of political manipulation. They are, in his terminology, 'totalizing without being totalized'.[16] Though this work clearly constituted an innovation in the philosophy of action in history, Sartre himself never completed the second volume, which was to reflect on the experience of group praxis.[17] That and the inherent complexity of the position he developed make it difficult, within the confines of this study, to assess the scope of the opening he made for a different rationality in human agency.

The work of Cornelius Castoriadis and Claude Lefort represents a different French development in the theory of social change and the role of human agency within it. They give full weight to the culture in social reality. They combine the logical or semantic level in political and historical discourses with the symbolic. To do this, they have developed a concept of the 'social imaginary', which has a direct role in interpreting the Revolution. (I shall return to that later in the chapter.) The social imaginary is the total of signifying resources available to a society in order to represent its relationship to itself, to historical change and to reality outside of it. It is culturally constructed and open to re-examination and choice. Yet it also refers to, interprets and constitutes an objective reality. The imaginary is therefore a field of signification which can develop creatively and attribute the characterization of 'objective' to various realities.

Like Sartre, Castoriadis's starting point was political and theoretical opposition to the French Communist Party. He attacked that version of Marxism which Popper had called 'holistic', that is, Marxism claiming to know the true nature and destiny of the whole of a society. This kind of thinking, Castoriadis argues, constructs a totality of fixed entities with fixed relations.[18] It is therefore inherently inclined to do violence (in all senses of the word) to the human reality that confronts it. So far, little difference from Popper. But Castoriadis does not reject the *language* of totality from the range of proper human discourse, as Popper had done. Politics entails directing one's actions towards society as a whole.[19] So, Castoriadis insists, totality is implicit in the very idea of politics and a necessary component of society's understanding of itself. The social imaginary must include the idea of totality. The imaginary also embraces the necessity for autonomous growth in time. In Castoriadis's words, the imaginary is 'the element that constitutes history as such'.[20] But because the symbolic system must embrace society's *changing* reality, the totality has to be an indeterminate idea, a free realm. The imaginary contains a society's judgement of what is real, what is possible and what is of value: it unites 'everything in the life of the subject which exceeds reality and history'.[21]

Once history has been defined in terms that include autonomy, Castoriadis can advance a notion of political praxis as 'that activity in which the other or others are seen as autonomous beings and considered as the essential agent of the development of their own autonomy'.[22] Autonomy and change, because they are inherent in the material of the imaginary, have been imported into history and human action within history. The problem of intervention in history is apparently solved by including autonomy as a necessary component of the symbolic system of historical agents.

Castoriadis's associate Claude Lefort argues that the possibility of historical change, though it is inherent in the imaginary, is suppressed in modern society. His theory is intended to show that change is *made* into a problem in modern culture. (It is a version of Marx's account of atomization, 'self-estranged individuality' and the 'terrible illusion' of the state in modern bourgeois society, see pages 178–80.) Generally, argues Lefort, discourses in modern society implicitly define the nature and role of individuals in society ('the identity of the social subject').[23] In doing this, they have to obscure the fact that, in reality, power limits the individual. So they exploit the difference between what is said (the content of a discourse) and the saying of it. The latter involves the extent of power held by the discourse and by those who utter it. But discourse has to *appear* not to be 'the product of power'.[24] For example, historical discourse has to suppress the fact of human power in history; that is, of historical agency. According to Lefort, each of the discourses of modern society delimits itself so as to 'dissimulate the historical'.[25] Any general discourse, covering all the discourses and indicating the creativity inherent in the character of an imaginary, has to be suppressed.[26] History, in the sense of a process in time in which the agents may act autonomously, is made to seem impossible.

Castoriadis and Lefort offer an idea of the totality of society as an object of thought and historical action without the determinism that many found unacceptable in earlier historicism. Hence Castoriadis's notion of praxis as 'an open unity making itself'.[27] Their idea of totality is reached by considering what must be included in the symbolic resources of a society — in other words, in its culture broadly understood. According to their view, discourse on the historical has to entail the possibility of total change and of autonomy. Their idea of discourses is wider than the logic-led scientific objectivity from which the possibility of self-conscious historical action was excluded by Popper and others. They therefore epitomize a trend (found also in Sartre) to attribute rationality afresh to agents of social change. But now the rationality of the agents is understood in terms of the meanings or representations they assign to themselves, to their social world and to their aims in it. The representations are particular and incomplete. They never succeed altogether in grasping and intervening as the agents wish in the objective social world they portray. But they are components in a rational apparatus to do so.

HISTORICAL SOCIOLOGY: MESSIANISM AND COMPARATIVE METHOD

Modern studies in the historical sociology of revolution have been quite as much influenced as philosophy by the experience of fascism and Stalinist communism. Of the two post-war tendencies I wish to identify, the first (like Popper) portrayed the pursuit of historical progress as irrational. J.L. Talmon and Norman Cohn considered it under a designation for a primal semi-religious urge, 'messianism'. More recent comparative accounts of revolution have placed it in sociological models which take precise account of a complex of conditions – though they have an inherent tendency to play down the conscious intentions of those involved.

The argument of Talmon's *The Origins of Totalitarian Democracy* (1952) was that a specific form of political messianism has been growing since the eighteenth century. This 'totalitarian democracy' cleaves above all to the salvation of human society in a union of perfect citizens. Identifiable in Rousseau's notion of a seamless General Will, messianism surfaced in the Jacobin movement. It has since gone on to guide modern-day communism, totalitarianism and organized anti-Semitism. It is profoundly illiberal, because of its hostility to real people's lapses from the ideal. According to Talmon, when they came to power, the Jacobins made use of the messianic postulate of social indivisibility for a strategy of wartime government.[28] In theory, political messianism was even admitted by the founding principle of the Revolution (as expressed by Sieyès) – that the only true source of law is the will of the people.[29] But it could not be confined within political tactics. Talmon regards the longing for a perfect union as something deeper than any strategy. Robespierre and Saint-Just expressed it in fervour for the purity of the humble poor. It naturally manifests itself in a loathing of the 'impurity' of the wealthy, who are regarded as outsiders. Messianism therefore drove the revolutionary state to control the economy, and oppress the wealthy in order to prevent inequality.[30] In this interventionist form, it has been bequeathed to modern socialism and fascism, and the xenophobia of anti-Semitism.[31]

Talmon presents political messianism as an underlying psychological impulse, which maintains an independent force through many historical transformations. In consequence, it is not at all clear whether we are dealing with the same continuous phenomenon throughout its many appearances, or why it should be more fundamental causally than factors such as social structure or political evolution. Though it does not cover the French Revolution as such, Norman Cohn's work on *The Pursuit of the Millenium* (1957) made up for this lacuna in the study of messianism.

Cohn, too, was preoccupied by the enormity of twentieth-century anti-Semitism, especially under fascism. But his analysis of the appearances of messianism, or 'millenarianism', in late medieval Europe, generated a more systematic account of the social conditions which provoke it to flare up. Messianism ceases to be an autonomous movement of the irrational, surging through European history since the eighteenth century and the French Revolution. It is a peculiar faith, a form of revolutionary chiliasm, which has 'a dim, subterranean existence down through the centuries'.[32] Minorities under pressure from terrifying social change surrender themselves to it from time to time, with the encouragement of *déclassé* intellectuals.[33]

The messianic impulse for unity in the French Revolution (as in later revolutionary movements) is a psycho-social response to a phase of profound social change. In short, Cohn incorporated messianism as an account of revolution into a more balanced, sociological model of change. The underlying impulse of revolutions is as deeply irrational as for Talmon, but the irrationality does not appear sweeping all before it, regardless of circumstances.

The more recent comparative approach to revolutions originated in de Tocqueville. It has not been as given to generalization as the historians of messianism. Rather, the method compares the variables and outcomes in a limited range of historical situations, as a way of identifying their objective dynamics. English, French, Russian and Chinese revolutions have been favourite cases for study.[34] The classic of the genre has been Barrington Moore's *Social Origins of Dictatorship and Democracy* (1966). Moore placed modern revolutions within the context of the passage to 'modern' social organization, with its characteristics of a central sovereign state and a commercial economy (especially in agriculture). According to Moore, there have been two routes to modernity: the democratic and the dictatorial, or totalitarian. Which route a society takes depends crucially upon the balance of social power held by the state, the nobility and the peasantry. When the peasantry is weakened or prised away from a landed nobility in decline, that can make way for the modern state and the commercialization of the land. But it can also produce peasant resistance to the reorganization of the countryside, which provokes dictatorship from the state.

Moore drew on twentieth-century French economic historians for his material on France. In his analysis, the situation prior to the Revolution lay in between two extremes.[35] The peasantry had not been abolished or the aristocracy integrated, as they had in England. Their resentment simmered in an otherwise stable rural society. When the absolutist state which had protected the nobility crumbled, the peasantry turned on the landed nobles. But the alliance of interests between the revolutionary state and the peasantry soon broke down. The Jacobins sided with the urban poor, and opted to expropriate food for them from the peasantry, who responded by resisting the Revolution altogether.

An influential variation on Moore's approach (with a greater debt to de Tocqueville, to Marx and to world system theory) was put forward in 1979 by Theda Skocpol.[36] She argued that modern revolutions in France, Russia and China arose from the collapse of a certain kind of state, usually under pressure in war from more advanced rivals. The so-called 'agrarian bureaucracies' are inherently unstable, because they employ the services of an unreliable landed nobility to contain a perpetually disgruntled peasantry. Breakdown releases the centrifugal urges of the peasantry. These are matched by the revival of the state in a form that, under the leadership of the marginalized intellectuals of the old regime, is more coercive and centralized than before.

Revolution emerges from these comparative analyses as a complex outcome in the delicate balance of certain societies in long-term historical processes. It is a hazardous business, practised within complicated objective parameters which are set by the major social classes and fractions as they develop over the longer term.

The comparative analyses do not by any means exclude the agency of those involved in revolutions. The Marxist historian, Eric Hobsbawm, is the author of an authoritative historical overview which described how the French and other early nineteenth-century revolutions brought the bourgeoisie to power.[37] Yet, taking stock of current research in 1975, he easily accepted the findings of comparative studies of revolution. But he pointed out the need to sustain a vital distinction between interests, intended goals and actual out-turns of action.[38] 'Those who seek for a self-conscious, let alone an organized "bourgeoisie" seeking to make a "bourgeois revolution" *before* such a revolution are likely to be disappointed.' The achievement of the organized agents of revolution, the 'revolutionary movement', 'lies in turning a changing situation to their advantage'.[39]

The long-term structural crisis of a social system, as analysed by comparative and sociological methods, is a historical fact. Within it, revolutionary collapses occur, and humans seek a direction. The modern sociological approach has, I infer, managed to analyse systematically the conditions of historical events. But it has still to leave space for the view of their situation taken by the humans involved, and their reactions as agents. Now let us turn to historians of the Revolution, with a particular eye on how they understand the human agents in history.

MODERN FRENCH MARXIST HISTORIOGRAPHY: LEFÈBVRE AND SOBOUL

In his most approachable work, *Quatre-vingt-neuf* (1939),[40] Georges Lefèbvre subdivided the Revolution thus: an aristocratic revolution (the reforms by the monarchy) which failed; a bourgeois revolution which succeeded, with the help of a popular urban revolution; and a peasant revolution which was suppressed by the bourgeois state. All the players in this history are social classes, operating through political transformation or insurgency. Lefèbvre embodied the authoritative post-war French Marxist account of the Revolution. The autonomous action of classes is the central element in this interpretation. It is a position that has set the terms for portrayal of the Revolution, both in France and elsewhere, since the Second World War. I contend that the most promising direction of historical portrayal today is a modified version of the French Marxist account. As in the case of sociological accounts, the role of culture in the self-identification of classes *and other* agents has to be taken fully into account.

202

For Lefèbvre the overall direction of history is with the bourgeoisie. This class was to impose its ascendancy upon the political structure and the aristocratic status hierarchy.

> The growth of commerce and industry had created . . . the bourgeoisie . . . it proved highly useful to the monarchical state in supplying it with money and competent officials . . . It had developed a new ideology . . . The role of the aristocracy had correspondingly declined; and the clergy found its authority growing weaker. These groups preserved the highest rank . . . The Revolution of 1789 restored the harmony of fact and law. The transformation spread in the 19th Century throughout the West.[41]

The French Revolution was 'the arrival of the bourgeoisie':[42] one of those moments when, via the rise and decline of social classes, the material world, in classical Marxist terms, imposed a new ideological order.

This view of the Revolution attributes to the social classes involved in the process a very real role as agents consciously bringing about the course that history is predisposed to take. As Lefèbvre put it:

> Between historical realities and economic and social ones, there is the human spirit, which must become conscious of the second in order to bring about the first. It is all the same true that the Revolution was only the crowning of a long economic and social evolution which made the bourgeoisie the mistress of the world.[43]

Many difficulties in this Marxist account have been exposed over the last three decades by various 'revisionist' historians. The English, with successful historical studies to their name (notably Alfred Cobban and Richard Cobb) attacked the Marxist view outright; while more recently a sophisticated strand of cultural history in France (represented by François Furet) has also undermined it from a standpoint which, for all that, owes much to Marx. I shall review the challenge made first by English, and then by French opponents of the Marxist account. Then, I shall consider what scope there is to salvage some sense that, within the Revolution, there are none the less human agents of some kind of progress. The overall sense of the chapter is that a shift towards analysing culture in historical writing produces an account that is more plausible in relation to the evidence. Moreover, it shows how those involved in the Revolution identified themselves as agents, through a culture or an ideology. Hence, this 'psycho-cultural' type of history indicates their rationality and limitations as agents.

Lefèbvre and Soboul, who became the doyen of French Marxist revolutionary history after Lefèbvre, had very much a *French* Marxist view. The special status and destiny of France, and of the Left in France, is at stake. In the early part of the twentieth century, Jaurès and Mathiez, from whom Lefèbvre took much, had added a socialist dimension to Michelet's enthusiasm for the people and the Revolution. From its inception in the 1920s, the French Communist Party had an interest in emphasizing its country's seniority in the business of making effective mass revolutionary movements. So Lefèbvre and Soboul were inclined to see the Revolution as France's peculiar gift to the cause of human progress. The storming of the Bastille, the Great Fear and similar *mass* movements became (as they were for Sartre) models of progressive political action.[44]

The empirical difficulties in the Marxist account were these. The active 'bourgeois' takeover in the National Assembly was short-lived in the first place, and in any case disputable. The economic outcome of the Revolution was industrial decline (partly the result of chronic warfare) and the installation of a bloc of backward-looking peasant agriculture. Politics soon turned into war abroad and mutual destruction by power-seeking factions at home. The state fell to arbitrary arrests and executions. From 1795, there followed chronic political instability, only brought to an end by a military dictator (Napoleon). Napoleon's time in charge dwarfs any spells of bourgeois power (or sansculotte struggle). What kind of bourgeoisie, the 'revisionist' historians could ask, would have wanted to make a revolution like that?

In his classic on *La Grande Peur* (1932), Lefèbvre himself, like other Marxist historians, tackled these empirical difficulties without departing from the orthodox concept of class conflict.[45] He employed voluminous data on their insecure economic and social conditions to account for the peasant disturbances which, at the crucial moment, undermined the legitimacy of the rural property structure. Later, Albert Soboul incorporated the urban poor into the class struggle in his *Les Sans-culottes parisiens* (1958).[46] But the integration of these discordant empirical elements into the Marxist account is not entirely satisfactory. After a description of peasant responses to often mistaken rumours of roaming brigands and aristocratic plots, the peasants appear more like catalysts *by default* than agents or beneficiaries of a revolutionary process. Yet, Lefèbvre tries to construe the Great Fear as a 'startlingly obvious' case of 'class solidarity' amongst commoners.[47] For his part, Soboul seemed inveterately thrown back upon the emotive

204

notion of class betrayal to account for the failure of the more radical classes to hold on to power.[48] Latterly, in order to incorporate the impact of the peasantry on the bourgeoisie's success, Soboul redefined the 'bourgeois' revolution as a 'bourgeois-peasant' revolution.[49] This incorporates the peasantry over their heads, emphasizing their objective role in breaking up large land-holdings to make way for the capitalization of land.

There was, then, no getting away from the theoretical aspect in the difficulties that confronted the Marxist account of the Revolution. Those difficulties amounted to this: In what sense can it be said that the bourgeoisie, the sansculottes, the peasantry, the people, anyone *made* the Revolution? For the evidence challenges the role of the bourgeoisie as the primary agent of the Revolution. It suggests rival agents in other classes, whose character and capacity to act need to be determined and explained. Or it points to forces beyond social classes and even deliberate intentions altogether: political institutions independent of class, the momentum of war, the driving force behind the Terror. Such forces appear to override all the participants.

ENGLISH PARTICULARIST HISTORY AND ITS IMPLICATIONS

The predominant English style of historical writing is staunchly empirical and suspicious of global theses. It prefers to build modestly from particular research. In a word, it is 'particularist'. In historical studies of the French Revolution, particularism generated effective attacks upon two weak points in the Marxist idea of the Revolution: the claim that the state changed at the bidding of social classes, and the role of bourgeoisie's lower-class supposed rivals, the sansculottes. At the same time, particularism produced alternative accounts which, if interpreted theoretically, are not in my view incompatible with some kind of Marxist account.

Alfred Cobban was the first to attack what he called the 'myth' of the Revolution: that is, the interpretation of it as the arrival of the bourgeoisie in power. In his view, the Revolution was a financial crisis of the *ancien régime* allowing 'officials and professional men to move up from the minor to the major posts in government'.[50] It was a 'revolution of place-holders', then, anxious to re-establish the kind of secure state power that benefited them.

In *The Social Interpretation of the French Revolution* (1964), Cobban pitched his attack more widely. This work uses a critique of sociological concepts in historical explanation to sustain a Tocqueville-inspired emphasis on the long-term *continuity* of power in France. It is heavily influenced by Popper's view of scientific rationality and historicism. Cobban argued that 'the sociological historian' corrupts 'the criterion for the selection of relevant historical facts' with a global theory of the nature of society, which cannot be tested because it is 'holistic'.[51] Marxist and other 'sociological' interpretations have failed to test their contention that specific classes rose or fell in the Revolution. More generally, Cobban casts suspicion on the use of *any* social categories that are not contemporary to the period under study.[52] The class ascendancy of the 'bourgeoisie' accordingly dissolves into the pursuit by various groups of town-dwellers of their particular, divergent interests. In Cobban's estimation, a good proportion of this alleged bourgeoisie had a financial or career stake in the old regime; while others operating in a capitalist market might have little to gain from 'bourgeois' economic liberalism.[53] As for the sansculottes, Cobban holds that they are too diverse to be drawn together by anything but political manipulation at the time and the enthusiasm of Marxist historians since.[54]

The Revolution emerges from this critique as a specifically political struggle over the particular interests of opportunists and functionaries. Far from being progressive in the Marxist sense, the Revolution is '*against* and not *for* the rising forces of capitalism'.[55] The greatest wish of those involved was open access to careers in a state that could provide for them and could sustain its own power:

> a struggle for the possession of power and over the conditions in which power was to be exercised. Essentially the revolution was the overthrow of the old political system of the monarchy and the creation of a new one in the shape of the Napoleonic state . . . The supposed social categories of our histories – bourgeois, aristocrats, *sans-culottes* – are all in fact political ones.[56]

In Cobban, particularism was predisposed to dissolve social movements and make them the creature of political calculation from above.[57]

The greatest and most influential of the English particularist historians, Richard Cobb, concentrated on the lower classes. He was quick to spot divergences between the detailed picture and the Marxist view of class struggle. But his work has been so subtle and sympathetic to his subjects that he may be interpreted as showing the complexity of active social movements within the revolutionary process.

Cobb's first point of entry into the history of the Revolution was to study the most organized manifestation of the sansculotte movement. His classic *Les Armées révolutionnaires* (1961) examined the 'revolutionary army', which was recruited to requisition food from the countryside. He described the establishment, personnel, organization and activities of the 'army' with a devoted attention to the details of individuals which was grounded in both methodological preferences and a self-effacing, affectionate style. There are countless stories of the careers of individuals; an analysis of the spatial deployment and organization of the army; and exhaustive accounts of its attitudes and those of the rural people. Cobb then concludes Book Two with a characteristic display of modesty *vis-à-vis* any big historical questions. He has, he writes, only 'tried to let the actors speak for themselves' and 'illustrate life as it was', drawing himself merely negative and imprecise conclusions.[58]

Cobb's better-known *The Police and the People: French Popular Protest, 1789–1820* (1970) was a longitudinal study of the personnel of the whole sansculotte movement, taking it as one instance of popular protest against the state. It exposed the weakness of Soboul's view, with its idolization of spontaneity in the movement, and its taste for identifying players in a stock drama of class conflict (what Cobb calls Soboul's 'ballet'[59].) The sansculotte movement appears subservient to the fear of famine and hence to the state, which alone can palliate that fear. For Cobb, the movement, whatever its claims, was merely a short-lived and myth-laden expression of age-old popular protest. It was only given substance and status by a central government suffering a temporary wartime crisis of authority. 'Its fragility, its incoherence, and its endless fractionalisation' made even its brief existence a miracle.[60] Its characteristic militant was no more than 'a political accident',[61] 'a freak of nature'.[62]

In Cobb's books the actors speak through a number of barely acknowledged categories of cultural explanation. In *Les Armées révolutionnaires*, Cobb is never afraid to use an effortless common-sense empathy to interpret his subjects: their inextinguishable enthusiasm for the cause; their naive self-importance, laced with the grandiose language of equality; their townies' gullibility in the countryside; their fear of famine; their 'habits of real soldiers throughout the ages: those of eating and drinking without paying';[63] their 'small consumers' prejudice against the dealer in foodstuffs'.[64] This common-sense manner of interpretation is certainly enlightening. Cobb can embrace non-commonsensical categories, too, such as the psychological meaning of the moustache[65] or the anxiety brought on by rural empty space.

But he plays with these illuminating categories of interpretation without admitting how he is doing so, or what its significance or limitations might be.

This is anthropological history, or 'histoire des mentalités',[66] without the name. The actors 'speaking for themselves' are being given a *cultural identity* by Cobb. He portrays them through their own meanings and representations. Differently understood, such representations can *constitute* a coherent, if complex, social movement in the Revolution. If we explicitly consider the implications of Cobb's engagement with the *culture* of the lower classes in the Revolution, he appears to be providing a more complex version of the struggle of the lower classes in the revolutionary process – even though his explicit statements deny it. Why should we not interpret Cobb's sympathetic account of the lower orders so as to see them as the embodiment of one, or more likely of a number of *lived* ideologies? In the historical conjuncture of the Revolution these come into conflict. As Cobb himself says – albeit ironically – 'the essence of sans-culotte "thought" was 'something behavioural rather than doctrinal'.[67]

In such an interpretation, the overarching fear of famine would appear as a site of *ideological* conflict between people and state. This would be mediated by historically specific representations of reality, such as the dispute between the absolutist regime's long-established practice of food management and the advocacy of a free market. The participants in this conflict do not divide along simple class lines, with the bourgeoisie opting for the market and the rest favouring the old *dirigisme*. Class conflict cannot therefore be seen as the opposition between clearly specifiable social groups. Instead, it takes place through ideological shifts *overlaying* given groups and movements. The sansculottes, for example, tried to obtain power, and to constitute *themselves as a movement*, in a setting determined from outside. They had to do this via representations, such as new, 'bourgeois' notions of equality and political representation, drawn from outside their immediate level of society. There is separate evidence for this.

Certainly, Cobb refuted Soboul's impression of a seamless, convivial 'mass movement'.[68] But he does not demonstrate that there was no such thing as a movement. A different movement emerges, made up of thousands of political beginners, who operated with the many ambiguities of their own ideology and of the symbolism of democracy, under political pressures from a central government which they could hardly imagine. The sansculottes are not shorn of all their role as agents in the Revolution, then. They merely appear in more realistic terms:

trying (inadequately) to determine their own identity in a movement made up of contradictory elements, and stumbling into temporary success which collapses after a spell.

Two other English language historians have contributed to an alternative account of the agents in play in the Revolution: Georges Rudé and Colin Lucas.[69] In my view, they, too, give undogmatic sense to *social* movements as agents in the Revolution.

Rudé acknowledged help from both the French Marxist historians and Richard Cobb for his 1959 study of *The Crowd in the French Revolution*.[70] In it, he reconstituted the make-up of the revolutionary crowds from police records. Ingeniously, he combines personnel, ideology and psychology in his picture. The crowds commonly gathered at familiar places of assembly such as wine shops or markets. They were then prompted to pass to public demonstration (or, on occasion, to riot) by a combination of rumour, progressive ideology filtering down from the literate sections of society, and well-founded fears for their economic survival. Rudé combines objective and subjective elements to show the particular and actively evolving character of the crowds. He observes, for example, that without 'the impact of political ideas, mainly derived from the *bourgeois* leaders, such movements would have remained strangely purposeless'.[71] But, on the other hand, 'had the *sans-culottes* not been able to absorb and adapt these ideas', they would have had far less impact. The sans-culottes emerge as convincing historical actors precisely *because* their identity is established in a fluid combination of conditions, action, *and* ideology.

In an article of 1973, Colin Lucas examined the complex meanings that the classes of the Revolution gave to their social world.[72] His initial contention is firmly anti-Marxist: the division between noble and commoner was of little significance for the well-to-do classes of late eighteenth-century France. It follows that they could hardly have engaged in a deliberate struggle to replace 'aristocratic' with 'bourgeois' power. Instead, according to Lucas, members of noble and non-noble strata competed for success in *the same* hierarchy of status and wealth. But, as the eighteenth century advanced, entry routes to the best positions were progressively closed by financial factors and by the insiders. When the Estates were summoned, the well-to-do classes were obliged to restate the meaning of nobility. The aspirants then fell out with the established aristocrats, who insisted on an already outdated categorization between the estates. In short, late eighteenth-century France was 'a hybrid situation in which men sought to express complex social realities in symbols and language whose connotations referred to a qualitatively different structure'.[73]

A rift between groups was produced by a conflict *within* an ideology of status, which fitted poorly to social reality. The upshot, according to Lucas, was that the commoners seized power, with some noble allies, in order to *re*institute free movement in the hierarchy. Lucas's argument, I would contend, makes the Revolution the result of a breakdown in the system of meanings. In order to reinstitute the free movement that had appeared to exist before, aspirants to status had to find a new system of meanings to describe what they wanted. The ideology of a political order with *no* aristocratic power came to hand.

In sum, when they confronted the previous Marxist orthodoxy, what I have called English 'particularist' histories challenged the Marxist account of class struggle in the Revolution quite seriously. But they may simply have shown how the role of classes as agents in the revolutionary process needs to be more subtly described — in terms of interlocking groups, institutions *and* ideologies. There have been a considerable number of valuable new works on the Revolution in English since those that I have examined. These have opened up two new areas in particular: the long-term effect of the lower classes' resistance to the Revolution; and the growth of new political institutions.[74] However, in the 1970s and 1980s, the debate over the Marxist view began to open up in France. A new style of analysis, explicitly focusing on the psycho-cultural level, came to prominence there (and also, to some extent, in North America). This development has recast the issue of agency in the Revolution more explicitly in terms of representations.

CLASSES OR REPRESENTATIONS: THE FRENCH DEBATE

François Furet's trenchant attack on the Marxist view, an essay entitled 'The French Revolution is over', announced the priority of representations in the course taken by the Revolution.

> If the Revolution . . . experienced, in its political practices, the theoretical contradictions of democracy, it was because it ushered in a world where mental representations of power governed all actions, and where a network of signs completely dominated political life.[75]

In the essay, Furet claims that, by arguing that the Revolution installed bourgeois power in France, the Marxist view merely added the gloss of 'bourgeois state' to the revolutionaries' own perception of themselves as creators *ab initio* of a historically necessary new political order. An objective history, by contrast, would analyse the nature and affects of the revolutionaries' self-perception. It would distinguish the causal nexus that brought about the Revolution from 'the Revolution as a mode of change, a specific dynamic of collective action'.[76]

Furet constructs his own analysis at the psycho-cultural level. The Revolution's dynamic of collective action was contained within its representations of politics and of society. It is these that steer it towards the Terror and the war, both factors in due course playing into the hands of Napoleon.

> There was behind that crescendo of events something never clearly conceptualised, unrelated to the circumstances, existing apart from them, though evolving with and through them. That force, which the historian calls an increasingly 'popular' power, because it *manifested itself* in that form, had no objective existence at the social level, it was but a *mental representation of the social sphere* that permeated and dominated the field of politics.[77]

In his explanation of the Revolution, Furet explicitly acknowledges the overwhelming influence of representations. Analysed as they are by Furet, the 'mental representations' of the Revolution are so fundamentally divorced from reality that its nature 'can be defined as dialectic between actual power and a symbolic representation of it . . . whose chief *outcome* . . . was the establishment, with Napoleon, of a democratic royalism'.[78] This is what makes the drift into Bonapartism inevitable. It predetermines that the 'democratic' revolution will, in the end, fall into the hands of autocracy. Furet seems to show here his acknowledged debt to de Tocqueville, with the latter's sceptical view of democracy and his emphasis on the supervening growth of the state.

According to Furet, the revolutionaries derived from the Enlightenment an aspiration for society to be freed from institutions, mechanisms and strategies of power. In short, they sought freedom from what is, for Furet, the essence of politics. They believed this would leave the way clear for history to be shaped by collective human action.[79] Their idea of 'democratic politics as a national ideology'[80] spread rapidly with Jacobinism to occupy the vacuum created when traditional, monarchical power collapsed. But, according to Furet, the inspiration of this idea is not, properly speaking, politics, but a seamless unity:

> a kind of spontaneous equivalence between the values of revolutionary

consciousness – liberty and equality – the nation that embodied those values, and the individuals charged with implementing or defending them. Indeed, it was this equivalence that *ipso facto* transformed those isolated individuals into a collective entity, the people, making the people the supreme source of legitimacy and the Revolution's sole agent.[81]

In other words, liberty and equality were erected as shared values. As such, they gave an *illusion* of active, transparent unity which was obligatory for all those identified as members of 'the nation'. Likewise, they shaped the revolutionaries' xenophobic obsessions with unmasking and punishing spies and traitors. Whereas the Marxists regarded Terror and mass participation as the 'radicalization' of the Revolution, according to Furet, these were the working-out of a powerful dynamic in the Revolution's way of construing politics.

Furet's account had enormous strengths with regard to those awkward aspects of the Revolution that undermined the Marxist interpretation. It explained how there could be an outcome which no class would have aimed for. It indicated that, because the new kind of political sociability was unsustainable, the state was bound to be the final beneficiary of the process. Finally, in analysing the culture embodied in the Revolution, it appeared to reveal a reality experienced by participants. But all this was bought at the price of presupposing the *impossibility* of the Revolution's enterprise. 'It was', wrote Furet, 'a pledge that no event could fully redeem.'[82] Whatever their political preferences, can historians fairly do justice to historical experience with such an explanation? It confines seemingly autonomous historical actors a priori within the very culture through which they try to realize themselves as agents. Their representations were apparently preset to make no effective contact with the other levels of reality in which they existed.

Furet's was the first comprehensive account of the Revolution to focus so explicitly on the psycho-cultural level. However, around that time and since, others in France have analysed particular aspects of the Revolution on the same level: Jean Starobinski's *1789: Les Emblêmes de la Raison* (1973); Mona Ozouf's *La Fête révolutionnaire* (1976); Michel Vovelle's *Les Métamorphoses de la fête en Provence de 1750 à 1820* (1976); and Maurice Agulhon's *Marianne au combat: l'imagerie et le symbolique de 1789 à 1880* (1979).[83] The trend towards psycho-cultural analysis has been evident in North America, too. In 1983, Ronald Paulson argued much as Starobinski had, but covered French, English and Spanish perceptions of revolution.[84] Lynn Hunt's 1984 essay complemented insights from Ozouf and Agulhon.[85] She linked a literary-psychological analysis of how the revolutionaries conceived the 'plot' of their own history, to a political sociology about the diffusion of Jacobinism in different regions of France. Finally, Brian Singer employed the Lefort–Castoriadis concept of the 'imaginary' for a version of the Talmon thesis.[86] Singer argued that the Revolution was bound to become the victim of its own discourse of legitimacy.

Even though the leaders of the school were perfectly capable of analysing cultural movements on this level,[87] French Marxist historians initially condemned it. To Soboul's way of thinking, it was not only that Furet contradicted the fundamental idea of the Marxist account, namely, that the Revolution produced, in the final analysis, the political and social regime that the bourgeoisie wanted.[88] For Soboul, they also failed to be sufficiently deterministic. Their account 're-introduced chance and the irrational into history, although the discipline is a proper object of thought and hence rational'.[89] Yet, in his way, Furet was all *too* deterministic. Soboul appeared to regard as no determination at all an explanation which indicated determination on some other level than the 'revolutionary thrust' of classes as such. For him, the Revolution was 'inevitable' only if it necessarily led to the creation of a bourgeois society. A 'slippage' of the revolutionary movement implied 'the contingent character of the Revolution'.[90] We can, however, ask if it was really necessary to reject that type of account in order to defend a theoretically viable role for classes as agents in the Revolution.

Claude Mazauric, on the other hand, has developed a more complex model for relations between various levels of analysis in history, including the psycho-cultural. Mazauric adopted from Althusser the idea of the relative autonomy of the political. From Gramsci, he took the idea that in the events of political history, we see the 'social formation' absorbing a new mode of production, with its associated balance of classes. Finally, he adopted Foucault's idea of 'discursive formation' – a concept very close in spirit to Furet. Bringing all these strands together yielded an analysis of the content of the discursive formations of the Revolution; of how they functioned in institutions; and of their 'mode of insertion' into the mode of production's gradual historical emergence in specific circumstances.[91]

These concepts take Mazauric to the following conclusions about the Revolution.[92] It was 'bourgeois" in the sense that it 'embourgeoisified' property. But the political 'front'[93] (or 'revolutionary bloc'[94]) that achieved the change was based on an unworkable compromise: a fudge over how property held under feudal terms would be converted into bourgeois property. As they stumbled over this ambiguity, both the aristocracy and the peasantry abandoned the political front. The urban poor were driven by a food crisis to challenge the political front at the same time.[95] In Mazauric's words, this account, rather than giving enlightenment culture the predominant role (as Furet had) shows how 'revolutionary politics' was:

> a concrete and continuous creation, the realisation of a mode of government and of action in a complex situation . . . not mechanically reducible to the ideology which founded it or the principles that informed it. The development of social struggles created an objective logic into which was inserted the political action of an elite imbued with the ideology of the Enlightenment.[96]

Michel Vovelle has embraced psycho-cultural history with greater confidence. He brushed aside fears of mystification and idealism in the history of *mentalités*, arguing that it had something to offer Marxist history because it indicates the 'complex mediations' between 'real life' and the life 'of images'.[97] He followed up his early work on the revolutionary festivals, religiosity and perceptions of death[98] with more comprehensive studies of the Revolution as such. In a work of 1986, he uses the history of *mentalités* without losing the reality of the Revolution in a long-term evolution, or turning it into a process predestined to futility by the resurgence of hidden, primitive strata in the popular mentality.[99]

Vovelle defines a number of strands, both psycho-cultural and material, which came together in the 'revolutionary mentality'. By extrapolating from the variety of data about matters such as divorce or the adoption of non-Catholic names, he situates the revolutionary mentality in the evolution of popular late eighteenth-century attitudes. It includes such things as a desacralized 'imaginary' concerning death; libertarian attitudes about marriage and the family; and a new kind of sociability (including political sociability) based on common affection. Vovelle also considers crowd vandalism, mass violence and the Terror; phenomena which were, for Furet, the products of a fatal dynamic in the Revolution's representations (or were, for many English theorists, signs of an underlying irrationality). They emerge as the product of a complex entwining of the cultural and the economic. It consisted of a genuine need for self-defence; cruelty learnt from the society of the day; popular resistance to the dignity and authority of their masters;

subversive humour; and an urge for renewal expressed in destruction, though modified by native soft-heartedness. [100]

At first glance, Vovelle appears to concede almost everything to Furet. However, the direction taken by the Revolution in Vovelle's account, is not, as it was in Furet's, the product of a *self-enclosed* dynamic. It arises, in part, from interactions *within* the psycho-cultural level: for example, that between ancient elements deep in the psyche and the diffusion of a new ideology. It arises also from interactions of the psycho-cultural with *material* changes in the social order outside. Demographic and economic changes, for example, dissolved the older peasant society and its inherited forms of sociability, which had been founded on common affection. [101] The conflict between the new ideology and the pre-existing *mentalité* represents the invasion of evolving *material* conditions, structuring social relations between *classes*. In Vovelle's account, the political ideology of the Enlightenment would not simply transmit to the Revolution the contradictions of a certain conception of politics. Unlike Furet, Vovelle grants that the Revolution's representations of politics are *trying* to connect with reality outside politics − even if they do so unsuccessfully. The revolutionary mentality attempts to represent social life while adapting to a class-related economic transformation. Vovelle's history of *mentalités* anchors the mental representation of political life to material class changes beyond the psycho-cultural sphere.

INTENTION, ACTION AND OUTCOME IN THE REVOLUTION

Over a couple of decades, historical writing has substantially undermined the Marxist account of the Revolution, which held it to be a social change fundamentally beneficial to the bourgeoisie and actively pursued by them and by other classes. But my explication of this trend indicates that the Marxist account can be modified without losing sight of social classes active and progressive in the Revolution − though not unambiguously so.

The psycho-cultural level, which was incorporated untheorized by Cobb, damaged Lefèbvre and Soboul's version of classes as agents in the Revolution. But, understood in different terms, it is by no means fatal to a convincing alternative conceptualization. That is why Vovelle can give an uncompromising, Marxist account of the intertwining strands of psycho-cultural and material levels in the revolutionary transformation. Properly incorporated, the psycho-cultural elements make the role of groups as agents in the transformation more realistic and more understandable.

In fact, when they incorporated ideology into the history of the Revolution as a moment of social progress and class conflict, the historians shadowed a shift in Marxist thinking, namely, the growing influence of Gramsci, which placed ideology centre stage. This influence is particularly evident in Mazauric. [102] In this shift, ideology becomes a site where political blocs form and negotiate over the transformation of the mode of production. Ideology readily occupies an autonomous role between classes and the outcomes of events. In this version of the Marxist perspective, a class does not have to rise economically or socially during the Revolution, or as a result of it. The Revolution can still be either instigated by it, or congenial to it, or undertaken on its behalf. Nor does a class have to be directly involved politically: the politicians or the intelligentsia may work to bring forward the new social environment suitable to it. Finally, there is no need to assume that a rising class will have a clear-cut victory in a revolution: some more or less temporary compromise is very likely. This new emphasis upon the political and intellectual struggle over how society is to be organized can obviate many of the difficulties posed to the older Marxist version of the French Revolution. It makes the *realization* of what is in the interests of a social class indirect, and far more hazardous. Social classes no longer figure as agents straightforwardly reorganizing society in their own interests.

The uncertain course of political changes, the role of subgroups such as public servants and intellectuals, and the ambiguous outcomes of the Revolution were all cited as empirical difficulties for the older Marxist view. Given the newer perspective, none of these need contradict the interpretation which takes the underlying character of the Revolution to be the transformation of society in terms set by the growth of the bourgeois social environment. The empirical difficulties merely suggest that, as putative agents of change, the bourgeoisie interacted in a complex fashion in their specific social, political and historical context. Other classes did likewise.

With a view like this, what sort of agents might the classes in the Revolution be? They have neither simple, clear-cut aims, nor a guarantee of realizing what aims they have. Instead, they proceed from conjuncture to conjuncture, in the thick of currents of ideological debate, trying to settle which short- and long-term objectives suit them. They then try to realize their purposes through, or in spite of, a number of political and historical contingencies. It follows that a given social class often may not have a clear grasp of what suits it, what it can achieve, or what it believes to be right. Other groups or individuals, with clearer objectives or a better tactical position, may represent the wishes and interests of a social class, or believe that they know what is best for it. The actual outcome may not be something which any of the historical agents wanted or can easily understand. It may be what they are prepared to settle for – or can persuade themselves they wanted. In short, social agents, including classes, do not understand their own identity fully, or realize their own aims straightforwardly.

But this complex picture of their action is no reason to deny that classes can be rational agents of social change. It describes their situation in terms which we have no difficulty in understanding when it comes to individual agents. It is common enough for individual human beings to act with an indistinct sense of their own character or interests, or to fail to see what they 'really' want. Often, they wind up with something approximating their original aims: something that is a product of their action and their circumstances, which they come to regard as acceptable. They may even believe the out-turn to be what they were aiming for in the first place. That is no grounds to deny that these individuals are rational agents. The complexities merely help to show how agency is articulated.

The concept of a 'social imaginary' can come to our aid in describing a social group's efforts to grasp its own identity as agents. To recap, the imaginary is the totality of representations to understand society in its relationship to itself, to historical change and to reality (see page 197–8). It is the equivalent for social groups of the cultural, cognitive and emotional resources an individual acquires from the environment. Like those personal resources, the role of the imaginary does not invalidate the idea of the agent. It fleshes it out.

To focus on the workings of the imaginary affects the conceptualization of agents in various ways. Firstly, it sets aside the notion that the bourgeoisie, or any other social group, can unhesitatingly pursue some transformative aims which it desires. Aims have to be identified within the cultural resources available to represent them, which circulate through various sub-groups and institutions. Secondly, aims are not identified, nor transformation pursued in a void, divorced from the objective realities of the given economic, political and social conditions. Thirdly, the imaginary itself has an objective organization, which it also tries to grasp. In short, the process of fixing and attaining objectives, with all its vicissitudes and shifts of direction, is not undertaken in an ideal world, set against the real one.

As regard the Revolution, this conceptualization produces a view similar to that which I attributed to Marx at the close of Chapter 6. It implies that the Enlightenment ought not to be seen as a factor *alternative* to the social conditions assisting the bourgeoisie. The Enlightenment provided resources to represent and foster those new conditions. But it also channelled their representation, and hence the reaction to them. The bourgeoisie can therefore be regarded as an agent in the transformation wrought by the Revolution, even though its attachment to the ideology of legality, national unity, centralization and economic liberalism was neither clearsighted nor unique in French society at the time. The bourgeoisie was realizing and pursuing its common identity and interests in a confused way, through the articulation of the imaginary. Other classes and groups, such as the sansculottes, were articulating *their* identities in the same setting, adopting comparable or compatible aims. The various groups latched on to a political upheaval which was not of their own making. All wound up with an objective outcome born of interractions between each other, and with the outside world: political confusion, war, a declining economy, an unsatisfactory redistribution of land. But none of this undermines the notion that the Revolution was an arena for social classes, and others, as agents in pursuit of a social transformation. What it does is to give a more complex and convincing picture of how they went about this pursuit.

NOTES

1. For a detailed exposition of Popper's philosophy of history, see B.T. Wilkins, *Has History any Meaning?* (Brighton: Wheatsheaf, 1978).
2. Karl Popper, *The Poverty of Historicism* (London: Routledge and Kegan Paul, 1957), p. 3.
3. Ibid., p. 80.
4. Karl Popper, *The Open Society and Its Enemies* (London: Routledge, 1945; Routledge and Kegan Paul, 1966), vol. II, ch.14.
5. Popper, *Poverty*, pp. 83–93.
6. Isaiah Berlin, *Historical Inevitability* (London: Auguste Comte Memorial Trust/Oxford University Press, 1954), pp. 5–9, 58–70 and 74. Compare Popper's view that 'universal laws' are 'so trivial . . . that we need not mention them, and rarely notice them' (*Open Society*, vol. II, pp. 143–5). The common source of this account of generalizations in history is the logical positivist Carl Hempel's 'covering law' theory.

7. Isaiah Berlin, *Two Concepts of Liberty* (Oxford: Clarendon, 1958), reprinted in *idem*, *Four Essays on Liberty* (Oxford: Oxford University Press, 1969).

8. Ernst Gellner, *Thought and Change* (London: Weidenfeld and Nicolson, 1964).

9. Ibid., ch. 2.

10. Ibid., p. 40.

11. Ibid., p. 60.

12. Raymond Boudon, *Theories of Political Change: A Critical Appraisal* (Cambridge: Polity Press, 1986).

13. This takes its general inspiration from the strategy of René Thom's mathematicization of the unpredictable in catastrophe theory, and its particular mathematical model from so-called 'Cournot effects', whereby modelling the impossibility of closure in a situation is no bar to its formal (hence logical) representation.

14. Jean-Paul Sartre, *Critique de la raison dialectique* (Paris: Gallimard, 1960), bk.2, p. 384.

15. Ibid., pp. 386ff.

16. Ibid., p. 754.

17. A summary and commentary on the material Sartre prepared appeared in Ronald Aronson, *Sartre's Second Critique* (Chicago: Chicago University Press, 1987).

18. Cornelius Castoriadis, *L'Institution imaginaire de la société* (Paris: Seuil, 1975), pp. 92–6.

19. Ibid., pp. 121–4.

20. Ibid., p. 225.

21. Ibid., p. 200.

22. Ibid., p. 103.

23. Claude Lefort, *The Political Forms of Modern Society: Bureaucracy, Democracy and Totalitarianism* (Cambridge: Polity Press, 1986), pp. 187–8.

24. Ibid.

25. Ibid., p. 203.

26. Ibid., p. 204.

27. Castoriadis, *L'Institution imaginaire de la société*, p. 123.

28. J.L. Talmon, *The Origins of Totalitarian Democracy* (Harmondsworth: Penguin, 1986), pt.2, ch. 2.

29. Ibid., p. 73.

30. Ibid., pt.2, ch. 2.

31. Talmon pursued the evolution of messianism since the French Revolution in *Political Messianism, the Romantic Phase* (London: Secker and Warburg, 1967) and the posthumous *The Myth of the Nation and the Vision of Revolution* (London and Berkeley: Secker and Warburg/ University of California Press, 1980).

32. Norman Cohn, *The Pursuit of the Millenium* (London: Heinneman (Mercury), 1962), p. 309.

33. Ibid., pp. 314–19.

34. Wider-ranging exercises in comparative study of revolutions can be

found in John Dunn, *Modern Revolutions, an Introduction to the Analysis of a Political Phenomenon* (Cambridge: Cambridge University Press, 1972), or Jack A. Goldstone (ed.), *Revolutions: Theoretical, Comparative and Historical Studies* (New York: Harcourt Brace Jovanovich, 1986).

35. Barrington Moore, *Social Origins of Dictatorship and Democracy* (Harmondsworth: Penguin, 1967; 1973), ch. 2.
36. Theda Skocpol, *States and Social Revolutions* (Cambridge: Cambridge University Press, 1979).
37. Eric Hobsbawm, *The Age of Revolutions: Europe 1789–1848* (London: Weidenfeld and Nicolson, 1962).
38. Eric Hobsbawm, 'Revolution' in R. Porter and M. Teich, *Revolution in History* (Cambridge: Cambridge University Press, 1986).
39. Ibid., p. 22.
40. Translated as *The Coming of the French Revolution* (Princeton, NJ: Princeton University Press, 1947).
41. Ibid., pp. 1–2.
42. The title given by Lefèbvre to Book 2 of his *La Révolution française* (Paris: Presses Universitaires de France, 1957), translated as *The French Revolution from its Origins to 1793* (London: Routledge and Kegan Paul, 1962).
43. Ibid., p. 246.
44. Tony Judt argues in *Marxism and the French Left* (Oxford: Clarendon, 1986) that the model of the masses combining to invade the seat of power has possessed symbolic force, because the political experience of the Left in France has been one of occasional incursions into a predominantly right-wing, centralist state. A particularly affectionate (and for that reason misguided) account of mass movements in the Revolution, and their defeat or betrayal, can be found in Daniel Guérin, *Luttes des classes sous la première république: bourgeois et 'bras nus' 1793–7* (Paris: Gallimard, 1946, 1968).
45. Georges Lefèbvre, *The Great Fear of 1789* (London: New Left Books, 1973); see also Lefèbvre, *Les Paysans du Nord pendant la Révolution française* (Paris: Colin, 1924).
46. Albert Soboul, *Les Sans-culottes parisiens en l'an II: mouvement populaire et gouvernement révolutionnaire* (Paris: Clavreuil, 1958); translated as *Parisian Sans-culottes* (Oxford: Clarendon, 1964). Soboul gives a fuller account of the classes and subdivisions of classes in conflict during the Revolution in his 'Classes et luttes des classes sous la Révolution', *La Pensée*, 53 (1954), reprinted in his *Comprendre la Révolution* (Paris: Maspero, 1981).
47. Georges Lefèbvre, *The Great Fear of 1789*, p. 204.
48. Albert Soboul, *Précis d'histoire de la Révolution française* (Paris: Editions Sociales, 1962); translated by Alan Forrest and Colin Jones as *The French Revolution 1787–1797* (London: New Left Books, 1974).
49. This is derived from the role of the peasantry as interpreted in an original, but still entirely Marxist way in the Russian study by A. Ado, *Krest'yanskoe dvizhenie vo Frantsii vo vremya velikoy burghiaznoy revoliutsii konstsa XVIII veka* (Moscow: 1971). For commentary, see Soboul,

'Georges Lefèbvre: historien de la Révolution française', *Annales historiques de la Révolution française*, no. 1 (1975), reprinted in *idem*, *Comprendre la Révolution*; and T.C.W. Blanning, *The French Revolution: Aristocrats v. Bourgeois?* (London: Macmillan Education, 1987), pp. 51–2. According to Ado, even though, subjectively, the peasantry conceived of its political purposes as quite different from capitalism, objectively it was contributing to the bourgeois revolution by attempting to break up the system of large aristocratic proprietors, such that a capitalist market would begin to operate.

50. Alfred Cobban, *The Myth of the French Revolution*, in *Aspects of the French Revolution* (London: Cape, 1968), p. 106.

51. Alfred Cobban, *The Social Interpretation of the French Revolution* (Cambridge: Cambridge University Press, 1964), ch. 2, esp. p. 13.

52. Ibid., ch. 3, esp. 16–17.

53. Ibid., chs 6 and 7.

54. Ibid., ch. 11.

55. Ibid., p. 168.

56. Ibid., p. 162.

57. Cobban may be challenged, with an almost Popperian argument. He employs an inflexible assumption which makes it inevitable that political categories and state power must be imposed from above. Because his theoretical scepticism excludes any social category without a contemporary designation, it is bound from the start to filter out from consideration any that lack an explicit identity – which is to say, in all probability, a *political* presence. The conscious, political arena is therefore tautologically likely to impose upon society, and social conflict to disappear into political manoeuvring.

58. Richard Cobb, *The People's Army*, trans. M. Elliot (New Haven, CT and London: Yale University Press, 1987), p. 512. This work was originally published as *Les Armées révolutionnaires: instrument de la Terreur, avril 1793–floréal An II* (Paris: Mouton, 1961).

59. Richard Cobb, *The Police and the People: French Popular Protest 1789–1820* (Oxford: Oxford University Press, 1970), p. 199.

60. Ibid., p. 199.

61. Ibid., pp. 199–200

62. Ibid., p. 200.

63. Cobb, *The People's Army*, p. 130.

64. Ibid., p. 132.

65. Ibid., p. 129.

66. By the time he wrote *The Police and the People*, Cobb was himself well aware of a 'histoire de mentalité' aspect to his writing, which he discusses on pp. 203–4.

67. Ibid., p. 132.

68. Ibid., pp. 122–6.

69. In addition, Norman Hampson, *A Social History of the French Revolution* (London: Routledge and Kegan Paul, 1963; 1966) gave a pluralistic account of the phases of the Revolution not unlike Lefèbvre's. Each

phase witnesses competition between political groupings to grasp and direct political power on behalf of various social classes. Classes emerge as agents in the Revolutionary process *through* the articulation given their aspirations by political institutions and personnel. Hampson portrays the politicians as position-players intent on gathering a coherent constituency of supporters from society at large. Hampson's subsequent studies of political leaders — *Robespierre* (London: Duckworth, 1974) and *Danton* (London: Duckworth, 1978) — show a personal sensitivity to the interaction of individuals with their institutional and ideological environment.

70. Georges Rudé, *The Crowd in the French Revolution* (Oxford: Oxford University Press, 1965). The writer who has most clearly followed in Rudé's footsteps is R.B. Rose. His *Les Enragés* (Melbourne: Melbourne University Press, 1965) and *The Making of the Sans-culottes* (Manchester: Manchester University Press, 1983) show how the sansculottes developed workable applications of direct democratic principles.

71. Rudé, *The Crowd*, p. 209.

72. Colin Lucas, 'Nobles, Bourgeois and the Origins of the French Revolution', *Past and Present*, no. 60 (1973), pp. 84–126.

73. Ibid., p. 99.

74. See, for example, D.M.G. Sutherland, *The Chouans: the Social Origins of Popular Counter-Revolution in Upper Brittany, 1770–1796* (Oxford: Clarendon, 1982); *idem, France 1789–1815* (London: Collins/Fontana, 1985); T.C.W. Blanning, *The Origins of the French Revolutionary Wars* (London: Longman, 1986). In addition, one recent discussion from George C. Comninel may carry the long-term influence of Cobban into Marxist histories in English. Comninel's *Re-thinking the French Revolution: Marxism and the Revisionist Challenge* (London and New York: Verso 1987) accepts the theoretical force of Cobban's critique, but rejects Cobban's own version on the grounds that it merely resituates the 'bourgeois' revolution. Comninel sketches a new, arguably Marxist view of the Revolution as a product of *intra*-class conflict over how to preserve the advantages of the *ancien régime*'s state-centred system of expropriation. This, according to Comninel, is a materialist account which would spike an attack like Cobban's because its categories are *not* anachronistic. Comninel directs his keenest theoretical attack, however, against a structuralist strategy which, in his view, merely aggravates with theoretical subtleties (not always correctly applied) the tendency to read back the presence of capitalism into the pre-revolutionary past.

75. François Furet, 'The French Revolution is over' in *idem, Interpreting the French Revolution* (Cambridge: Cambridge University Press, 1981), p. 48. The essay was written originally as a *post hoc* defence of the book that Furet had published, with Denis Richet, in 1965: *La Révolution française* (Paris: Hachette). This reflects the same emphasis on the culture, with its inheritance from the Enlightenment, plus the crucial role of Terror and war in diverting the course of the Revolution. Richet himself separately argued the case for the Enlightenment roots in his

'Autour des origines idéologiques lointaines de la Révolution française: élites et despotisme', *Annales, ESC* (1969).

76. Ibid., p. 18.
77. Ibid., p. 63.
78. Ibid., p. 78.
79. Ibid., pp. 24–5.
80. Ibid., p. 28.
81. Ibid., p. 29.
82. Ibid., p. 7.
83. For details, see Chapter 2, note 34 and Chapter 3, note 22.
84. Ronald Paulson, *Representation of Revolution (1789–1820)* (New Haven, CT and London: Yale University Press, 1983).
85. Lynn Hunt, *Politics, Culture and Class in the French Revolution* (Berkeley and London: University of California Press, 1984).
86. Brian J. Singer, *Society, Theory and the French Revolution* (London: Macmillan, 1986).
87. Apart from Lefèbvre's *The Great Fear of 1789*, see, for example, his 'The Murder of the Comte de Dampierre'; Soboul's 1957 essay, 'Religious Sentiment and Popular Cults during the Revolution' (both reprinted in J. Kaplow (ed.), *New Perspectives on the French Revolution: Readings in Historical Sociology* (New York: Wiley, 1965)); and Soboul's chapter on the popular *mentalité* in his *La Civilisation et la Révolution française* (Paris: Arthaud, 1982), vol. 2, pp. 217–37.
88. Albert Soboul, 'Historiographie révolutionnaire classique et tentatives révisionnistes', *La Pensée*, no. 177 (September–October 1974), reprinted in his *Comprendre la Révolution*. References below are to the reprinted edition.
89. Ibid., p. 341.
90. Ibid., p. 338.
91. See Claude Mazauric, 'Peut-il y avoir des événements non politiques?' in *Actes du colloque 'L'événement'* (Aix-en-Provence: Université de Provence, 1984) reprinted in Mazauric, *Jacobinisme et révolution* (Paris: Messidor/Editions Sociales, 1984), esp. pp. 134–5 and 138–40.
92. Claude Mazauric, '1974: Quelques voies nouvelles pour l'histoire politique de la Révolution française' in *idem, Voies nouvelles pour l'histoire de la Révolution française* (Paris: Comité d'histoire économique et sociale de la Révolution, 1978), reprinted in Mazauric, *Jacobinisme*. References are to the latter.
93. Ibid., p. 85.
94. Ibid., p. 90.
95. Ibid., pp. 81–4.
96. Ibid., p. 86.
97. Michel Vovelle, *Idéologies et mentalités* (Paris: Maspero, 1982), pp. 12–26 (translated as *Ideologies and Mentalities* (Cambridge: Polity, 1988)). In general, Vovelle claims, the history of *mentalités* is a 'study of the mediation and the dialectical relationship between objective conditions of human life and the way humans describe and even live it.

At this level, the contradictions between . . . ideology on one side and *mentalité* on the other dissolve. Mapping out *mentalités*, far from being a mystificatory procedure . . . broadens the field of research' (p. 17).

98. Michel Vovelle, *Piété baroque et déchristianisation en Provence au XVIIIme siècle: les attitudes envers la mort d'après les clauses des testaments* (Paris: Plon, 1973); *idem, Religion et Révolution. La Déchristianisation de l'an II* (Paris: Hachette, 1976); *idem, Mourir autrefois* (Paris: Gallimard, 1974); and *idem, La Mort en l'Occident de 1300 à nos jours* (Paris: Gallimard, 1983).

99. Michel Vovelle, *La Mentalité révolutionnaire* (Paris: Messidor/Editions Sociales, 1986).

100. Ibid., pp. 86–95.

101. Ibid., pp. 52–3.

102. Mazauric, '1974', p. 101. For Gramsci's own account of the Revolution, see *Selections from the Prison Notebooks*, ed. Q. Hoare and G. Nowell-Smith (London: Lawrence and Wishart, 1971), pp. 77–82. For discussion of his views see A. Tosel, 'Gramsci face à la Révolution française: la question de jacobinisme' in Tosel (ed.), *Philosophies de la Révolution française* (Paris: Vrin, 1984); and Alain Goussot, 'Gramsci, la Révolution française comme révolution culturelle', in proceedings of the conference 'La Révolution française et le processus de socialisation de l'homme moderne' (Rouen: IRED, University of Rouen, 1989).

Conclusion:
Action and Culture in the Revolution

The French Revolution is an event which strains our ability to understand the nature of history and of social action. This book has tried to pick a path through the efforts to understand something so literally *extra*ordinary. It has revealed some of their submerged structures of thought and of image, some of their ambiguities and tensions. Not the least consequence of this study of the portrayal of the Revolution in different cultural forms and moments, is to confirm just how difficult an event it is for culture to represent. It was difficult for the revolutionaries themselves; it is difficult for those who have reflected on it since.

At the heart of that difficulty is the sense, which the revolutionaries themselves had, of the power of the united community. If they were united, they felt, they had the capacity to restart the social-political order – indeed, the whole of historical time – from scratch. Their perception of themselves as a powerful union of free agents focuses all that is hardest to grasp about the Revolution. We have seen how the culture of the revolutionary period itself tried to deal with this: by language that played up the listeners' common identity in a collectivity with the speaker at its centre; by performances that tried to exemplify the power of the community acting together; by portrayals which projected the members of the community on to a higher moral and historical plane. Ultimately, these efforts seem to have been limited by a difficulty that was both historically real and theoretical – that is, the 'classical' abstraction of ideals, such as the nation, from the human beings that were supposed to realize them. Many cultural forms attempted to incorporate the people into the active political union. But from the start, the people were, in a sense, set aside by the conception of the ideal that was in play. With changes in the political balance of power, they were soon to be excluded in fact as well as in image.

The historical and theoretical writings of the Revolution's aftermath tended to replay that movement in reverse. That is to say, they started out by excluding several connected ideas from their portrayal of the Revolution: the people, collective power of action, free human agency. But they gradually reintegrated these things on other terms. Early historical and theoretical writing put the mass of the people beyond the pale (both of reason and of coherent action), or saw the Revolution as governed by something distant from society itself. For some, the Revolution was directed by a mysterious destiny, which was imposed by the obscure inertia of the given society, or by the power of the Ideal in the human spirit, or by God himself. For others, the driving force behind the Revolution was the long-term historical progress of a culture of liberty, originating in corporate life of the bourgeoisie during the Middle Ages or in earlier times.

But by the time of the later romantic historians and the fusion of Hegelian idealism and socialism, the mass of society regained a central place in the portrayal of the Revolution. Though in a highly qualified way, the real existence and active role of the people are portrayed in the later histories. That romantic empathy, which embraced only a narrow range of historical actors in the writing of de Staël or Thierry, was extended. In Michelet, it embraced the whole of the French people – past, present and future. Meanwhile, more theoretical writings were trying to define what levels of a society's existence determine the process of change. They also included an explanation of how the culture of a society could bring social groups together – or fail to do so. The best of them took a wide range of social elements, in complex inter-relation, and managed to include human agents as well.

Out of this there re-emerges a conception of the role of human beings as historical agents in the attempt to transform society through the Revolution. But the human role is limited by two dimensions: the inherent difficulty of finding representations in culture which can portray a large number of real people as a body; and an awareness of various phenomena covered by the term 'atomization'. That term refers to the way social processes place the members of society in opposition to each other, dividing them from any sense of shared identity or united action.

Modern general theories of revolution and modern historical writing on the Revolution itself seem to till over this ground yet again – without apparently absorbing fully the lessons of the nineteenth-century struggle with the same problems. Prominent post-war theories of social change gave weight to inchoate forces in the outcome of social upheaval, in a way that denied all rationality to collective action aimed at social transformation. They seemed to express a dread of the pursuit of social change — which was understandable given the historical experience in the first half of the twentieth century. Later investigations, however, have arranged the forces provoking revolutions and determining their outcome in models of supervening structures. The structures are systematic, predictable and objective to those involved. Human agents operate within them. Historical writing on the Revolution, on the other hand, has displayed a tendency to give a prominent place to the culture of those involved in the upheaval. As I have analysed it, the nineteenth-century debate indicates that culture should have such prominence. In modern historical writing, the evolution of culture has been partially integrated into an understanding of the actions of collective agents in the Revolution. Increasingly, history places culture at the centre of the agents' self-identification. That kind of thinking has diverted historical writing away from both grand claims about the action of classes and from an insistence on the inchoate primacy of individuals or small groups.

The running theme of this study has been how culture integrates the members of a society into an active, common identity. Yet I have not attempted to define what type of culture does this best. There is no reason to believe we could decide in advance on a single culture, or a limited number of cultures, best able to perform that task. Instead, I have tried to pass in review various styles and forms of culture that belong to or address a particular historical moment. The study provides a critical investigation of how others have attempted to portray the unusual historical experience of a society self-consciously transforming itself. It shows how different forms of culture implicitly conveyed a representation of the collectivity in the historic upheaval of the Revolution. At the very least, the analysis confirms the crucial and varied role of culture in constituting agents in history, in their own eyes or in the eyes of others.

What follows from the crucial role of culture for groups active in a historical situation? Not only does culture constitute those involved in their own eyes, it constitutes an understanding of the objective reality of which they are a part. The abstract ideal deployed in revolutionary culture failed precisely in this way: it portrayed a people made up of moral heroes who could not exist in objective reality. In spite of romanticism's taste for the historically specific, Michelet's romantic portrayal of the people exhibited the same shortcoming. A further implication of this study then is that culture in a social upheaval such as the Revolution has to reflect two realities. There is the reality of the world that is objective to the historical actors. Then there is the reality of the complex and ambivalent collective identity of those actors, *in* that world. The culture which drastically misrepresents either of these objective realities will undermine those involved. It will encourage them to confront the world not as it is but as it is misrepresented to them. Or it will suppress their complex reality as agents in the world.

Portrayals of the French Revolution – or situations of social change more generally – could be asked to fulfil three tasks. They had to draw fully on the cultural resources available. They had to portray the objective conditions of the situation human agents were participating in. And they had to convey to those involved their own identity as agents. The shortcomings of the culture portraying the self-identity of those involved in the Revolution crucially affected its objective outcomes. In studying or assessing portrayals of the Revolution (or of social change generally), we need, therefore, to observe how they drawn on cultural resources, portray objective conditions and convey the self-identity of those involved. We can be best assured that we have understood the portrayals thoroughly when we can, in addition, explain how they were constrained by the real mechanisms of cultural resources.

Appendix 1: Chronological Chart

1788

January–August: Provincial riots and disputes with courts (*parlements*) over monarchy's long-running efforts to reform legal and tax systems and overcome bankruptcy. King gives in to pressure to summon the ancient representative assembly, the Estates General.

1789

January–May: Widespread disputes over the manner of election to the three different chambers of the Estates. Publication of Sieyès' *What is the Third Estate?*, asserting the priority of the commoners' (Third) chamber (see Chapter 3).

May: Formation of Jacobin Society (known initially as the Society of Friends of the Constitution).

May–July: Assembly of Estates, disputes over voting, etc., Oath of the Jeu de Paumes by the Third Estate (vowing to draw up a new constitution), other chambers forced to join the Third, renamed 'National Assembly', then 'National Constituent Assembly'.

July: David's *Brutus* appears at Paris Salon (see Chapter 3).

July–August: Disturbances in Paris; suspicions that the king will use the army to subdue Paris and his short-lived dismissal of his reforming director of finance, Necker, spark off the attack on the Bastille. General breakdown of order in the countryside as peasants form bands to defend themselves against supposed marauding soldiers, brigands or agents of the nobility, etc., and attack strangers and châteaux (known as 'the Great Fear'). In Paris and the provinces, local authorities form 'civic' or 'national guard' units, taking over from the royal army.

August: Assembly abolishes feudal rights and the exemptions from taxation, and passes a declaration of the Rights of Man.

September: First issue of *L'Ami du peuple* by Marat, demagogic anti-government journalist (see Chapter 1).

229

October: Parisian marchers bring the king to Paris from Versailles.

December: First presentation of Chénier's *Charles IX* (see Chapter 2).

1790

April: Formation of the radical Cordeliers Club.

July: First *Fête de la Fédération* in Paris and the provinces, to celebrate the new-found unity of the nation (see Chapter 2).

July–November: A new 'Civil Constitution' for the Clergy makes them subject to secular national sovereignty.

November: Publication in England of Burke's attack on the Revolution (*The Reflections on the Revolution in France*) (see Chapters 4 and 5).

1791

January: Appearance of regular journal of Père Duchesne, by Hébert (see Chapter 1).

April: Death of Mirabeau (leading constitutional monarchist in the Assembly).

June: King's unsuccessful flight to join anti-constitutional emigrants. He is captured at Varennes. Voltaire's remains become the first of a national figure to be interred in the Panthéon in Paris.

July: Formation of moderate 'Feuillant' club by dissatisfied elements from the Jacobins. Massacre by national guard of petitioners for a republic gathered at the Champ de Mars.

July–August: Threats of military intervention from Austria and Prussia.

September–October: King agrees to '1791' constitution, in which he becomes an executive agent of laws approved by the legislature; Legislative Assembly (replacing National Constituent Assembly) meets.

1792

March: Formation of moderate, pro-war, 'Girondin' administration.

April: War with Austria and Prussia.

June: Girondin administration replaced by moderate 'Feuillant' group in government.

June–August: Crowds invade the Tuileries Palace (twice), where the king is being held. Legislative Assembly dissolved.

September: Constitutional Convention meets, a Republic is declared.

September–October: French defeats at Longwy and Verdun, panic and massacre of prisoners in gaols of Paris, French victories at Valmy and Lille.

1793

January: Execution of Louis XVI. Murder of pro-execution deputy, Lepelletier. First production of Laya's *Ami des Lois* (see Chapter 2).

February: Formation of first coalition of European monarchies (Austria, Britain, Holland, Prussia, Sardinia, Spain) to defeat the Republic militarily. Food riots in Paris.

March: Start of the Vendée uprising against the republic and its religious legislation (till February 1795). Also first anti-government, 'Chouan' disturbances in Brittany and Normandy (till March 1796). Girondins' journals attacked in Paris. Establishment of first committees of surveillance (afterwards revolutionary tribunals).

April: Defection of Dumouriez, senior general, to the Austrians.

April–June: Establishment of executive Committee of Public Safety (initially dominated by Danton); uprising against Girondins leads to their removal from Convention and arrest; populist 1793 constitution approved (though not brought into force).

April–July: Unsuccessful trial of Marat. Marat's assassination leads to his burial in the Panthéon and a public cult of him.

August: General registration for military service (*Levée en Masse*) introduced.

September–December: Radical uprising in Paris, led by Hébert; Law to confine and confiscate the property of suspected counter-revolutionaries; price controls (*Maximum général*); execution of Girondins; 'revolutionary' government (with extensive emergency powers to the Committees of Public Safety and General Security) decreed until the end of the war.

October: Adoption of revolutionary calendar to run from the foundation of the Republic in September 1792 (see Chapter 2).

November–December: Start of Dechristianising movement, to turn churches over to secular or public use. Festival of Reason held in Notre Dame de Paris (see Chapter 2).

December: First issue of Desmoulin's *Vieux Cordelier* (see Chapter 1).

1794

March–April: Execution of Hébert and his group, followed by that of Danton and his followers (including Desmoulins).

May–June: Deistic worship of the 'Supreme Being' officially introduced, Festival of the Supreme Being, led by Robespierre (see Chapter 2).

June: Extension of revolutionary tribunals' powers.

July: Fall and execution of Robespierre and his associates ('Thermidor')

August: Reorganization of Committee of Public Safety.

October: Ecole Normale Supérieure and National Conservatory for Arts and Crafts established.

November–December: Closure of Jacobin Club of Paris, suppression of *Maximum*.

1795

April, May and October: Suppression of 'Germinal', 'Prairial' and 'Vendémiaire' uprisings in Paris.

May–June: 'White Terror' against supporters of previous revolutionary government.

July–November: Establishment of 'Directorial' constitution.

1796

May: Babeuf arrested and executed for unsuccessful conspiracy against government.

1796–7

Napoleon's successful campaign in Italy.

1797

September: 'Fructidor' purge of royalists in the legislature ('Councils') by executive ('Directory').

1798

French military successes in Italy and Switzerland; Napoleon begins Egyptian campaign.
May: 'Floréal' annulment of elections by Directory to unseat Jacobins.

1799

June: 'Jacobin' Councils unseat Directors.
October–December: Napoleon returns to France and seizes power ('18 Brumaire') in new, consular constitution.

1802

May: Education reform establishes lycées.
August: Napoleon made first consul for life.

1804

May: Napoleon crowned emperor; systematic legal reform ('Code Napoléon').

Appendix 2: Biographical Index

Babeuf, François Noël ('Gracchus') (1760–97): Journalist and revolutionary. In 1796, he created a secret movement to carry out a democratic egalitarian uprising. The members were betrayed and arrested. Babeuf himself was executed. He and his followers subsequently came to be thought of as professional revolutionaries *avant la lettre*.

Bara, Joseph (1779–93): Boy soldier in the Republic's army fighting in the Vendée. Bara was shot down in cold blood by the rebels when, allegedly, he cried *'Vive la République'* instead of *'Vive le roi'*, as instructed by his captors. He became a republican hero, whose picture was sent to all primary schools as a lesson for French children.

Barère de Vieuzac, Bertrand (1755–1841): Lawyer and member of both the Assembly and the Convention. He supported the Montagnard party and joined the Committee of Public Safety, but was instrumental in bringing about the fall of Robespierre, which preceded the dissolution of the Committee itself.

Barnave, Antoine Pierre Joseph Marie (1761–93): Lawyer and member of the Estates General/Constituent Assembly, where he defended a constitutional monarchist line. He retired from politics in 1791 and wrote his *Introduction à la Révolution française*. In 1793, he was arrested and executed for his part in an alleged royalist conspiracy.

Brissot de Warville, Jean-Pierre (1754–93): Lawyer, writer and member of the National Assembly and the Convention. He was the leading light in the Girondin tendency, enjoying the temporary support of the king. He was executed with his fellow Girondins.

Carmontelle (real name: Louis Carrogis) (1717–1806): Graphic artist, pamphleteer and comic playwright.

Carnot, Lazare Nicolas Marguerite (1753–1823): General and member of the Assembly, the Convention and the Committee of Public Safety. He was Minister of War in the mid-1790s and a vital architect of the success of France's new revolutionary armies. He subsequently served as Minister of War under Napoleon.

Carra, Jean-Louis (1742–93): Librarian, novelist, historian, journalist and member of the Convention. He was executed with the Girondins.

Chalier, Marie Joseph (1747–93): Merchant and radical revolutionary. He took part in the attack on the Bastille. Subsequently, he led the repressive Montagnard leadership in Lyon, when it was overthrown by the Girondin party, in revolt against the central government. He was executed by the Girondins of Lyon.

Chénier, Marie-Joseph Blaise (1764–1811): Dramatist, poet and member of the Convention. He belonged to both the Committee of Public Safety and the Committee of General Security. His writing included revolutionary hymns as well as the liberal-minded *Charles XI*.

Condorcet, Marie-Jean-Antoine-Nicolas Caritat (1743–94): Mathematician, philosopher, biographer, member of the Legislative Assembly and Convention. He was the last great member of the eighteenth-century *philosophe* circle. He was active in proposals for educational reform and the preparation of the 1793 constitution. He fell under suspicion because of his links with the Girondins and killed himself in prison. In hiding, however, he wrote the optimistic *Sketch for an Historical Picture of the Progress of the Human Mind*, which was published after his death and became the basis of the educational and epistemological thinking of the *idéologue* movement.

David, Jacques Louis (1748–1825): Painter, member of the Convention and the Committee of Public Safety. He had already distinguished himself before the Revolution as the leading French advocate of the neo-classical revival. He dominated the politics of republican-minded artists during the early 1790s, and created many of the finest works of the Revolution, both in paint and in the staging of festivals. After that period, he continued as a successful portraitist and became the court painter to Napoleon.

Desmoulins, Camille (1760–94): Journalist, political militant and member of the Convention. He was associated with Danton when the latter opposed the Committee of Public Safety's policy of rigorous suppression. He was executed with Danton.

Diderot, Denis (1713–84): Philosopher, writer and art critic. Over two decades, he held together the project of the *Encyclopédie*, a highly influential compendium of up-to-date technical knowledge and progressive ideas. His often subtle views on the important place of art and enlightenment in society were a source of both revolutionary and post-revolutionary thinking.

Fabre d'Eglantine, Philippe François Nazaire (1750–94): Playwright, poet, journalist and member of the Convention. He was executed with the associates of Danton.

Fauchet, Claude (1744–93): Priest and member of both the Assembly and the Convention. He took part in the attack on the Bastille. In 1791, he became bishop of Caen under the new clerical regime. An opponent of the Montagne in the Convention, he was executed for alleged complicity in the murder of Marat.

Fréron, Louis Marie Stanislas (1754–1802): Journalist and son of Elie-Catherine Fréron, whose *Année Littéraire* he edited from 1776. As representative of the Convention in Toulon and Marseilles after their uprisings in 1793, he made himself notorious for the severity of the reprisals. He became a leading anti-revolutionary after 1795, and died as a colonial official in the West Indies.

Girondins: Moderate republican party in the Assembly and the Convention, so called because many of them came from the Gironde. Dominant in the government during 1792–3, they were overthrown and arrested in a mass coup encouraged by the Jacobins, and subsequently executed.

Gorsas, Antoine Joseph (1752–93): Teacher, journalist, member of the Convention, where he opposed the king's execution. For a short time, he was a member of the Committee of General Security. In July 1793, after a public campaign against his supposed royalism, he was arrested and executed, the first member of the Convention to die in this fashion.

Gossec, François-Joseph (1734–1829): Composer and first master of the Paris Conservatory. He composed music for republican performances in the theatre and the open air, including the standard arrangement of the 'Marseillaise'. His music contributed to the development of the symphony.

Hébert, Jacques René (1761–94): Journalist (writing in the name of an imaginary *alter ego*, *Le Père Duchesne*) and prominent Parisian sansculotte leader. He was associated with the prison massacres, the dechristianizing movement, and a coup attempt by Paris militants in 1793, which led to his execution.

'Jacobin' Society: Formed in May 1789 to discuss political business associated with the Estates General, the society became known as 'the Jacobins' when it took over a former Jacobin monastery for its headquarters. On the model of literary corresponding societies, it established a nationwide network of affiliated societies. It rapidly became an organized movement to foster 'public spirit' and support for the Republic, promoting candidates for election, commentating or affirming the policies of the authorities, and monitoring the actions of civic and national officials. Many of the leaders of the revolutionary governments rose and had to defend themselves in the society – rather as politicians in the meetings of a modern parliamentary caucus. Hence, the regime of 1792–4 is known as the 'Jacobin' government, and the society was closed by those who took over from it in 1795.

Laclos, Pierre Choderlos de (1741–1803): Officer in the *ancien régime* army and author of the realist, epistolatory novel *Les Liaisons dangereuses* (1782), which attacked aristocratic idleness and voluptuousness. He was active in the Jacobin Society and briefly editor of the Society's first journal in 1790.

Lafayette, Marie Joseph Paul Yves Roch Gilbert de Motier, Marquis de (1757–1834): Soldier and politician. He took a leading part in the French military support for the American colonialists in their uprising against the British. He was a member of the Estates General and the Assembly, and first commander of the new National Guard, where he was responsible for the shooting of protesters at the Champs de Mars in July 1791. In 1792 he fled the country fearing punishment for the failure of his military campaign for the Republic. Though he returned in 1799, he took no more part in politics until the 1830 Revolution.

Laya, Jean-Louis (1761–1833): Playwright, critic and journalist. Author of pro-enlightenment dramas before the Revolution. After the controversy of his *L'Ami des lois*, he wrote other tragedies in the late 1790s. Subsequently, he became a professor at the Sorbonne and member of the Académie française.

Lepelletier de Saint Fargeau, Louis Michel (1760–93): President of the Paris Parlement and member of the Estates General and the Constituent, of which he was president when it tried the king. He supported the death penalty. He became a republican hero when a soldier of the king's guard assassinated him on the eve of the king's execution.

Marat, Jean Paul (1743–93): Physician, journalist and demogogic politician. From September 1789, he published *L'Ami du peuple*, which set an example of vitriolic attack on public authority from a standpoint of the rights of the downtrodden people. After being unsuccessfully indicted by the authorities in 1793, he was murdered. He was commemorated in two remarkable pictures by David, and his funeral became the centre of a brief pseudo-religious cult.

Maréchal, Pierre Sylvain (1750–1803): Lawyer, librettist, playwright and revolutionary journalist and writer. Apart from *Le Jugement dernier des rois*, he produced a secular almanach and a parody of the Bible. He drew up the *Manifeste des Egaux* of Babeuf's conspirators, though he was not arrested with the others.

Mercier, Louis Sebastian (1740–1814): Literary journalist and realist comic playwright.

Mirabeau, Honoré Gabriel Riqueti, Comte de (1749–91): politician and member of the Third Estate/National Assembly. An impressive orator, he was a crucial figure in many of the Assembly debates of the 1789–91 period, advocating reforms that would not alienate the nobility, and constitutional limitations on the monarchy in the manner of the English parliamentary system. He secretly negotiated to bring the king round to accept constitutional monarchy. His death through illness robbed this political current of an essential supporter.

Montagnard/Montagne: Name, meaning the mountain, given to the radical deputies who sat on the left of the Assembly and the Convention, in the higher seats. This tendency was dominant in the Convention during the period of 'revolutionary' government in 1792–4.

Necker, Jacques (1732–1804): Swiss financier and politician. From 1777 to 1789 the king repeatedly brought him into the government as a reformer and guarantor of financial soundness. His reputation stood so high in 1789 that his dismissal contributed to the rumours of impending reaction by the king which provoked the storming of the Bastille. By 1790, however, the direction of politics had left him behind and he retired to Switzerland. The writer and historian, Madame de Staël, was his daughter.

Paine, Thomas (1737–1809): English pamphleteer and politician. He emigrated to North America in the 1770s and published a defence of the American colonies' demands under the title of *Common Sense*. He then became a state official in Pennsylvania, but returned first to England and then to France in the late 1780s. He published *The Rights of Man*, a famous

236

defence of the Revolution against the charges of Burke in *Reflections on the Revolution in France* – for which he was subsequently tried for treason in his absence. As an elected member of the Convention, he took an active part in constitutional debates, but was imprisoned for a spell as a result of his moderation. In 1802, he retired disillusioned, and went back to live in America, where he died in poverty.

Quatremère de Quincy, Antoine Chrysostome (1755–1849): Writer on the arts, member of the legislative assembly and the legislative Council of the late 1790s. His royalist politics led him to two close shaves with the guillotine, but he survived to obtain public honours under the restored monarchy.

Robespierre, Maximilien François Marie Isadore de (1758–94): Lawyer and member of the Assembly and the Convention. He rose to prominence in the Jacobins and in the Convention through his independent-minded republicanism in debates over the war and the king's trial. He then became the dominant figure in the executive Committee of Public Safety, promoting the rigorous suppression of opponents of the central government, populist policies on price controls and education, and a deistic national religion. In 1794, he found himself politically isolated and outmanoeuvred, and was summarily executed after becoming embroiled in an attempted coup by his supporters in Paris.

Roland de la Platière, Manon, Jeanne Philipon (Madame Roland) (1754–93): Wife of the Girondist politician and hostess of an influential salon where progressive, republican politics was discussed and developed. She was executed shortly after her husband.

Rousseau, Jean-Jacques (1712–78): Francophone Swiss composer, writer and philosopher. He was associated with the progressive *philosophe* movement, but broke with them over their materialism and their irreligion. His *Social Contract*, with its account of popular sovereignty, greatly influenced the thinking of radical democratic republicans. His reflective autobiographical writings and his posture as a pure, uncorrupted soul were taken as models for the rhetoric of politics and public debate, and the nascent romanticism of many revolutionaries.

Saint-Just, Louis Antoine Léon Florelle de (1767–94): Writer and member of the Convention, where he espoused a diehard romantic republicanism. He was appointed by Robespierre to act as an agent of the revolutionary government at the front, and afterwards became a close associate of Robespierre's in the Committee of Public Safety. He was executed alongside Robespierre.

Sansculottes: Name adopted in the early 1790s by radical republican militants from the common people and their supporters. It proclaimed their modest decency, and their indifference to self-interest and the finery of aristocratic manners and dress – such as *culottes*.

Sieyès, Emmanuel-Joseph, Abbé, Comte (1748–1836): Author of renowned pamphlets on the eve of the Revolution, Sieyès was a moderate member of all the representative assemblies of the period and took a leading part in the preparation of many of the constitutions. He co-operated with

Napoleon in bringing the latter to power in 1799, but was rapidly set aside thereafter.

Simoneau (?–1792): Tradesman and mayor of Etampes who refused to impose price controls in the town and was consequently murdered by rioters.

Talleyrand-Périgord, Charles Maurice de (1754–1838): Bishop of Autun at the time of the Revolution, he was prominent in the Estates General/National Assembly before resigning in deference to the current view of the church and becoming a diplomat and subsequently Foreign Minister and adviser to Napoleon, who appointed him to various senior imperial offices and distinctions, finally making him Prince de Benavento.

Vergniaud, Pierre Victurnien (1753–93): Leader of the Girondin tendency in the Assembly and Convention. He was executed with them.

Volney, Constantin François de Chasseboeuf, Comte de (1757–1820): Journalist, writer and public official under Louis XVI. He was arrested in 1793 because of his links with the Girondins, but survived to become a senator opposing Napoleon under the empire. He made a crucial contribution to the linguistic and historical thinking of the *idéologue* movement.

Voltaire, François Marie Arouet de (1694–1778): Liberal philosopher and writer. His progressive ideas were highly influential in the decades up to the Revolution, which adopted him as a founding father.

Index

239